The Impact of ICT on Work

Jungwoo Lee
Editor

The Impact of ICT on Work

Springer

Editor
Jungwoo Lee
Center for Work Science, Yonsei University
Seoul, Korea, Republic of (South Korea)

ISBN 978-981-10-1249-5 ISBN 978-981-287-612-6 (eBook)
DOI 10.1007/978-981-287-612-6

Springer Singapore Heidelberg New York Dordrecht London

Softcover re-print of the Hardcover 1st edition 2016

Printed on acid-free paper

Springer Science+Business Media Singapore Pte Ltd. is part of Springer Science+Business Media (www.springer.com)

Acknowledgements

This work was partially supported by the National Research Foundation of Korea Grant funded by the Korean Government (NRF-2012S1A3A2033474). I would also like to acknowledge with much appreciation the crucial role of the researchers at the Center for Work Science in Yonsei University, especially Hyejung Lee, Jun-Gi Park and Seyoon Lee.

Contents

Chapter 1
Impact of ICT on Work: Introduction

Jungwoo Lee

The age of industrialized work is ending (Rifkin 2004). Various reasons have come together impacting the changing nature of work such as high performance expectations (Burke and Cooper 2006), demographic and cultural changes (Cox and Blake 1991), globalization and international competition (Cartwright and Holmes 2006), and economic pressure (Guevara and Ord 1996). Information and communication technology (ICT) is underpinning all of these reasons of transformation, because ICT provides the technological backbone for new organizational structures and new ways of working enabling above reasons (Heerwagen et al. 2010; Landry et al. 2005; Robey and Sahay 1996; Wallace 2004; Winter and Taylor 2001).

Industrialized technologies made workers come to work and remain at the workplace 5 days a week, 8 h a day. However, in the early days of the Industrial Revolution, it was common to abuse workers, such as underage children working at the factory 20 h a day, 7 days a week (Nardinelli 1990). It took more than a century to stabilize and institutionalize the work practices as commonly practiced in business today (De Vries 1994). Now, the emerging ICT economy allows greater possibility in terms of place and time of work as well as content, structure, and process of work. Over past decades, new patterns of work are emerging as the knowledge economy realizes the full potential of both new technologies and new organizational models. Many routine jobs are on their way to being replaced by numerical machine and electronic processors.

As Wallace (2004) described, ICT is changing work and employment. New patterns of communication are emerging with new work practices, business boundaries are being blurred, hierarchical structures are being reduced, etc. (Burke and Cooper 2006; Cartwright 2003; Landry et al. 2005; Nolan and Wood 2003). Work is now more cognitively complex, more team based, more dependent on social skills, more dependent on technological competence, more time pressured, and more mobile (Cartwright and Holmes 2006; Cronshaw 1998; Guion and Landy 1972;

J. Lee (✉)
Center for Work Science, Yonsei University, Seoul, Korea, Republic of (South Korea)
e-mail: jlee@yonsei.ac.kr

J. Lee (ed.), *The Impact of ICT on Work*, DOI 10.1007/978-981-287-612-6_1

Hackman and Oldham 1976; Nolan and Wood 2003). It is argued that workers in this new work environment require kaleidoscope thinking (Kanter 1999), the ability to see different angles, and integrated fragmented perspectives into new patterns propelling innovations. These changes require us to rethink our working environment (Heerwagen et al. 2010) as well as processes and content of work (Cartwright 2003; Huws 2006).

However, these predictions are decades old (DeCarlo 1967). Predictions for the changing nature of work in connection with the coming of knowledge-based society and ICT have been here for quite a while, and academics and practitioners have almost lost interest as the progress was not as eminent as predicted, until recently. It is the rapid and recent proliferation of smart devices connected via the Internet since the advent of iPhone in 2007 that rekindled and renewed the interest in this transformation of work. Predicted transformations are actually being implemented in a wide scale in a fast pace. Knowledge fication, projectification, and virtualization of work is now happening across almost all the domains and all the jobs and produces outcomes and consequences that may have been not anticipated in full, such as jobless growth (Dolphin 2015). Though ICT is moving toward CASMIT[1] in a fast pace, the potential effect of ICTs on work is still suffering from the rather polarized views (Rubery and Grimshaw 2001) as can be seen in Table 1.1.

This volume on "Impacts of ICT on Workplace" brings together the work of experts from eight different research institutes in seven countries across five continents. They are the ones involved in research on transformation of work. The first three chapters – 2, 3, and 4 – are focusing on drivers, consequences, and shape of transformed work while other chapters are focusing on real world cases.

In Chap. 2, "The New Way of Working: Bricks, Bytes and Behavior" by Kok from the Netherlands, three pillars of the New Way of Working (NWoW) emerging in the Netherlands are presented as *Bricks, Bytes and Behavior*, with several industry cases. Attention is given to what is happening in the physicals of offices. Radical redesign of office space is bound to permanently change how we work. Case descriptions are supplemented with literature review highlighting critical differences between NWoW and telework in the past. Effects of NWoW are discussed concerning knowledge sharing, flexibility, satisfaction, and work–life balance. Outcomes of organizational transformation into NWOW are discussed with possible drawbacks.

Chapter 3, "Telecommuting: What, Why, When and How?" by Nicklin, Cerasoli, and Dydyn in USA, presents an interesting summary of literature on telecommuting. Starting from an updated model of factors in defining telework (what), benefits and drawbacks of telecommuting (why and why not), context of telecommuting (when), and practical methods for implementing telecommuting (how) are presented in detail. The framework presented at the end is geared toward guiding practitioners to refer when implementing telecommuting in their organizations.

[1]This acronym summarizes recent trends of ICT applications: Cloud, Analytics, Social, Mobile, and Internet of Things.

Table 1.1 Scenarios of ICT impacts on workplace

	Negative/pessimistic	Positive/optimistic
Employment	Jobs are destroyed by automation and rationalization	New jobs are created by developing new markets and human capital
Employment relations	Lower trust as workers are monitored real time with ICT	Higher trust as knowledge work increases
Career	Career ladders are disrupted by unexpected competition	Opportunities for new boundaryless careers
Job prospects	Increase 'dead-end' jobs with surveillance and outsourcing	Expand career opportunities among connected and open organizations
Skills	Downgraded to personal services and machine tending tasks	Upgraded for multi-tasking and creative knowledge based tasks and job
Workplace relations	Isolate workers and impose stress on individuals	Interconnect and stimulate individuals
Life balance	Work takes over life, any time any where	Work is integrated and harmonized with daily life
Work intensity	Lead to work intensification work in multiple jobs	Provide opportunities to reduce work efforts with the help of machines
Compensate/pay	Reduce pay with downgraded skills and weak bargaining power	Increase pay for individuals with talents and knowledge based skills
Social structure	More divided society with centralized power and control	Increase individual flexibility and freedom of choice

Adopted from Rubery and Grimshaw (2001, p. 166)

Chapter 4, "Drivers and Consequences in Transforming Work Practices" by Jungwoo Lee in Republic of Korea, reports on related variables found in a systematic review of literature concerning the work transformation in the academic research. The focus was to identify and surface critical variables involved in implementing and executing new practices of work. Review of 913 research articles revealed a total of 37 drivers and consequences of work transformation: 16 individual-level variables, 15 organizational-level variables, and 6 societal-level variables. These variables are framed into a series of relational diagrams depicting work transformation processes that may guide managers and executives in planning for the future.

The next four chapters – from 5 to 8 – are reports on industry case studies identifying issues involved in ICT implementations of various kinds: techhelp in a knowledge-intensive service firm, traveling teachers in an educational firm, implementation of social collaboration infrastructure, and gamification of service desk.

Chapter 5, "Future of Work and Work Skill in Knowledge Intensive Service: Impact of New Media and Technologies" by Bandi and Shah from India, reports on two case studies in implementing coordination technologies in a knowledge-intensive service firm. Anecdotal evidences are presented arguing that almost everyone – even people with mundane tasks – is becoming a knowledge worker today and work is increasingly becoming knowledge intensive, requiring interactions with individuals at remote locations. Two cases described the changing nature of work, and the kind of capabilities required for the knowledge workers, managers, and organizations to be successful in this context.

Chapter 6, "Seeing is Belonging: Remote Working, Identify and Staying Connected" by Dery and Hafermalz from Australia and USA, examines how workers in a distributed environment use technologies to overcome the isolation and invisibility of virtual work. Qualitative data analyses revealed how the remote workers struggle with maintaining the connections with the organization. Identified are the new practices used to engage technologies in maintaining social and visible linkage across the organizations, building an identity and a presence.

Chapter 7, "Smart Workplace Technology Buzz" by Schallenmueller from Germany, describes a real-world case of the social collaboration infrastructure rollout in a large firm. A multidimensional view on technology and organizational aspects, both on the team and the individual level, is proposed as necessary in the journey to a digital workplace with social collaboration infrastructure. This framework captures various dimensions and provides a platform for discussion.

Chapter 8, "Gamification of Service Desk Work" by Conger in USA, is making a case of gamification as an emerging tool to redesign work processes to resemble game play, injecting game elements into work situations to make boring or mundane work more interesting. Details of gamification in redesigning the work of IT service desk workers are presented with process and element frames. Communal quality metrics and rewards are also presented in detail.

The last two chapters – 9 and 10 – are reporting on empirical studies related to the changing nature of work: differences in work design characteristics between mobile and stationary workers, and gap theoretical analyses on actual and desired working time in different cultures.

Chapter 9, "Work Design Characteristics of Mobile Intensive Workers: Implication for Future Work Design" by Lee and Park from Republic of Korea, uses the modern work design theory (WDT) to empirically investigate the work design characteristics of mobile intensive workers. WDT is empirically tested against user groups of instant messengers – mobile messenger group against stationary messenger user group. Mobile messenger user group represents the mobile intensive workers, expecting that mobile intensive users are more subjected toward new ways of working. Interestingly, job autonomy and interdependence are found to be much higher for mobile workers while complexity of work is found to be much higher for stationary workers. Moreover, job satisfaction is critically high for mobile intensive workers.

Chapter 10, "Work Longer or Live Smarter? Striving for Desirable Work Time Arrangements in Diverse Cultural Contexts" by Lu from Taiwan, reports on a study analyzing the data collected in the International Social Survey Program (ISSP). Data from 8,525 employees in 9 countries revealed the fit between desired and actual working hours is associated with higher job satisfaction and organizational commitment. However, this association did vary across different social welfare regimes. Logistic regression further revealed that compared against the East Asian welfare regime, employees in countries with social democratic, conservative, and liberal welfare systems were more likely to experience a fit between personal preferences and actual choices of working hours. Furthermore, interestingly, after controlling for the macro-level social institutional factors and micro-level demographics, personal financial needs of "wanting to earn less" could still predict the state of misfit.

Acknowledgments This work was partially supported by the National Research Foundation of Korea Grant funded by the Korean Government (NRF-2012S1A3A2033474).

References

Burke RJ, Cooper CL (2006) The new world of work and organizations: implications for human resource management. Hum Res Manag Rev 16(2):83–85. http://dx.doi.org/10.1016/j.hrmr.2006.03.013

Cartwright S (2003) New forms of work organization: issues and challenges. Leadersh Org Dev J 24(3):121

Cartwright S, Holmes N (2006) The meaning of work: the challenge of regaining employee engagement and reducing cynicism. Hum Res Manag Rev 16(2):199–208. http://dx.doi.org/10.1016/j.hrmr.2006.03.012

Cox TH, Blake S (1991) Managing cultural diversity: implications for organizational competitiveness. Executive 5:45–56

Cronshaw SF (1998) Job analysis: changing nature of work. Can Psychol/Psychologie canadienne 39(1–2):5–13. doi:10.1037/h0086790

De Vries J (1994) The industrial revolution and the industrious revolution. J Econ Hist 54(02):249–270

DeCarlo CR (1967) Systems design and nature of work. In: Seminar on manpower policy and program, Washington, DC, 17 November 1966

Dolphin T (ed) (2015) Technology, globalisation and the future of work in Europe: essays on employment in a digitized economy. Institute for Public Policy Research, London

Guevara K, Ord J (1996) The search for meaning in a changing work context. Futures 28(8):709–722. http://dx.doi.org/10.1016/0016-3287(96)00030-4

Guion RM, Landy FJ (1972) The meaning of work and the motivation to work. Organ Behav Hum Perform 7(2):308–339. http://dx.doi.org/10.1016/0030-5073(72)90020-7

Hackman JR, Oldham GR (1976) Motivation through the design of work: test of a theory. Organ Behav Hum Perform 16(2):250–279. http://dx.doi.org/10.1016/0030-5073(76)90016-7

Heerwagen J, Kelly K, Kampschroer K (2010) The changing nature of organizations, work, and workplace. Retrieved March 22, 2015, from http://www.wbdg.org/resources/chngorgwork.php. 15 December 2010

Huws U (2006) The transformation of work in a global knowledge economy: towards a conceptual framework. Final thematic report of the WORKS-project, Leuven

Kanter RM (1999) The enduring skills of change leaders. Lead Lead 13:15–22. doi:10.1002/ltl.40619991305

Landry BJL, Sathi M, Hartman S (2005) The changing nature of work in the age of e-business. J Organ Chang Manag 18(2):132–144

Nardinelli C (1990) Child labor and the industrial revolution. Indiana University Press, Bloomington

Nolan P, Wood S (2003) Mapping the future of work. Br J Ind Relat 41(2):165–174. doi:10.1111/1467-8543.00267

Rifkin J (2004) The end of work: the decline of the global labor force and the dawn of the post-market era. Jeremy P. Tarcher/Penguin, New York

Robey D, Sahay S (1996) Transforming work through information technology: a comparative case study of geographic information systems in county government. Inf Syst Res 7(1):93–110

Rubery J, Grimshaw D (2001) ICTs and employment: the problem of job quality. Int Labour Rev 140(2):165

Wallace P (2004) The internet in the workplace: how new technology is transforming work. Cambridge University Press, New York

Winter SS, Taylor SL (2001) The role of information technology in the transformation of work: a comparison of post-industrial, industrial, and proto-industrial organization. In: Yates J, Van Information technology and organizational transformation: history, rhetoric, and practice. Sage, Thousand Oaks, pp 7–33

Part I
Looking Back Past for Future: Reviewing Researches

Chapter 2
The New Way of Working: Bricks, Bytes, and Behavior

Arjan de Kok

Abstract The world in which we work is changing. Information technologies transform our work environment, providing the flexibility of when and where to work. With the changes in the way we work, the role of the workplace is changing as well. Offices transform from dull production facilities to inspiring meeting places, in which no effort is spared to create a new sense and experience of work. Employees engage in a working relationship that suits them best in terms of ambition, skills, lifestyle, and stage of life. The New Way of Working is a relatively new phenomenon that provides the context for these developments. It consists of three distinct pillars that are referred to as Bricks, Bytes, and Behavior: the work location, use of ICT, and the employee-manager relation. The New Way of Working employees have the freedom to work when and where they are most productive. This freedom is based on mutual trust instead of managerial control and on results instead of presence. Research shows that after the implementation of the New Way of Working, employees experience more job autonomy, a higher level of job satisfaction, decreased levels of stress, and a more peaceful family life. Though the New Way of Working may not be a cure for all organizational illnesses, organizations need to realize that in an ever-changing world, changes in the way we work are inevitable.

Keywords The New Way of Working • New World of Work • NWOW • Work flexibility • Telework

2.1 Introduction to Chapter

In the past decades, information technologies have changed the way we work, and they will continue to do so in the decades to come. These changes not only affect individuals but also organizations that are challenged to change the way they are organized and work. This chapter is about the New Way of Working, a relatively new phenomenon that has gained a lot of interest in the past years and is

A. de Kok (✉)
Utrecht University, Utrecht, The Netherlands
e-mail: a.dekok@uu.nl

J. Lee (ed.), *The Impact of ICT on Work*, DOI 10.1007/978-981-287-612-6_2

increasingly impacting organizations. The aim of this chapter is to describe what the New Way of Working entails and increase awareness of what is happening in our work environment.

After a brief review of the history of work, and the challenges twenty-first century companies face, the emergence of the New Way of Working, specifically in the Nordic countries and the Netherlands, is discussed. Because of this "local" setting, the question is raised whether cultural aspects played a role in the readiness of these countries for the New Way of Working.

The next section elaborates on the definition of the New Way of Working and the three main pillars: Bricks, Bytes, and Behavior. Special attention is given to what is happening in our offices. The radical redesign of office space, which is also taking place outside the realm of the New Way of Working, is bound to permanently change the physical infrastructure of organizations.

Based on a literature review, the differences between the New Way of Working and Telework are highlighted. The concepts of the New Way of Working are not new as such; many authors have written about new ways of working, and Telework has been around for decades. However, organizations that implement the principles of the New Way of Working still go through a transformation process, even when Teleworking arrangements were already in place. After this comparison, the effect of the New Way of Working on knowledge sharing, and the effect of schedule- and time flexibility on employee satisfaction and work-life balance, is discussed.

The chapter closes with the expectations companies had when implementing the New Way of Working and results that were actually realized. Also, the drawbacks of the New Way of Working are discussed. The New Way of Working may not be a cure for all organizational illnesses, but in a world that is continuously developing, a change in the way we work is inevitable.

2.2 The Challenge of the Twenty-First Century

The advancement of information technologies is conceived as one of the major causes for the changing nature of work. Work is no longer restricted to a certain time or place. Work may even cross the traditional boundaries of organizations. As information has become available to everyone anywhere, companies are placed in a global playing field. Offshoring of activities and technological innovations changes the work that has to be performed and puts higher demands on skill and knowledge levels of employees. Also, a new generation of workers is entering the work arena, the Net generation: a multitasking generation that grew up in the digital age and for whom networking is a lifestyle (Tapscott 1998; Veen and Jacobs 2004). Organizations need to attract, inspire, and motivate current and future work generations. These challenges force companies to rethink the way they are organized and the way work is organized, as new ways of working are needed.

Where many authors have envisioned a new future of work and new ways of working, the question remains: What is "new work"? What makes "new work" different from “old work”? This apparently simple question is harder to answer than one would expect; a clear-cut distinction can often not be made between new and old work. Yet, the challenges companies face in the twenty-first century force them to act and work differently from the traditional, early twentieth century, work principles of the Industrial Revolution. Bryan and Joyce (2007) state: “Trying to run a company in the twenty-first century with an organizing model designed for the twentieth century places limits on how well a company performs. It also creates massive, unnecessary, unproductive complexity; a condition that frustrates workers and wastes money.” Something therefore has to change in the way we work and organize ourselves, but the question is: what and how? As in all change processes, the first step is awareness: When we realize the world around us is rapidly changing, we realize we need to find new ways of working.

2.3 A Brief Review of the History of Work

In past centuries, apart from slavery, people worked on the land or in crafts in a relatively independent way. Knowledge-intensive work was learned in a master-apprentice relationship and often performed in guilds or other professional associations. It was not until the Industrial Revolution that began in the nineteenth century when major changes in work and the way we work occurred. The ability to mechanize simple or complex work tasks dramatically changed the role of the worker. The principles of Frederick Taylor, as described in the Scientific Management theory (1911), defined the worker as being an integral part of a well-oiled machine. The division of labor into small repeatable tasks became a way of increasing worker productivity. To control the worker output, management layers were created, resulting in a hierarchical top-down organization; the Machine Bureaucracy was born (Mintzberg 1978).

Taylor’s principles did not restrict themselves to industrial production facilities; also offices were seen as “paper-processing-and-production” facilities, leading to a deeply embedded industrial mind-set that this is the way work should be done (Fig. 2.1).

The result of Scientific Management was low-level employee control with virtually no opportunities for personal development. Though the Hawthorne studies in the mid-1920s already suggested social factors were more important predictors of employee performance than physical ones, it was not until the 1960s that job enrichment – giving employees some of the responsibilities that used to belong to their supervisors – started to emerge. In 1966, Herzberg defined job autonomy as one of the most important motivators. Things started to change: employees were no longer considered to be machines, but creatures with needs and desires, such as autonomy and responsibility; individuals, who become motivated by need fulfillment. The Job Characteristics model from the 1970s gave notice to the fact that employees’ needs were important predictors of employees’ responses to their work environment (Hackman and Oldham 1976). In the 1980s and 1990s, the increased industrial

Fig. 2.1 Industrial Revolution and mind-set

competition fueled the notion that organizations needed to drastically change the way they operated; business processes became a focal area. When describing a "new world of work", with process-based tasks and a flat, non-hierarchical, organization model, Hammer and Champy (1993) define information technology as rule breaking for the way business processes would radically change. One of the breaking rules they mention is information being available on multiple places at the same time, even on portable devices.

By the end of the 1990s and early 2000s, the concept of virtual, boundaryless, high performance, and collaborative organizations emerges, abandoning all traditional organizational forms (e.g., Ghoshal and Bartlett 1997). A schematic outline of these developments is shown in Table 2.1 (Child and McGrath 2001).

Even though work has changed in the past decennia, the changes have occurred in a slower pace than often anticipated. Due to the cost and functionality of ICT systems, many of the early expectations only partly became reality. Meel (2011) states that at that time, technologies were not yet able to provide the speed, power, and ease of use that people need for mobile and flexible work styles, or they were just too expensive.

History has shown that remote working, Teleworking, or Telecommuting has failed to live up to its initial expectations (Pyöriä 2011). In 2005, the most advanced countries, like Finland and the UK, showed figures of around 8 % of the employees

Table 2.1 Conventional and emerging perspectives on organizational form (Child and McGrath 2001)

	Conventional perspective - Traditional hierachical forms	Emergent perspective - New organizational forms
Goal Setting	Top-down	Decentralized
Power	Concentrated	Distributed
Size of units	Preference for large	Preference for small
Leadership function	Control and monitoring of specific objectives through formal authority	Guidance, management of conflicts
Vision	Dictated	Emergent
Structure	Hierarchy	Team and work groups
Primary unit of analysis	Firm	Production system or network
Boundaries	Clearly specified and durable	Permeable and fuzzy
Objective	Reliability and replicability	Flexibility
Regulation	Vertical	Horizontal
Integrity	Rule-based	Relationship-based
Assets	Linked tot organizational units	Structure independent of assets
Functions and roles	Specialized	General
Uncertainty	Try to absorb	Try to adapt
Rights and duties	Relative permanence	Impermanence
Governance	Efficiency oriented	Innovation oriented

Teleworking (Ruiz and Walling 2005). The number is however growing; according to the US Census Bureau, home-based work in the USA in fields of computer, engineering, and science has risen to 69 % between 2000 and 2010 (Gillen et al. 2013).

Global research by Forrester (2014) shows the number of employees that work one day a week, of a few times or more per month, continued to grow between 2010 and 2013 (see Fig. 2.2).

2.4 The Emergence of the New Way of Working

The New Way of Working, also called the New World of Work, has gained a lot of interest in the past years, especially in Scandinavian countries and the Netherlands. In 2005, inspired by the book "The World is Flat" (Friedman 2005), Bill Gates lectures on the "New World of Work" (Gates 2005). He launches a vision on the future of work and the role software technology plays in it. Gates argues that over the last decades, software has been used to build bridges between disconnected information islands, but access to information is no longer the main problem. The new challenge is how to make sense of all this information that tends to overload the modern information worker. In the New World of Work, information-worker software should help the information worker adapt and thrive in an ever-changing work environment. In his view, the future of work and work spaces is not only a major challenge for the world's largest software company but for almost any company and any employee in the world.

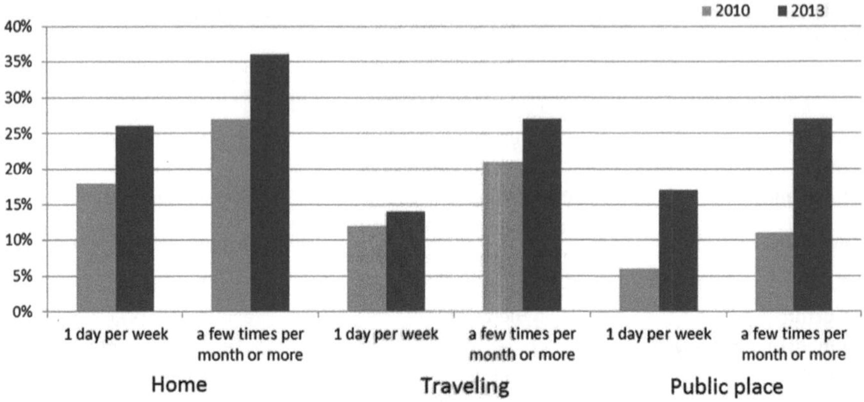

Fig. 2.2 Growth of remote working 2010–2013 (Forrester 2014)

Following the Executive Briefing, Microsoft releases a White Paper titled: "Digital Work Style: The New World of Work" (Microsoft 2005), providing an overview of trends affecting work, workers, and the work environment and painting the role of ICT in a world where knowledge is the most important asset of organizations. Microsoft writes: "Empowering people to work more efficiently and effectively in the 'digital work style' of the New World of Work should be at the center of any organization's strategy as it addresses the coming era of rapid change and increasing global integration." The Dutch version of the paper is called "Digitale werkstijl, het nieuwe werken," or: Digital Work Style: the New Way of Working, marking the beginning of the term the New Way of Working (MicrosoftNL 2005). The management of Microsoft Netherlands is convinced of the importance of the New Way of Working and decides to personally coach the project for the new Microsoft head office building on Amsterdam Airport Schiphol. In doing so, they actually relate the New Way of Working concept to a movement that was already going on for almost a decade: the radical redesign of traditional offices and the creation of new, flexible, work environments.

In 1995, the Dutch architect Erik Veldhoen was asked by Interpolis, a Dutch insurance company, to design their new head office building. Inspired by modern offices in Finland of Ericsson and Digital, where status symbols for the executive board had been completely eliminated, Veldhoen suggests to completely abandon the traditional office layout (Veldhoen 1995). Instead of the management residing on the top floor in their own luxury offices, he designs an open office with the executive board visible on the first floor, sitting among their employees. In the new head office, there would be no more fixed offices or workplaces, but concentration and communication workplaces, room for leisure and catering, wireless telephones and networks, and paperless working with all documents digitally available. The completely digital environment enabled employees to work at any desk, but also at home or elsewhere (Fig. 2.3).

Because this new concept also almost halved the number of workplaces and square footage needed, Interpolis did not need to build a twin tower but only a single

Fig. 2.3 Impressions of Interpolis' new office design (Photography: Jonathan S. Igharas, Morley Von Sternberg)

office tower: a direct saving of 55 million euro. Instead of employees leaving the company, because they had no more personal workspace, people lined up to start to work for Interpolis. The new work environment, at that time called "flexible working," propelled the desired entrepreneurship. By 2001, the revenue of Interpolis had tripled and the company had moved from the 11th to the 4th place on the ranking of insurance companies in the Netherlands. Customer satisfaction rose from 6.1 in 1996 to 7.4 in 2000 and 8.4 in 2008 (on a scale of 10). Between 2006 and 2010, Interpolis was chosen five times in a row as the Netherlands' favorite and most trustworthy insurance company. The Interpolis case did not remain unnoticed; over one hundred thousand visitors from the Netherlands and abroad came to the office, and in the following years, new initiatives at several companies and local governmental organizations proved the "new work" concepts were universally applicable (Pous and Wielen 2010).

Also, the new Microsoft head office broke with all traditional settings; the largest and most popular room in the building is taken by a grand café with lounge seats where people can meet in an informal setting. To obtain scientific metrics, Microsoft asked Erasmus University to perform research before and after the move to the new office. In 1994, employees rated their work-life balance with a 5.4 (on a scale of 10); in 2008 this had changed to 8.3 (Heck et al. 2011). For 3 years in a row (2009–2011), Microsoft Netherlands won the "Great Places to Work" award. Though Microsoft does not publish any internal financial data, the Facility Manager mentions savings of around 500.000 euro per year on internal moves and another 500.000 euro on telephone and travel costs for an 800 staff organization (Lonkhuyzen 2009; Bijl 2011). Again, many visited, and still visit, the Microsoft office and the number of companies and governmental organizations that decided to implement the New Way of Working and the Netherlands began to accelerate. Examples are Philips, Hewlett Packard, Vodafone, Getronics (an ICT company), KPN (Dutch Telephone), and TNT (Dutch mail). The acquaintance of the Dutch employees with the term the New Way of Working (Het Nieuwe Werken) was 96 % in 2011; in Belgium this was 42 % (Kluwer 2011). The Belgium number may seem relatively low, but the percentage of the acquaintance with the New Way of Working in other countries is expected to be much lower. The changes did not restrict themselves to the office itself; besides the restructuring of traditional office buildings, many third-place work locations arose, sometimes complete with high-tech videoconferencing equipment.

An example of an implementation of the New Way of Working worth mentioning is Rabobank's Unplugged project. In 2007, Rabobank, a triple A-rated bank with 60.000 employees, decided to build a new head office completely in line with the concepts of the New Way of Working. The preparations were thorough; they first renovated an empty office completely in the style of the new head office to allow departments to get used to the new working environment, before actually moving to the new head office (Bijl 2011). The "Rabo Unplugged" project introduced result contracts with employees describing the output of their work. As the employees needed to get used to this phenomenon and had to learn to stand up for themselves, trainings were organized. The first results showed an increase of employee satisfaction of between 20 and 30 % and a significant and structural saving on accommodation facilities (Bijl 2011).

The past years have shown an enormous increase in the spread and impact of the New Way of Working. Many companies and (local) governmental organizations have implemented, or are in the process of implementing, the concepts of the New Way of Working. The Dutch government is establishing legislation to regulate the new labor conditions. In a macroeconomic survey, PricewaterhouseCoopers states they expect the Dutch Gross Domestic Product (GDP) to grow by 1 % because of the New Way of Working related increased labor productivity. In the projected growth scenario, the total benefits of the New Way of Working in the period 2012–2015 for the Dutch economy are estimated between 5.6 and 8.7 billion euro (PWC 2011). The effect of the New Way of Working in organizations did not remain unnoticed in the rest of the Dutch society. The term "The New Way of …" has become a popular way of promoting innovation in any area. For example, the project to innovate the way children learn at school is called "The New Way of Learning."

2.5 Cultural Aspects and the New Way of Working

Examples like Ericson, Interpolis, and Microsoft Netherlands have been important triggers in the growth of the New Way of Working, but without a "fertile ground," these initiatives would have never been able to make such a large and broad impact for the New Way of Working. The question is therefore: Why is the New Way of Working so successful in the Scandinavian countries and the Dutch setting? Is culture one of the aspects why the New Way of Working is accepted more easily in one country than in another country, or should we be looking at other antecedents? And if culture indeed plays a role: which cultural treats are the ones that support the New Way of Working best?

Hofstede uses four cultural dimensions that define cultural differences between countries and organizations (Hofstede et al. 2010). These four cultural dimensions are: (1) Power distance, the degree of hierarchy and acceptance of autocratic leadership; (2) Individualism vs. collectivism, the degree of group/family thinking; (3) Masculine vs. feminine, the degree of role thinking and caring; and (4) Uncertainty avoidance, the degree of desired safety and rules. When taking a closer look at these four dimensions, the following picture emerges: (1) Power distance: Countries with a low power distance tend more toward dialog than obedience. The manager is not seen as the boss but as the coach. Nordic countries and the Netherlands score low on power distance, as do the USA, Australia, and Canada. Eastern European countries like Russia and Asian countries like China have a high power distance. Latin and South European countries are somewhere in the middle. (2) Individualism vs. collectivism: Workers in individualistic countries tend to be better able to take care for themselves and be less dependent on the group. Scandinavians and the Dutch are individualistic, as are most Anglo-Saxon countries. Latin and Asian countries are more collective in their thinking and working. (3) Masculine vs. feminine: In masculine countries, men are competitive and assertive. Countries like Italy, Japan, and Australia are typically masculine countries. Nordic countries and the Netherlands are more feminine, i.e., people do not like boasting but prefer equal treatment and respect. (4) Uncertainty avoidance: Greece, Portugal, Belgium, and South American countries score high on uncertainty avoidance. In these countries, people are more precautious. Nordic, Anglo-Saxon, a number of Asian countries, and, to a large extent, the Netherlands and the USA deal more effectively with uncertainties and risks. For a limited number of countries, from different regions and cultural backgrounds, Fig. 2.4 gives an overview of the cultural differences (Hofstede et al. 2010).

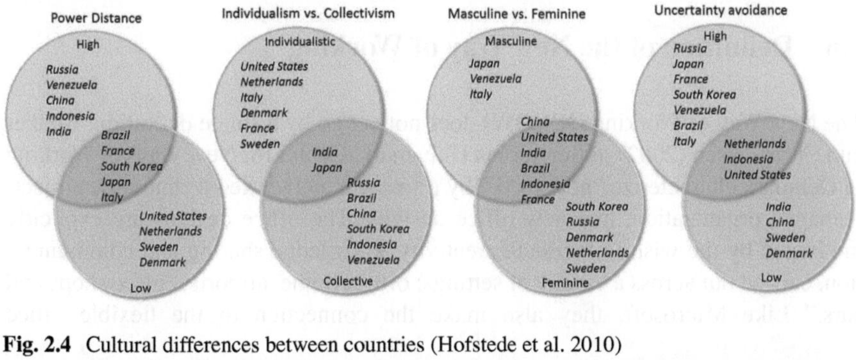

Fig. 2.4 Cultural differences between countries (Hofstede et al. 2010)

Looking at the overall picture, culturally, the Nordic countries are close to the Netherlands. Their cultures are based on dialog and consensus, personal responsibility, mutual respect, and entrepreneurship. These treats seem to have a good fit with the concepts of the New Way of Working. From a cultural point of view, Belgium – though partly Dutch speaking – is closer to France than the Netherlands. This does not mean that countries with another cultural spectrum are not suitable for the New Way of Working. It does mean that in those countries, certain aspects may need to be adjusted to make implementations of the New Way of Working a better fit and success.

For example, in the "Work Place Innovation" project of Philips, the 120,000 employee multinational aims to implement the New Way of Working worldwide in over 100 countries. For the technological support, a special program suite was introduced, providing workers with various technological resources to do their work optimally and ensure they are as connected as possible. As Philips wanted to keep a close watch on the cultural differences, local teams were set up in every country and office location to tailor the implementation. The Hong Kong team decided that the complete removal of the offices of managers, forcing them to sit among their staff, would be too much of an initial step for the high power distance Asian culture. Managers were allowed to keep their own private desk or office, but the name and function plates were removed, making the offices flexible to use when the manager was not present. Dutch managers, working in Hong Kong but often traveling and away from the office, could however not persuade employees to sit on their desk or in their office when they were not in the country.

Of course, cultural aspects are likely to not be the only reason for the New Way of Working to become successful in a certain country. Other conditions that may also positively influence the climate for the New Way of Working are the spread of (mobile) devices, (wireless) networks, and the demographics of the workforce. In the Netherlands, over 90 % of the households have one or more computers, and almost 80 % have a broadband Internet connection, ranking Holland in the top of the word. Also, the female participation in employment is at 68 %, among the highest in the world (Bijl 2011). This increases the need for flexible work and improving the work-life balance for both men and women, drivers for the New Way of Working.

2.6 Definition of the New Way of Working

The New Way of Working (NWOW) does not yet go by a single definition. Bødker and Christiansen (2002) of the Aarhus University' Center for New Ways of Working in Denmark characterize "new work" by a "mobile, networked technology, project-managed organization, and new office designs. The office designs are explicitly motivated by the wish to facilitate creativity, knowledge sharing and communication, carried out across a variety of settings: office, home, airports, coffee shops and cars." Like Microsoft, they also make the connection to the flexible office environment that is meant to inspire the employees. Bijl (2011) defines the New Way of Working as "a vision for making work more effective, efficient, pleasurable and valuable for both the organization and the individual. This is achieved by placing people center-stage and, within limits, giving them the space and freedom to determine how they work, where they work, when they work, what they work with and with whom they work. The New Way of Working aims to touch people's intrinsic motivation and entice them into giving their best in their work." Baane et al. (2010) argue that "The New Way of Working is an umbrella term, which organizations variably use to state their social innovation initiatives." They observe four work principles in the New Way of Working: (1) Time and location free work, "Anytime, anywhere"; (2) Steering workers toward achieving results, "Manage your own work"; (3) Free access to and use of knowledge, experiences, and ideas, "Unlimited access and connectivity"; (4) Flexible work relations: "My size fits me." The work principles mean to give maximal freedom to employees, based on mutual trust. This trust is expressed in the freedom that employees have for carrying out their work in ways and at times and locations that suit them best. Employees are evaluated based on their personal or team contribution, and on results, rather than their presence in the office. In this way, employees can engage in a working relationship that suits them best in terms of ambition, skills, lifestyle, or stage of life. In summary, the New Way of Working can best be defined as "a vision for the organization of work and the work environment in such a way that employees are enabled and motivated to work in an optimal way, that suits them best, in order to improve employee satisfaction and work-life balance. Key elements in this vision are the freedom and trust to be able to work anyplace and anywhere, a result oriented way of working, and offices with activity-based workplaces, that are designed to enhance interaction, engagement and creativity."

2.7 Bricks, Bytes, and Behavior

Baane et al. (2010) found the implementation of New Way of Working at organizations is characterized by the combination of the aspects on three dominant levers. They state: "The breaking down of traditional concepts of work is taking place on the basis of three dominant levers of business: Housing, ICT, and behavior, in other words: Bricks, Bytes, and Behavior." These three levers could been seen as the three dimensions that define the New Way of Working: (1) Bricks, the Physical dimension or the work environment; (2) Bytes, the Technological dimension or the use of information technology; and (3) Behavior, the Personal dimension or the organization of work and work relations. Though the third dimension also includes organizational aspects, e.g., management and control, the dimension is not called the organizational dimension to emphasize the pivotal role of the employee in the New Way of Working. In the following section, these three dimensions will be discussed in more detail.

2.7.1 Bricks, the Physical Dimension

This dimension contains the aspects that deal with the work environment and facilities. The new work environment focuses on flexible work and activity-related or activity-based workplaces. In practice, this means that the office is (re)designed in such a way that there are concentration places to support quiet and concentrated work and meeting places where workers can discuss issues. But there may also be brainstorm places, chat places, and relax places. In the Netherlands, the (re)design of offices and the work environment experiences a huge revival because of the New Way of Working. Organizations often directly relate the implementation of the New Way of Working to the opening of a new office building or the redesign of their existing office space. Without this simultaneous change of the office and work environment, the concepts of the New Way of Working are almost never implemented.

2.7.2 Bytes, the Technological Dimension

This dimension contains the aspects that deal with the use of information technology and sharing data: the hardware, software, information use, storage, and sharing of data and knowledge. The most important characteristics are the real-time availability of information and the access to all data via networks, or "the Cloud" at all places, preferably on multiple devices. The use of information technology enables the creation of a virtual work environment including virtual communication capabilities. Johns and Gratton (2013) describe this as the "third wave of virtual work": after the virtual freelancer and virtual corporate colleague, the virtual coworker arises, the untethered knowledge worker that can perform tasks anywhere at any time. They state that "presenteeism" has come to mean showing up at an office even when you could be more productive elsewhere. ICT systems should be intuitive and based on the activities and tasks that need to be performed "work-the-way-you-want," rather than force the user to work in a way the environment predicts. The use of work-related devices can enhance productivity. Laptops, tablets, and smartphones are better equipped for mobile work than desktop computers. The virtual environment also enables the use of personal hardware: consumerization or bring your own device (BYOD). Though many companies do not yet have a BYOD program in place, the reality is that employees already bring their personal devices to work (Gillett 2012; Citrix 2013). Forrester Research found that 52 % of the information workers use three or more devices for work. They predict that by 2016, there will be 760 million tablets in use, most for use both at work and at home (Gillett 2012). Though the security aspects of protecting business data fragmentation on a broad range of personal devices is a challenge, (ICT) managers increasingly realize this trend cannot be stopped and therefore needs to be managed. Because of the security aspects, a number of organizations have implemented a choose your own device (CYOD) policy, allowing employees to choose from a range of mobile devices with preinstalled security management software.

2.7.3 *Behavior, the Personal Dimension*

The third dimension contains the broad scope of aspects that deal with the organization, the manager- employee relation, and the human-work relation. Research from the Hay Group showed that highly engaged employees are on average 50 % more likely to exceed expectations than the least-engaged workers. Companies with highly engaged employees outperform firms with disengaged workers by 54 % in employee retention, 89 % in customer satisfaction, and fourfold in revenue growth (Goffee and Jones 2013). In the New Way of Working, the most important aspects in the personal dimension are trust and autonomy of the employee, delegation of responsibilities (empowerment), and result-based work agreements. Freedom and mutual trust form the basis for the new work relation, instead of hierarchy and managerial control. Activities may be performed in different work settings and communities inside and outside the organizational boundaries. These new work forms may also impact the conditions under which workers are employed and rewarded. As the worker has the freedom to choose when and where to work, the balance between work and personal life becomes an important aspect for the individual employee.

2.8 Inspiring Offices

With the changes in the way we work, the role of the workplace is changing too. One of the most visible effects of the implementation of the New Way of Working in organizations is the radical redesign of office space, or the creation of new office space that is breaking with all traditional rules and design concepts. The office, as we know it, has not kept up with the pace of the transitions of the tools we use every day. Offices therefore need to transform from dull "production facilities" to inspiring meeting places, in which no effort is spared to create a new sense and experience of "work." Creating inspiring offices also happens outside the realm of the New Way of Working. Companies like Google and Virgin use their office design as a way to inspire employees and increase creativity (Groves et al. 2010). Creating inspiring offices does not have to come at a great cost. While gaining on attractiveness and efficiency, the actual cost per employee may even go down. After their redesign, a pharmaceutical company saved $ 16.000 in capital cost per employee. The time lost on distractions was reduced from 19 to 7 min per employee per day (Laing et al. 2011). Table 2.2 shows similar numbers for US- and UK-based companies in the energy and financial sector (Gillen and Jeffery 2014).

In general, the use of office space is very inefficient; most desks are unoccupied for most of the day. Research shows that office utilization peaks at only 42 % on any given day (Laing 2013). This could imply that, using the logic of an industrial mindset, the best solution is to eliminate "wasted" office space by compressing activities into a flexible, smaller, office. Though flexibility does improve efficiency and reduce

Table 2.2 Characteristics of workspace before and after redesign

	Before	After
Workspace is an atractive aspect of the job	21%	58%
Workspace creates a stimulating atmosphere	18%	45%
Total square footage per employee	212	156
Furniture cost per employee	$ 9.100	$ 4.900
Capital cost per employee	$ 34.000	$ 18.000
Hours lost per employee per year to noise	32	22.8
Hours lost per employee per year to drop-by-visitors	34.4	22.8

cost, this is by no means the objective of creating inspiring offices. The real challenge is that office space will boost creativity, eliminating or transcending the need to reduce costs. The office of the future has inspirational, wireless networked, shared, multipurpose spaces that redefine organizational boundaries. It creates intentional or unintentional collisions and collaboration between people from different disciplines and backgrounds. The logic behind this is that when people collide and have encounters and unplanned interactions, performance improves and creativity and innovation are triggered. Spaces that are designed to promote such encounters increase the likelihood of collisions, and data show that more collisions create positive outcomes (Waber et al. 2014). In fact, money spent on improving personal productivity could better be used to design workspaces that promote collisions, which will make organizations – not individuals – more successful.

No matter how well technology supports working in a virtual world, physical face-to-face interactions have not lost their importance. The most valuable form of communication remains face to face, followed by phone. The least valuable forms of communication are e-mail and text. Research found that 35 % of the variation in a team's performance can be accounted for simply by the number of face-to-face exchanges among team members (Pentland 2012). Too much communication will however decrease performance, as it consumes too much of the "working time." Informal communication also remains important: the best predictors for the productivity of a team are the team's energy and engagement outside the formal meetings. Together, these two factors explain one third of the variations in group performance. The coffee machine is not a cost but a gain. Teams with denser, more frequent, and more diverse interaction patterns are more productive as a whole (Reagans and Zuckerman 2001).

Proximity boosts communication; we are four times as likely to communicate regularly with someone sitting six feet away from us, as with someone sixty feet away, and almost never communicate with colleagues on separate floors or in separate buildings (Allen 1977). Distance-shrinking information technologies have not bridged this gap. Colocated workers e-mail each other four times as frequently as colleagues in different locations, leading to 32 % faster project completion times (Waber et al. 2014).

In the past decade, digital-savvy workers, escaping from the office but also avoiding the isolation of working at home, found a solution for their need to interact:

coworking spaces. The initial organic growth of coworking locations, also called third-place offices, has by now become one of the new ways to encounter and engage. And with success, in a survey under 1500 coworkers, 75 % of them report an increase in productivity, and 80 % an increase of their business network (Foertsch and Dullroy 2012).

Even though work has become mobile and distributed, physical interactions and work environments remain vital. The question is how to optimize the range and variety of the work environment, so it may become an instrument for workers to encounter and engage. The answer seems to lie at hand: create inspiring coworking spaces and increase the chance of collisions. As coworking locations are open to anyone, organizational boundaries within offices are likely to fade. New offices will support cohabited workspaces: coworking locations not only for own personnel but also for workers from outside the organization. In the future, offices may become small cities, neighborhoods, where communities encounter and engage, and in which the probability of many different kinds of interactions (i.e., social, intellectual, commercial) is enhanced and facilitated.

2.9 Differences between the New Way of Working and Telework

The concepts behind the New Way of Working are not new as such. The ideas of mobile working, desk sharing, video conferencing, and paperless, open offices originate from the 1970s or before (Meel 2011). Though the ideas were there, Meel states that they were by no means common or widely adopted at that time. Some industries and companies were more progressive than others, but in general, office organizations were command-and-control structures, characterized by hierarchy and rigidity, with limited freedom for individual employees. He warns however that we should not to be too quick to denounce new ways of working as recycled old 1970s ideas.

Similar to the New Way of Working, Telework, or Telecommuting, also has several definitions. In 1993, Gray defines Teleworking as "working remotely for an employer, involving electronic processing of information, and using telecommunications to keep the remote employer and employee in contact with each other." Ten years later, Sullivan states "there is a growing consensus that, in general terms, Telework is remote work, that involves the use of information and communication technologies (ICTs)." Though Teleworking plays a role in the New Way of Working, the primary focus is on the fundamental change in the way the work is done. In the New Way of Working, remote working is not primarily meant for being able to work at home; it is used as one of the tools to maximize work flexibility and effectiveness. Coming to the office at 11 instead of 8 or 9 o'clock and doing your e-mail at home are more effective than losing unnecessary time in traffic congestions. However, you may also choose to bring the children to school in the morning, or go to the gym, and finish work later that evening. Employees that choose not to work remote are free to come to the office at the normal office hours. The New Way of Working can therefore exist without Teleworking.

Baruch (2000) defines Telework as (1) Location of the workplace, which means it is partially or fully independent from the location of the employer, contractor, client etc.; (2) Use of information technology (IT), mainly personal computers, e-mail, faxes, and telephones; and (3) Organizational form and communication link to the organization. The last one may consist of several modes – home based, mobile working, and Telework centers. The definition Baruch uses has similarities with the three dimensions of the New Way of Working: Bricks, Bytes, and Behavior. In the following section, these three dimensions will be used to highlight a number of differences between Telework and the New Way of Working.

1. Bricks, the Physical dimension: In Telework, the location of the workplace mostly refers to working either at home or at the office, or in some cases a third-place office. In the New Way of Working, the Physical dimension mostly refers to the rearrangement of the work environment, the drastic redesign of the office to activity-based workplaces with concentration and meeting places. When the work can best be performed at another location than the office, workers are free to do so, but remote working is not the standard option.
2. Bytes, the Technological dimension: In Telework, information technology is used to enable remote working. In the New Way of Working, information technology is used to create the freedom to work anywhere at any time, but what is more important is that information technology should enable knowledge sharing and enhance (virtual) communication and collaboration. The information systems should be intuitive and facilitate activity-based working, to support the worker optimally and improve productivity.
3. Behavior, the Personal dimension: In Telework, the Personal dimension often refers to the employee-manager arrangements for remote working. These may include agreements on flexibility, autonomy, and supervision and control. In the New Way of Working, the personal view is pivotal; the utilization and development of the human potential are center stage. The New Way of Working is not just about making work more efficient; it is about making work more enjoyable and improving the employee satisfaction and work-life balance. Freedom and trust are the key ingredients to reach these goals. In the vision of the New Way of Working, direct supervision and control belong to the past and are replaced by result agreements or result contracts.

A literature study on the topics and themes that are addressed in both New Way of Working, NWOW, and Telework literature resulted in a classification, or breakdown, of themes and topics under the three dimensions of the New Way of Working (de Kok and Helms 2012). See Table 2.3.

Figure 2.5 shows the (relative) number of references to these themes and topics in NWOW and Telework literature.

The figure shows that for "Bricks," there is clearly more focus in NWOW literature on workplace and office design. For "Bytes," NWOW literature more

Table 2.3 Dimensions with themes and topics

Bricks Physical dimension	Bytes Technological dimension	Behavior Personal dimension
Flexible workplace	Devices	Trust & autonomy
Office design	Information technology	Results & accountability
Workplace design	Virtual work environment	Productivity & performance
Costs & savings	Any time any place	Managerial control
Environmental effects	Knowledge sharing	Social relations
	Social media	Flexibility & freedom
		Work-life balance
		Satisfaction & development
		Culture & motivation

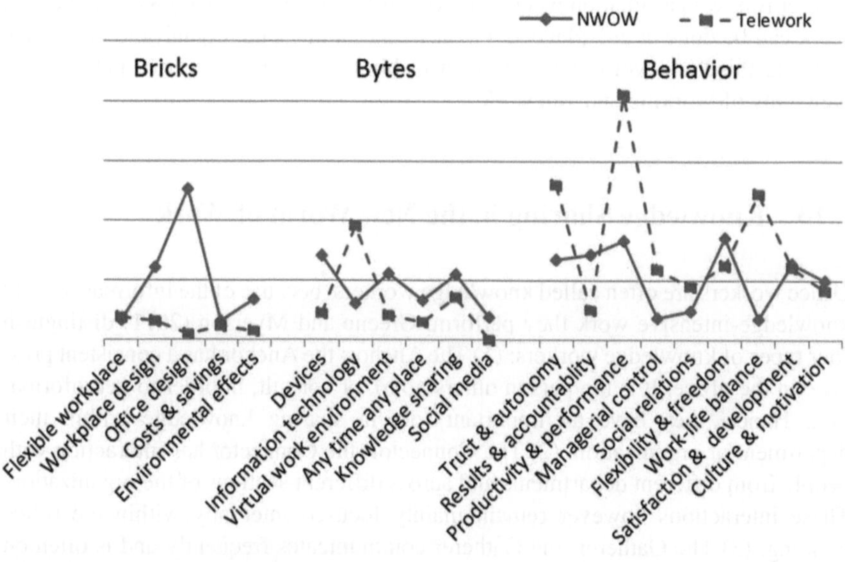

Fig. 2.5 References to themes and topics in NWOW and Telework literature

often mentions mobile devices and the virtual work environment, while Telework literature more often addresses information technology as an enabler in general.

For "Behavior," there is more attention in Telework literature for themes like trust and autonomy, productivity and performance, and work-life balance. These themes are also addressed in NWOW literature, but relatively less often. NWOW literature has more references than Telework literature to results and accountability.

In summary, there are overlaps in Teleworking and the New Way of Working, but the focus often differs. The most evident differences are the focus in the New Way of Working on the office (re)design and the breaking with hierarchical command-and-control structures and the focus in Telework literature on the performance and productivity of remote workers. Baane et al. (2010) found in their research that it is the combination of work principles of the New Way of Working that makes the difference. They concluded that the principles as such are not new, but organizations who consistently apply them in a combined way certainly go through a transformation process, even when Telework arrangements were already in place (de Kok et al. 2014).

Perhaps, the difference between Telework and the New Way of Working can best be explained in the following way: In Telework, the worker is confronted with two worlds: the "new world" outside the office, with a perceived form of freedom, and the "old world" inside the office. From a managerial point of view, the work has however not changed: working remote only changes the location where work is performed, not the supervision and control over the work. The New Way of Working brings the new world inside the office and replaces managerial control and supervision by trust and responsibility for results. As the work itself changes, the worker is now in a situation where the two worlds are almost seamlessly connected; work can be done at any place and at any time in the same organizational setting. Creating this "one-world concept" is probably the biggest difference between the New Way of Working and Telework.

2.10 Knowledge Sharing in the New World of Work

Office workers are often called knowledge workers, because of the information- and knowledge-intensive work they perform. Greene and Myerson (2011) distinguish four types of knowledge workers: (1) The Anchor: the Anchor has a consistent presence in the office. It is the person others go to, or consult, in order to get information. Hence, they have an important role in sharing knowledge within their department or organization. (2) The Connector: the Connector has interaction with people from different departments and across different sections of the organization. These interactions however remain mainly focused internally within the office building. (3) The Gatherer: the Gatherer communicates frequently and is often on the move. Often, the Gatherer communicates through mobile devices and works with wireless technologies. To the Gatherer, the office is a resource, a place where he or she can distill, process, and review information and have face-to-face contact with colleagues. (4) The Navigator: Navigators are rarely in the office at all. The Navigator works for the organization at arm's length, e.g., a contractor who is employed on a project basis, a nomad salesman who attends the office a few times a month, or a consultant who arrives for a meeting and temporarily needs access to a space to work on his or her laptop (Fig. 2.6).

An organization can be seen as a "system" of individuals with expertise. In psychology, such a system is called a Transactive Memory System (TMS); a TMS is a set of individual memory systems in combination with the communication that takes place between individuals (Wegner 1987). In a TMS, individuals are the "external memory" for other individuals who, in turn, encode "metamemories" (i.e., memories about the memories of others). In other words, a TMS refers to a

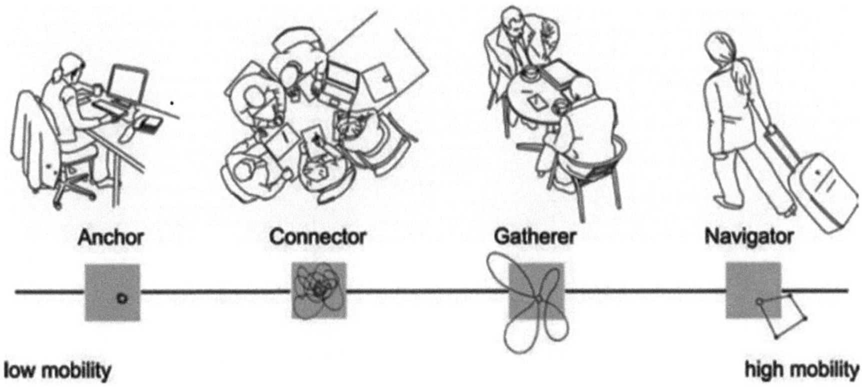

Fig. 2.6 Types of knowledge workers (Greene and Myerson 2011)

collective's shared knowledge of who knows what and the processes to retrieve, share, and apply. Studies have shown a positive relationship between group effectiveness and transactive memory (Brandon and Hollingshead 2004).

The question is whether and how the New Way of Working affects knowledge sharing in organizations.

Ipe (2003) distinguishes four major factors that can influence the level of knowledge sharing within an organization and between individuals:

1. Nature of knowledge: is tacit or explicit knowledge shared? Tacit knowledge is know-how acquired by personal experience that is hard to communicate; explicit knowledge is easy to store and communicate. Also, the value attributed to knowledge may influence its sharing. For example, when employees think their knowledge is an asset, that once shared makes it less valuable, the chance of knowledge sharing reduces.
2. Motivation to share: these are internal factors, e.g., willingness to share, power attached to knowledge (keep or share), and reciprocity (give and take); and external factors, e.g., the relationship with the recipient (familiarity, trust, power, and status) and the perceived rewards or penalties for sharing or not sharing knowledge.
3. Opportunity to share: this is the formal or informal communication setting. Formal communication settings are intentionally created opportunities to share knowledge. These may include training programs, IT possibilities, or structured work teams. Informal communication settings are unintentionally and unplanned opportunities to share knowledge, e.g., by personal relationships or social networks.
4. Culture of the work environment: the influence of the organizational culture of the unit or organization at large. Culture also influences all abovementioned factors (Fig. 2.7).

Van den Hooff argues that the nature of knowledge will not change by the New Way of Working; most knowledge is tacit, while explicit knowledge is a facilitating

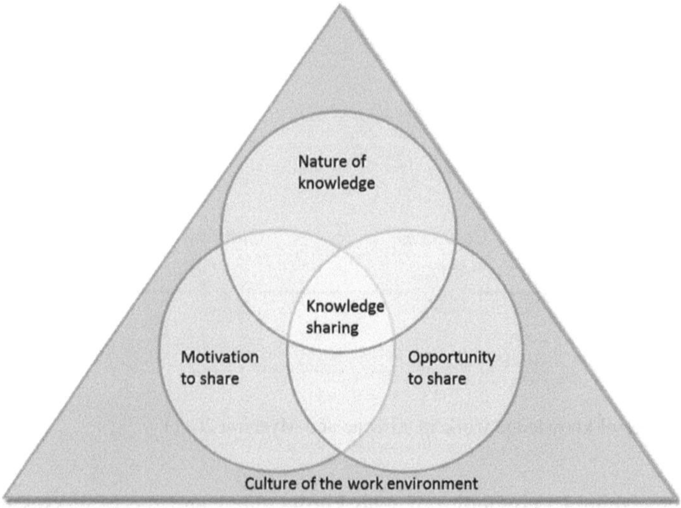

Fig. 2.7 Factors that influence knowledge sharing (Ipe 2003)

factor (Bellefroid 2012). It makes no difference whether this knowledge is transferred through the old, often more physical way, or the new, often more virtual way of working. He states the motivation to share knowledge will remain very personal. The new work setting may however demotivate some employees, having lost their own workplace, and the clarity on their work and the times they should work. Others may however become motivated due to the fact that they can work when and where they want. The opportunity to share will most likely be influenced by the New Way of Working. Because people meet less face to face, this is an important obstacle to overcome. Information technologies will play an important role in facilitating new opportunities to share. By making visible what employees are doing, and which employees are working when on a specific project, new opportunities to share knowledge can be created. This may even result in more opportunities to work together, with employees one did not know before, enabling also more diverse groups to be formed. Because of the New Way of Working, the culture of the work environment will, or should, become more informal and open. Boundaries fade away, and employees will more often have contact through social media. The culture of the work environment should however be ready for the New Way of Working, as old formalistic cultures probably will not adopt the New Way of Working at an early stage or easily.

Other factors that may influence knowledge sharing in the New Way of Working environment are vertical and horizontal interactions and the sensitivity of information. De Long and Fahey (2000) found that the impact of the culture can be assessed along three dimensions: (1) Vertical interaction with (senior) management, (2) Horizontal interaction with individuals at the same level in the organization, and (3) Special behavior for teaching and dealing with mistakes. Snyder and Lee-Partridge (2009) add: "Knowledge sharing may not only be influenced by the organizational levels, but also because knowledge is shared about general or sensi-

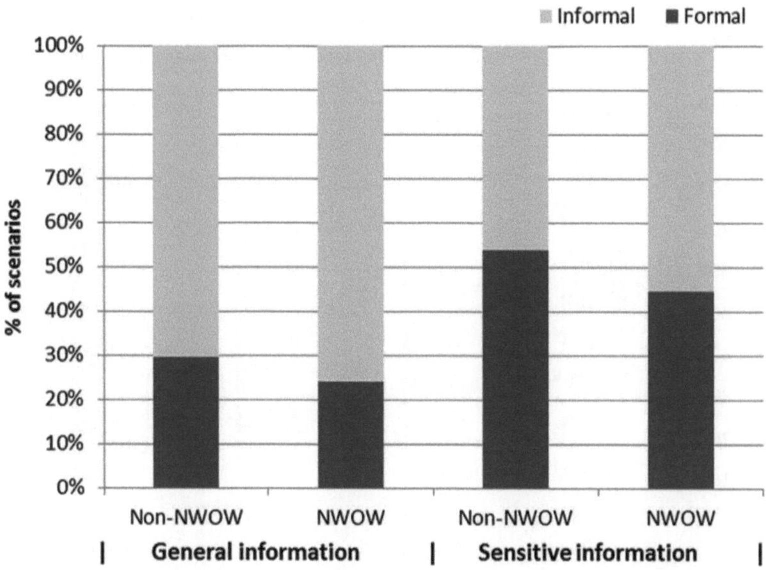

Fig. 2.8 Formal vs. informal communication in relation to sensitivity of information

tive information." They found that the level of sensitivity was of major influence on the channel choice for team knowledge sharing.

To determine differences in the sharing of knowledge by employees working in a traditional setting (non-NWOW workers) and employees working in an environment where the New Way of Working is implemented (NWOW workers), research was done in organizations that were in the process of implementing the New Way of Working (de Kok et al. 2013). As these organizations were in the process of implementing the New Way of Working, they had departments that had gone through the transition to the New Way of Working, as well as departments that still worked in the traditional way, making it possible to explore differences in knowledge sharing within the same organization. A number of scenarios were created to investigate how knowledge was shared in both environments. The scenarios included aspects such as the familiarity with the superior or coworker, the organizational level, the sensitivity of information, the formal or informal communication setting, the channel choice, and the reason for the channel choice.

Data shows the familiarity with the supervisor or coworker, and the organizational levels, does not really change the way knowledge is shared in the NWOW environment, compared to the traditional environment. NWOW workers do however prefer to communicate in a less formal way than workers in the traditional setting, though the difference is not significant.

Figure 2.8 shows that both groups will share knowledge in a more formal way when it comes to sharing knowledge on sensitive information. To a limited extent, NWOW workers do this in a less formal, i.e., intentionally planned, way.

Looking at the channel choice, overall, NWOW workers use a broader palette of communication channels for sharing knowledge than "traditional" workers.

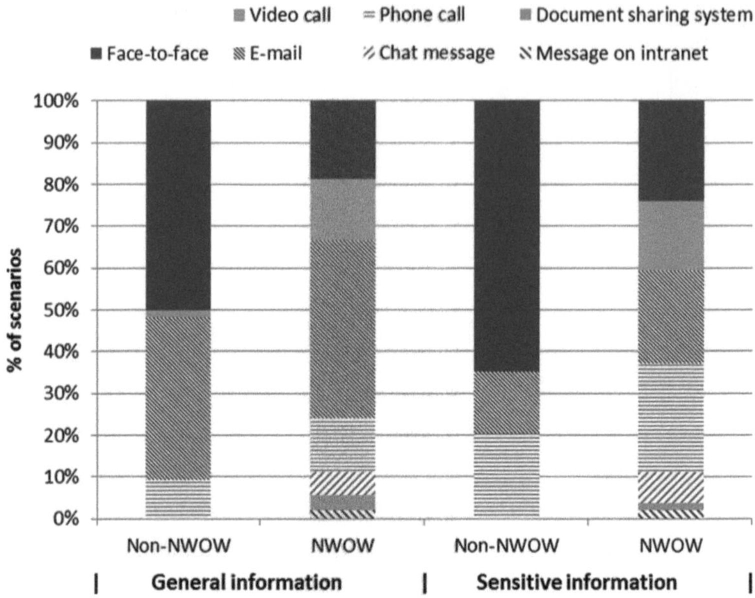

Fig. 2.9 Channel choice of traditional and NWOW workers

Face-to-face communication seems to be partly replaced by video calls, chat messages, and other means of communication.

When it comes to sharing knowledge on sensitive information, Fig. 2.9 shows that traditional workers have a strong preference for face-to-face meetings. Interestingly, the NWOW workers use much less face-to-face communication, even when sharing knowledge on sensitive information. They use video calls, e-mails, and chat messages instead, and note that video calls can also be used in a personal way.

The results show that traditional ways of sharing knowledge change when the New Way of Working is implemented. Organizations that want to implement the New Way of Working therefore need to realize that a new infrastructure is needed to facilitate and manage the changing preferences in sharing knowledge in the new world of work.

2.11 Effects of Schedule and Location Flexibility

With the changing nature of work, work flexibility becomes more important. Employees who are confronted with the new world of work expect they will be enabled to bring more flexibility in the way they work. In a multiyear global study under their workforce, PricewaterhouseCoopers found that 64 % of the "millennials", employees born between 1980 and 1995, would like their job to be more flexible and work occasionally from home; 66 % of them would like to be able to shift their work hours (PWC 2013).

Work flexibility can be divided into two aspects: schedule flexibility and location flexibility. Schedule flexibility is the ability to rearrange one's work hours within certain guidelines offered by the organization. Location flexibility is giving the employee varying degrees of control over where their work can be done (Hill et al. 2001). One could argue, the New Way of Working is about the freedom to work when and where, while Telework, in its essence, is only about the flexibility of work location: either at home or at the office. Though Telework offers some opportunities to shift tasks during the day, the freedom to postpone work and reschedule at the last minute is much bigger in the New Way of Working setting.

Research shows that the freedom when to work (schedule flexibility) and the freedom where to work (location flexibility) have different effects on aspects such as work-life balance and job satisfaction (Possenriede 2014). Though the two seem to be very interrelated, the actual effects differ.

Schedule flexibility is positively associated with both work-life balance and job satisfaction. Employees with more control over their work are better able to match paid work with other activities. Data show the effects are the same for men and women and employees with or without children at home. Schedule flexibility has a positive effect on work-life balance as well as job satisfaction for all employees, not only those with family responsibilities.

Location flexibility, Teleworking, is also associated with higher job satisfaction, though to a smaller extent than schedule flexibility. Also, the relation is more positive for men than women. Surprisingly, location flexibility does not have a positive relation on the improvement of work-life balance. Working one day at home, away from the office, does not seem to support the ability to combine work with private life significantly.

Table 2.4 gives an overview of the effects of schedule and location flexibility.

Schedule flexibility, being at the office at irregular times, appears to have no negative (nor positive) effect on career development. Frequent Teleworking, however, does have a negative effect on one's career. The probability of a promotion or employer-paid training is significantly reduced for (male) workers who work at home more than once a week. Apparently, employees who display less face-time in the office than expected, are perceived to be less dependable and committed to their

Table 2.4 Effects of schedule and location flexibility

	Schedule flexibility	Location flexibility
Work-life balance	++	o
Job satisfaction	++	++
Career development	o	–
Absenteeism	––	–
Working hours	o	o

Note: +, – and o indicate a positive, negative, or no significant association between the flexibility and the outcome variable. ++ and –– indicate a strong and highly significant association work. Occasional Teleworking does however not negatively affect career development.

Schedule flexibility, the ability to adjust working hours, reduces both the frequency and – in particular – the duration of absences. Employees with flexible work arrangements experience less stress and call in sick less quickly, less often, and are sick for less longer. Location flexibility also has a negative effect on the frequency of absences, but not on the duration. Dealing with unexpected situations or minor health problems seems to improve, but not the employee's overall health. Overall health and the feeling of well-being are often related to the perception of work-related stress. The stress of a job does not depend on the nature of the job; it depends on whether employees believe that they have the ability to control the stressful aspects of the job. Halpern (2005) found that time-flexible policies, offered by the employer, directly affect work-related stress and commitment to the employer.

Finally, on the number of working hours, in general, there does not seem to be a significant change in the number of working hours flexible workers invest in their work. One may argue that employees tend to put in more hours to compensate for their "absence" in the office, but often the extra working hours away from the office are overtime hours that would otherwise have also been spent at the office. Overall, both schedule and location flexibility seem to benefit both the employee and employer (Hill et al. 2001). Employees may not be so much more "productive" in the sense of working hours in the short run per day or week, but the overall ability to perform their tasks increases in the long run, because of their better health, fewer absences, and increased commitment.

2.12 Expectations and Obstacles

Organizations may implement the New Way of Working for various reasons. Research of Erasmus University found organizations often do not have one, but a number of aspects they want to address when implementing the New Way of Working (Meulen 2014). The five most mentioned aspects by organizations are: (1) Enabling flexible (home) work, (2) Creating a paperless office with digital document management, (3) Creating an open, flexible, office environment, (4) Activity-based working, and (5) Stimulating improved knowledge sharing. Figure 2.9 shows the top 10 aspects companies expected to realize and the percentage of aspects that were actually realized, after implementing the New Ways of Working.

Figure 2.10 shows that the expected aspects were often realized once the New Way of Working was implemented, though improving knowledge managements is lagging. Data also show there are relationships: aspects, e.g., flexible work was realized in combination with the new IT environment (68 %) and the flexible office was realized in combination with flexible (home) work (93 %).

The top 5 expectations on the expected effects of the implementation of the New Way of Working are (1) Increased employee satisfaction, (2) Improved work-life

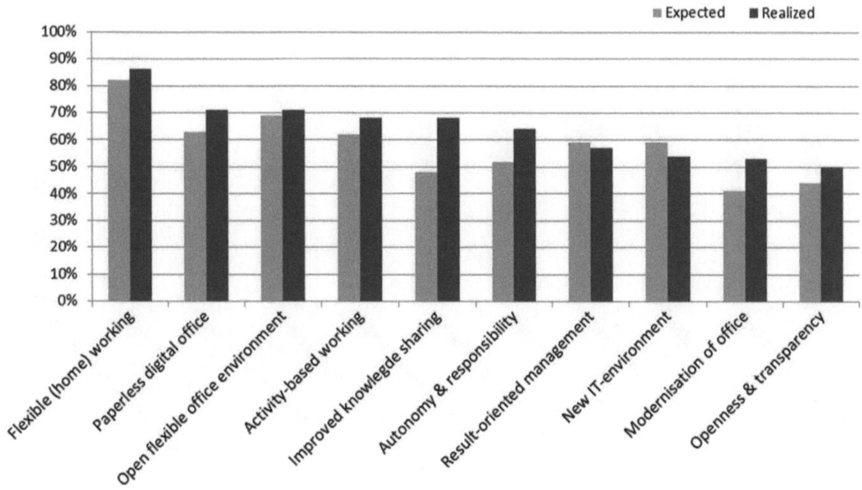

Fig. 2.10 Aspects when implementing the New Way of Working

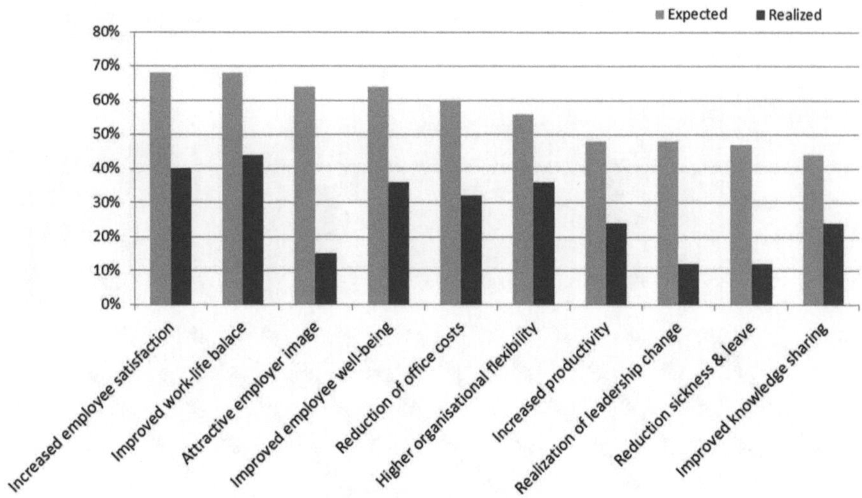

Fig. 2.11 Expected effects from the New Way of Working

balance, (3) A more attractive employer image, (4) Improved employee well-being, and (5) Reduction of office costs.

Figure 2.11 shows most expectations are realized in only a number of organizations. Most organizations only realize ¼ of the expected effects. On the positive side, over 40 % of the organizations that implemented the New Way of Working report an increased employee satisfaction and work-life balance.

The top 5 obstacles against the New Way of Working are (1) Fear of losing one's own workplace, (2) Non-fit with the management style, (3) Non-fit with the

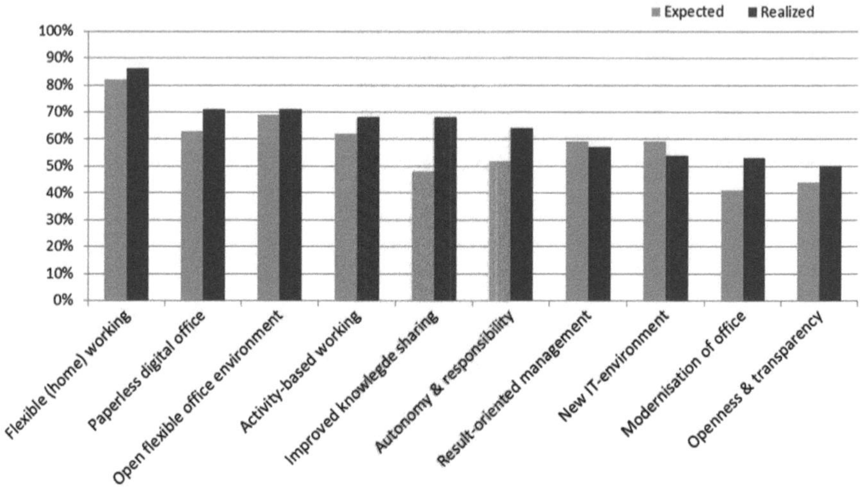

Fig. 2.10 Aspects when implementing the New Way of Working

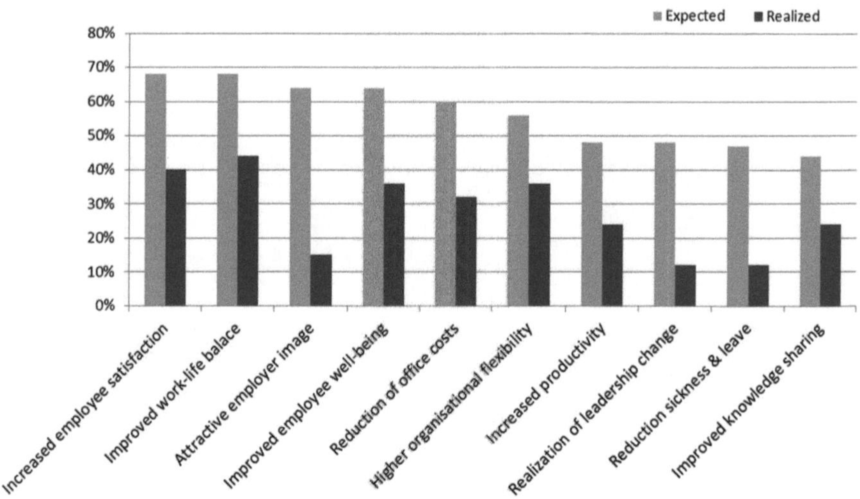

Fig. 2.11 Expected effects from the New Way of Working

balance, (3) A more attractive employer image, (4) Improved employee well-being, and (5) Reduction of office costs.

Figure 2.11 shows most expectations are realized in only a number of organizations. Most organizations only realize ¼ of the expected effects. On the positive side, over 40 % of the organizations that implemented the New Way of Working report an increased employee satisfaction and work-life balance.

The top 5 obstacles against the New Way of Working are (1) Fear of losing one's own workplace, (2) Non-fit with the management style, (3) Non-fit with the

Neufeld (1999) did note, however, that managers and coworkers felt uncomfortable phoning remote workers at home. Probably, with the present use of social media (e.g., WhatsApp Messenger), also in professional settings, boundaries in this area have been broken.

Erasmus' research shows that an increase of productivity is realized in only half of the companies that actually expected them (Meulen 2014). Apart from being more or less productive, one of the possible downsides of the New Way of Working is not knowing when to stop working. When workers put in more hours of work, they may become more productive, but their efficiency is not going up. Being always connected and constantly having the opportunity to perform small or bigger tasks put a strain on the employee's discipline to draw the line between working and not working.

Being able to work in a result-oriented way and carrying out tasks autonomously, instead of being managed in an autocratic and controlling way, bring great freedom to the worker. In 1966, Herzberg already defined job autonomy as one on the most important motivators. Research under almost 800 employees shows that after the implementation of the New Way of Working, 74 % of the employees experience more job autonomy, higher levels of job satisfaction (56 %), decreased level of stress (39 %), and a more quiet and peaceful family life (38 %) (Koenen et al. 2010). Although most employees enjoy this freedom, not all benefit from it. Slijkhuis (2012) found that there are employees who have difficulties coping effectively with the uncertainty and ambiguity of the newly gained freedom. These individuals with a "high personal need for structure" (high PNS) flourish in well-organized jobs in a hierarchical organization, whereas "low-PNS" individuals would pine away in these jobs. The uncertainty of what is expected from them has a counterproductive effect on their work and motivation. This puts an extra load on the manager, who not only needs to be the "coach" for most of his "independent" employees but also needs to recognize those individuals in need of more structure and guidance in the new work environment.

Not being interrupted, being able to work in a concentrated way may still be one of the main reasons for employees to work remote. In 1999, Perlow suggests the establishment of "quiet times" in the office to reduce interruptions and improve productivity (Perlow 1999). This could provide the benefits of remote working without experiencing the disadvantages of it. Though Perlow realized that quiet times in an office would probably be hard to keep, the new office design, in line with the concepts of the New Way of Working, includes quiet concentration places for those who wish to have an "uninterrupted time of productivity."

The number one objection employees have against the implementation of the New Way of Working, and the introduction of activity-based workplaces, is the fear of losing their own desk and working space. Employees are often of the opinion that their work requires a concentration workplace and that the "new office" does not facilitate this to a satisfying extent. The question is whether this argument is 100 % legitimate.

Research by the Danish Center for New Ways of Working has shown there is often a difference in the way people perceive their work and the reality of the work they actually do (Bjerrum and Aaløkke 2005). The reason for this misperception may lie in the "industrial mind-set" of employees and managers: one has to produce visible results; hence individual and concentrated work is essential. In that mind-set informal meetings, telephone calls, and other "disturbances" are not seen as "real" work and tend to be "forgotten" or eliminated from the perceived work activities. In their research, Bjerrum and Aaløkke (2005) found that there can be major differences between the perception and the actual observation of work. In an IT company, where workers claimed to be working concentrated on their workplaces all day, the actual presence in workplaces, over an observed period of 14 days, was only 45 %. Almost the same figure appeared in an Australian desk utilization study: the perceived time spent at desks was 81 % and in reality was only 40 % (Laing and Wittenoom 2013). This misperception of work may also cause complaints to the management, e.g., "I cannot work in this environment," and even impact the work satisfaction outside the office: at home or in a third workplace. When the employee works outside the office, in order to avoid interruptions, all perceived "not-real-work" activities may cause irritation and lead to stress for the worker and his or her environment and/or family. This may again result in a lower satisfaction of the employee and a worse work-life balance, while a large part of the dissatisfaction is caused by a misperception of work activities, because of an imprinted industrial mind-set. Awareness at the management and workers for the effects of the industrial mind-set and misperception of work, and proper action to change this mind-set, may lead to greater work satisfaction and success in implementing the New Way of Working. Possibly, the opposition against new working methods is not only fed by a misperception of work, or an industrial mind-set, but simply by the tendency of people to resist change.

2.14 Concluding Remarks

In the past decades, information technology has changed our lives and the way we work, and it will continue to do so in the decades to come. New generations will be entering the work arena: generations who grew up with tablets and smartphones, games, and social media. For them, working "differently" is not new but normal and logical. The New Way of Working offers opportunities to those who want to combine work with family life in a more natural flow. Reducing stress, living healthier, and enjoying life and work will become key elements in a world where working becomes fully integrated with everyday life and retirement shifts to the age of seventy plus. Organizations, and even societies, will need to realize that the nature of work has changed and will continue to change, requiring new approaches to issues like: What is free time? And how do you count the number of days off? Or how many vacation days am I entitled to? Microsoft calls their implementation of the New Way of Working a journey they embarked on: a start without a clear endpoint.

Relativism is at its place: the New Way of Working is an exciting new phenomenon, but it is not a cure for all organizational illnesses. It is a vision, and a concept, that helps organizations on their journey toward a new future of work. Though

Baane et al. (2010) are convinced of the importance to embrace the New Way of Working, their research also shows that "old way of working" can, to some extent, still be functional. They conclude the key to success is in finding the right mix between the "old world" and the "new world" in which, depending on the situation, the consideration has to be made which work principles best fit the gradually ever-changing organization of work in an ever-changing world. Probably, the New Way of Working is just a small first step toward the new future of work, but it is definitely a journey that is worth embarking on.

References

Allen TJ (1977) Managing the flow of technology: technology transfer and the dissemination of technological information within the R&D organization. MIT Press, Cambridge. ISBN 0262010488

Baane R, Houtkamp P, Knotter M (2010) The new way of working unraveled: about bricks, bytes & behavior – Het nieuwe werken ontrafeld: over bricks, bytes & behavior. Koninklijke Van Gorcum BV, Assen, the Netherlands, pp 1–168, ISBN 9789023245858

Baruch Y (2000) Teleworking: benefits and pitfalls as perceived by professionals and managers. N Technol Work Employ 15(1):34–49

Bellefroid B (2012) The new way of knowledge sharing: the effects of NWOW on knowledge sharing. Center for Organization and Information, Utrecht University, Utrecht, the Netherlands

Bijl DW (2011) Journey towards the New Way of Working – creating sustainable performance and joy at work. Par CC, Zeewolde, the Netherlands, ISBN 978-94-90528-00-3

Bjerrum E, Aaløkke S (2005) Working together: work space, organization and conception of work. The International Telework Conference 2005. Alexandra Institute. Center for New Ways of Working. Aarhus University, Denmark, pp 1–13

Bødker S, Christiansen E (2002) Lost and found in flexibility. Center for New Ways of Working. University of Aarhus, Aarhus, Denmark.

Brandon DP, Hollingshead AB (2004) Transactive memory systems in organizations: matching tasks, expertise, and people. Organ Sci 15(6):633–644. doi:10.1287/orsc.1040.0069

Bryan LL, Joyce CI (2007) Mobilizing minds: creating wealth from talent in the 21st-century organization. McGraw-Hill Education, Hoboken

Child J, McGrath RG (2001) Organizations unfettered: organizational form in an information-intensive economy. Acad Manag J 44(6):1135–1148

Citrix (2013) Best practices to make BYOD simple and secure. Citrix Systems

de Kok A, Helms RW (2012) The New Way of Working versus telework: definition and positioning. Research paper on 148 literature sources. Center for Organization and Information, Utrecht University, Utrecht, the Netherlands

de Kok A, Bellefroid B, Helms RW (2013) Knowledge sharing and channel choice: effects of the New Way of Working. In: Proceedings of the 14th European conference on knowledge management, ECKM 2013

de Kok A, Koops J, Helms RW (2014) Assessing the New Way of Working: bricks, bytes and behavior. In: Proceedings of the 18th Pacific Asia conference on information systems, PACIS 2014.

De Long DW, Fahey L (2000) Diagnosing cultural barriers to knowledge management. Acad Manag Exec 14(4):113–127

de Pous V, van der Wielen JMM (2010) Visions from the practice on The Way of Working – Praktijkvisies op Het Nieuwe Werken. Telewerkforum. Ten Brink, ISBN 978-90-79272-16-7.

Duxbury LE, Neufeld D (1999) An empirical evaluation of the impacts of telecommuting on intra-organizational communication. J Eng Technol Manag 16:1–28

Foertsch C, Dullroy J (2012) 2nd annual global coworking survey. Deskmag, Berlin, Germany

Forrester, Forrester Research (2014) In AppSense whitepaper: *what you should know before you start with virtualization* – Wat u moet weten voor u aan virtualisatie begint. Forrsights Workforce Employee Survey Q3 2012, Q3, 2013. (n=5519, 9766)

Friedman TL (2005) The world is flat – a brief history of the twenty-first century. Farrar, Straus and Giroux, New York. ISBN 0-374-29288-1

Gajendran RS, Harrison DA (2007) The good, the bad, and the unknown about telecommuting: meta-analysis of psychological mediators and individual consequences. J Appl Psychol 92(6):1524–1541

Gates B (2005) The New World of Work. Microsoft Executive Briefing

Ghoshal S, Bartlett CA (1997) The individualized corporation. A fundamentally new approach to management. Harper Collins, New York. ISBN 0-88730-806-6

Gillen N, Jeffery H (2014) The pursuit of happiness: how does the workplace influence productivity? See Further, The next generation occupier issue, Issue 01, Aecom

Gillen N, Jeffery H, Shani S (2013) Productivity: a homemade recipe? Aecom

Gillett FE (2012) Tablets will rule the future personal computing landscape. Forrester Research

Goffee R, Jones G (2013) Creating the best workplace on earth: what employees really require to be most productive. Harv Bus Rev Vol. 91:98–106

Gray M, Hodson N, Gordon G (1993) Teleworking explained. Wiley, Chichester

Greene C, Myerson J (2011) Space for thought: designing for knowledge workers. Facilities 29(1/2):19–30

Groves K, Knicht W, Denison E (2010) I wish I worked there! A look inside the most creative spaces in business. Wiley, Hoboken, New Jersey, USA. ISBN 978-0-470-71383-9

Hackman JR, Oldham GR (1976) Motivation through the design of work: test of a theory. Organ Behav Hum Perform 16:250–279. doi:10.1016/0030-5073(76)90016-7

Halpern DF (2005) How time-flexible work policies can reduce stress, improve health, and save money. Stress Health 21(3):157–168. doi:10.1002/smi.1049

Hammer M, Champy JA (1993) Reengineering the corporation: a manifesto for business revolution. Ch. 4 & 5. HarperCollins Publishers Inc., New York, USA, ISBN 0-06-662112-7

Herzberg F (1966) Work and nature of man. World, Cleveland, USA

Hill EJ, Hawkins AJ, Ferris M, Weitzman M (2001) Finding an extra day a week: the positive influence of perceived job flexibility on work and family life balance. National Council on Family Relations 50(1):49–58. Jstor

Hofstede G, Hofstede GJ, Minkov M (2010) Cultures and organizations – Software of the mind. McGraw-Hill, Cambridge, MA. ISBN 978-0-07-166418-9

Ipe M (2003) Knowledge sharing in organizations: a conceptual framework. Hum Resour Dev Rev 2(4):337–359

Johns T, Gratton L (2013) The third wave of virtual work. Harv Bus Rev, January-February 2013, pp. 66–73

Kluwer (2011) National Investigation on the New Way of Working – Nationaal Onderzoek Over Het Nieuwe Werken. Kluwer Publishing, pp 1–81

Koenen B, Vieira V, Verhue D (2010) The Netherlands ready for the New Way of Working – Nederland klaar voor het nieuwe werken: Onderzoek in het kader van de week van het nieuwe werken. TNS NIPO Publication No. 5475

Konradt U, Hertel G, Schmook R (2003) Quality of management by objectives, task-related stressors, and non-task related stressors as predictors of stress and job satisfaction among teleworkers. Eur J Work Organ Psychol 12:61–79

Laing A (2013) Work and workplaces in the digital city. Center for Urban Real Estate. Columbia University, USA

Laing A, Wittenoom S (2013) The emerging city workscape: propositions for Sydney. Strategy+Aecom

Laing A, Craig D, White A (2011) Vision statement: high-performance office space. Harv Bus Rev Vol. 89:32–33
Microsoft (2005) Digital workstyle: the new world of work. A Microsoft White Paper
MicrosoftNL (2005) Digitale werkstijl: het nieuwe werken. Een Microsoft white paper
Mintzberg H (1978) The structuring of organizations – a synthesis of research. Pearson Education. ISBN-13: 978-0138552701
Pentland A (2012) The new science of building great teams. Harv Bus Rev Vol.90 (4) Apr, 2012:60–70
Perlow L (1999) The time famine: toward a sociology of work time. Adm Sci Q 44(1):57–81
Possenriede DS (2014) The economics of temporal and locational flexibility of work. Utrecht University. Utrecht.the Netherlands, Ridderprint, ISBN 978-94-91870-07-1
PWC, PricewaterhouseCoopers (2011) A macro-economic survey for the effects of The New Way of Working, Een verkennning van macro-economische effecten van Het Nieuwe Werken. PricewaterhouseCoopers Accountants N.V.
PWC, PriceWaterhouseCoopers (2013) PwC's NextGen: a global generational study. PriceWaterhouseCoopers, the University of Southern California and the London Business School
Pyöriä P (2011) Managing telework: risks, fears and rules. Manag Res Rev 34(4):386–399
Reagans R, Zuckerman EW (2001) Networks, diversity, and productivity: the social capital of corporate R&D teams. Organ Sci 12(4):502–517
Ruiz Y, Walling A (2005) Home-based working using communication technologies. Labour Market Trends 113(10):417–426
Slijkhuis M (2012) A structured approach to need for structure at work. Groningen University, Ridderprint BV, ISBN 978-90-367-5387-6
Snyder JL, Lee-Partridge J (2009) Understanding choice of information and communication channels in knowledge sharing. In Proceedings of the international conference on information systems. Phoenix, pp 1–9
Sullivan C (2003) What's in a name? Definitions and conceptualisations of teleworking and homeworking. N Technol Work Employ 18(3):158–165. Blackwell Synergy
Tapscott D (1998) Growing up digital: the rise of the net generation. McGraw-Hill Education, New York, USA
Taylor F (1911) The principles of scientific management. Harper & Brothers, New York/London
van der Meulen N (2014) Status of the New Way of Working: Results of the National NWOW Barometer 2013 – De staat van Het Nieuwe Werken: Resultaten van de Nationale HNW Barometer 2013. Rotterdam School of Management, Erasmus University, Rotterdam, the Netehrlands
van Heck E, van Baalen P, van der Meulen N, van Oosterhout M (2011) Sustainable work innovation – measuring the impact of the New Way of Working at Microsoft Netherlands. Rotterdam School of Management. Erasmus University, Rotterdam, the Netherlands
van Lonkhuyzen P (2009) Microsoft looks boundaries of 'new work'- Microsoft zoekt grenzen 'nieuw werken' – Rinsema wil méér. MT Management. November 2009
van Meel J (2011) The origins of new ways of working: office concepts in the 1970s. Facilities. Emerald Group Publishing Limited
Veen W, Jacobs F (2004) Learning from the youth – Leren van jongeren: Een literatuuronderzoek naar nieuwe geletterdheid. Stichting Surf, Utrecht, the Netherlands
Veldhoen E (1995) Offices don't exist anymore – Kantoren bestaan niet meer. 010 Publishers, the Netherlands, ISBN 90-6450-272-2
Waber B, Magnolfi J, Lindsay G (2014) Workspaces that move people. Harv Bus Rev Vol.92 (10):68–77
Wegner DM (1987) Transactive memory: a contemporary analysis of the group mind. In: Mullen B, Goethals GR (eds) Theories of group behavior. Springer-Verlag, New York, pp 185–208

Arjan de Kok is PhD researcher at the Center for Organization and Information of Utrecht University in the Netherlands. Before becoming a PhD graduate, he obtained his Master of Business Administration degree from the University of Liverpool. He co-authored two books on Product Life Cycle Management and (guest) lectures at Utrecht University. He has over 20 years of experience in business consulting, and is Partner Industry Consulting at Ordina.

Chapter 3
Telecommuting: What? Why? When? and How?

Jessica M. Nicklin, Christopher P. Cerasoli, and Katie L. Dydyn

Abstract Given changing work demands, organizations are increasingly reliant on the use of telecommuting. The overarching goal of this chapter is to provide organizations with evidence-based actionable tools for effective telecommuting arrangements. Although telecommuting has grown over the past several decades, scholars and practitioners have not yet developed a comprehensive understanding of *what* telecommuting is, *why* it should (and should not) be used, *when* it is appropriate, and *how* it can be successfully implemented. Therefore, the purpose of this chapter is to review (1) the concept of telecommuting and its various forms (*what?*), (2) the consequences of telecommuting, both positive and negative for employees and organizations (*why?*), (3) antecedents of effective telecommuting (*when?*), and (4) recommendations for best practices (*how?*). We conclude the chapter with considerations for the future of telecommuting.

Keywords Telecommuting • Telework • Teleworking • ICT • Best practices • Autonomy • Work-life balance • Work-family balance

The CEO of Yahoo! Marissa Mayer created an uproar in 2013 when she banned home-based work, forcing all employees to return to the office. Mayer suggested that people are "…more collaborative and innovate when they're together [and that] the best ideas come from pulling two different ideas together" (c.f., Tkaczyk 2013). Mayer's move was counter to prevailing trends, given the increase in the number of companies offering telecommuting (SHRM 2013). Telecommuting has been accepted by many organizations because it has directly lead to increased productivity among employees (e.g., Kurland and Bailey 1999). It can also reduce employer costs, promote flexibility and autonomy, and improve work–life balance.

J.M. Nicklin (✉) • K.L. Dydyn
University of Hartford, West Hartford, CT, USA
e-mail: nicklin@hartford.edu; dydyn@hartford.edu

C.P. Cerasoli
The Group for Organizational Effectiveness, Inc. (gOE), Albany, NY, USA
e-mail: chris.cerasoli@groupoe.com

J. Lee (ed.), *The Impact of ICT on Work*, DOI 10.1007/978-981-287-612-6_3

Yet, some organizations remain hesitant to embrace telecommuting. In some cases, this may be due to lingering concerns surrounding accountability, isolation, collaboration, and control. We suggest a lack of understanding is the main reason some organizations approach telecommuting with trepidation. There are many different types of telecommuting arrangements, and not all approaches are appropriate for all circumstances. Therefore, given the prevalence of information and communication technology (ICT) use around the globe, it is important to explore *what* telecommuting is, *why* it is effective (and sometimes ineffective), and *when* it is most appropriate. The purpose of this chapter is therefore to explore telework and provide actionable recommendations (*how?*) for managers and employees who wish to implement telecommuting as a viable workplace arrangement.

3.1 *What* Is Telecommuting?

3.1.1 Introduction

Telework[1] has been broadly characterized as an arrangement in which employees perform at least part of their responsibilities outside the confines of their organization's physical boundaries using various forms of ICTs to maintain a virtual presence (e.g., Fay and Kline 2012). In some form, telecommuting has been around for well over a century. However, it wasn't until the height of the oil embargo in the 1970s that Jack Nilles coined the term *telecommuting* (Nilles 1975). In the ensuing years, telecommuting has become increasingly commonplace in organizations, and this is due in large part to the rapid evolution of ICTs that facilitate remote collaboration (e.g., personal computers, Internet, mobile phones, fax, videoconferencing), permitting employees to fulfill their work-related obligations from just about anywhere.

The percent of individuals who telework is substantial. In 2010, 20 % of American employees reported working remotely for an entire day at least once a month (World at Work 2011). A survey conducted by Robert Half Singapore (2012) reported that 79 % of companies across 13 countries provide telecommuting opportunities in order to improve recruitment and retention (Koh et al. 2013). A recent Reuters poll (Reaney 2012) indicated that approximately one in five workers telecommute, with the highest prevalence in the Middle East, Latin America, and Asia. While telecommuting has clearly been embraced in some countries, international adoption of telework policies is not uniform. European countries such as Sweden, France, Germany, Greece, Italy, Portugal, and Spain report using telework options far less (e.g., Peters and den Dulk 2003; Reaney 2012) than their international partners. The acceptance and prevalence of telecommuting may vary in part due to a number of unsubstantiated assumptions and fears concerning telecommuting adoption, as well as the

[1] Given their use in the literature, we use the terms *telecommuting* and *telework* interchangeably.

plethora of definitions, frameworks, and theoretical approaches used to conceptualize telecommuting. Therefore, we begin by discussing: *what is telecommuting?*

3.1.2 *Defining Telecommuting*

In the broadest sense, *telecommuting*, also known as *telework*, can be defined as working from anywhere at any time (Kurland and Bailey 1999), or completing work beyond the confines of a traditional office setting (e.g., Coenen and Kok 2014). Unfortunately, however, it is not that simple—there is no universally accepted definition of telework, and there are many inconsistencies in the literature concerning what qualifies as telework. Given that the concept of telework has evolved tremendously in recent years and modern telework relies heavily on ICTs, it is necessary to update the definition to match current and future trends and technology. Therefore, in this section, we first discuss some of the conflicts in the literature with regard to telecommuting terminology, criteria, and arrangements. Then, in consideration of these conflicts, we offer an updated and comprehensive definition of telework.

3.1.2.1 Terminology

Over the years, telework has been referred to as telecommuting, teleworking, remote work, virtual work, home-work, distance work, distributed work, and flexible work (e.g., Lautsch et al. 2009; Morganson et al. 2010). Multiple terms can misrepresent the nature of telework. For instance, telework typically involves an absence from the traditional office for some days during the week, whereas "virtual workers" are primarily away from the traditional office full time (e.g., Golden and Fromen 2011). Similarly, it should not be assumed that telework is always "flexible work." While working from a location outside of the central office may permit some flexibility to employees, telework arrangements can vary in terms of structure and flexibility. As a final example, "home-work" is often used synonymously with telework. While a majority of teleworkers do indeed work from home, it should not be assumed.

Despite some arguable differences among terms, they share in common more than they diverge upon. Namely, they all refer to work that (1) occurs outside the traditional workplace and (2) uses ICT equipment to maintain some level of presence. Given this, we use the terms *telework*, *telecommuting*, and *teleworking* interchangeably, but caution readers to avoid using these terms synonymously with home-workers, virtual workers, and flexi-workers.

3.1.2.2 Telework Criteria

In addition to the terminology, there is some disagreement as to what qualifies as telecommuting. Broadly speaking, some scholars argue that telework occurs whenever an employee is paid for work completed at a secondary location (e.g., Mariani

2000). Others are more specific in duration, indicating that to be considered a teleworker, employees must work outside the office for at least *1 full day per workweek* (e.g., Anderson et al. 2001) or *1 full day per month* (World at Work 2011). Similarly, some authors suggest that to be considered a telecommuter, one must be an organizational employee (e.g., Hartman et al. 1991) and exclude self-employed persons (e.g., Gibson et al. 2002), freelancers (Hartig et al. 2007), and independent contractors (Gajendran and Harrison 2007). Conversely, other scholars include several non-traditional employees in the category of telecommuters, such as individual entrepreneurs, freelancers, and mobile workers (e.g., Fetzner 2003). Time spent traveling has been included in some definitions of telework (e.g., Bricout 2004; Coenen and Kok 2014); while others suggest that work that is regularly performed outside of the office is not considered telework (e.g., Gajendran and Harrison 2007).

Thus, *what* is considered telework is not well defined. This is further complicated by the fact that those who classify themselves as non-telecommuters often report bringing work home or working at other locations, at least some of the time (e.g., Hartig et al. 2007). However, the literature is rather consistent in that most individuals who identify as telecommuters do so part time (e.g., Bailey and Kurland 2002), and most companies initiate telework on a part-time basis (e.g., Standen et al. 1999). Nevertheless, telecommuting is a multifaceted approach to meeting demands of the modern workplace, and as such, there are a number of different types of telecommuting arrangements to meet various demands.

3.1.2.3 Telework Arrangements

As discussed thus far, the field of telework is fragmented. Further, many frameworks have been proposed to organize research surrounding telework and examine various telework arrangements, each of which suggests a set of "core" components. A list of existing frameworks is shown in Table 3.1. Some of the first and more recent models have limited the definition of a teleworker to the location of the worker, while others have also outlined the hours, contract, and schedule of the employee.

With so many frameworks available, the field lacks a unified approach to telework. There are several commonalities among the frameworks: for example, most reference the proportion and location of telework. There are also many important factors unique to each framework: for example, autonomy is a critical consideration in any telework arrangement, yet it is only mentioned by Feldman and Gainey. Given that none of these can serve as a comprehensive framework, we suggest it may be appropriate to create a new model that combines all of these components.

3.1.3 An Updated Framework and Definition

The aforementioned frameworks attempt to take into account certain aspects of telework, such as *where* the work is being conducted, or the ability for workers to "mix and match" telecommuting arrangements. Based on our experience and research,

Table 3.1 Prior models of telework

	Feldman and Gainey (1997)	Kurland and Bailey (1999)	Peters et al. (2004)	Taskin and Devos (2005)	Garrett and Danziger (2007)	Pearce (2009)	Golden (2012)
Proportion	Full time			Full time	Full time	Full time	
	Part time			Part time	Part time	Part time	
Location	Home based	Home based	Home based		Home based	Home based	
	Satellite	Satellite	Multi-site/Fully mobile		Satellite	Work center	
		Work center			Fully mobile	Fully mobile	
		Fully mobile					
Schedule	Fixed						During work
	Flexible						After work
Autonomy	Voluntary						
	Job mandated						
Technology					Importance of ICT		
Contract status			Regular employee		Regular employee		
			Contract worker		Contract worker		

we have consolidated and clarified the existing frameworks from Table 3.1 into a comprehensive framework in Table 3.2. Employees can telework on a part-time basis or a full-time basis and from home or satellite offices (or from cars, trains, planes, or coffee shops!). Some telecommuting arrangements are flexible, whereas others are more rigid. Some jobs and projects are better suited for certain forms of telework than others, and hence there is no clear definition of telecommuting. We suggest several factors, and their considerations can help organize these perspectives and provide organizations with a way to think about factors surrounding telework.

Given that telecommuting can vary widely in terms of proportion, location, schedule, collaboration, synchrony, and autonomy, we believe that a telecommuter is any employee working outside of the main office on at least one occasion each month, and using information and communication technologies (computer and network hardware and software, cellular devices, satellite systems, etc.) to complete work-related responsibilities. Given these points, we forward an updated and comprehensive definition of telework:

Table 3.2 An updated model of factors to consider when defining telework

Factor	Considerations
Proportion: Part to full time	*Part time teleworkers:* periodically perform job functions outside the established base of operations *Full time teleworkers:* usually perform most or all job functions outside the established base of operations
Location: Fixed to mobile	*Fixed location:* employee predominantly works at one off -site location (e.g., home) *Mobile location:* employee can/does work in multiple locations outside the established base of operations *Note: field -based assignments would not be considered telework – they reflect a mobile assignment away from the established base of operations.*
Schedule: Fixed to varied	*Fixed schedule:* employee has set days/hours that job functions will be performed away from the established base of operations *Varied schedule:* days/hours that job functions are performed away from the established base of operations vary
Collaboration: Low to high	*Low collaboration:* employees require low interaction with co-workers at the established base of operations *High collaboration:* employees require high interaction with co-workers at the established base of operations
Synchrony: Serial to concurrent	*Serial:* employees' interdependent tasks proceed *sequentially* (e.g., e-mail, fax) *Concurrent:* employees' interdependent tasks proceed in *unison* (e.g., conference call, video conference)
Autonomy: Low to high	*Low autonomy:* employees have low choice over whether, when, and how to telework *High autonomy:* employees have high choice over whether, when, and how to telework

Note: These factors should be viewed as continua. For example, there are varying degrees of the extent to which telework occurs part-time or full-time, and this can also vary depending on the day or work being conducted. Similarly, the extent to which the location telework occurs at can vary (and likely will, as communication and collaboration technology continues to develop). Further, these are not fixed and likely vary both within employee over time and between various employees as organizational needs dictate

> Telework refers to the proportion of job function(s) performed by an employee away from both other employees and the organization's established physical base of operations, using various forms of information and communication technologies to maintain a virtual presence. Telework typically does not refer to: travelling assignments, work at multiple sites, on-site customer work, a total lack of virtual presence, or remote assignments including more than one employee. Telework can be described in terms of six continua: proportion, location, schedule, collaboration, synchrony, and autonomy.

3.2 *Why* (and *Why Not*) Institute Telework Programs?

A rise in dual-income households and unique child- and elder-care responsibilities, coupled with a competitive economy, require that organizations around the globe remove the physical and time-related boundaries surrounding work. Rapid

Table 3.3 Promises and pitfalls of telework

	Promises	Pitfalls
Society	Environmentally friendly	
	Reduce infrastructure stress	
	Global collaboration	
	Improved disaster preparedness	
	Better for disabled individuals	
Organizations	Reduced overhead	Different (albeit usually lower) expenses
	Increased margins	Increased ICT demands
	Lower turnover	Security issues
	Greater talent pool	May not work for some tasks
	Inexpensive, desirable benefit	Some loss of control
Individuals	Save resources	Added family → work conflict
	Living choice flexibility	Working on vacation
	Dependent care flexibility	Difficult to "unplug" from work
	Higher autonomy	Social and professional Isolation
	Higher job satisfaction	Missed opportunities
	Lower stress	
	Lowered work-family conflict	

developments in communication and information technology have enabled organizations to meet employee demands for flexibility and mobility (e.g., Coenen and Kok 2014; Lundberg and Lindfors 2002). Removing these boundaries also allows organizations to cast a wider net when recruiting and retaining top employees. However, telecommuting can introduce unique challenges that must be considered. For example, telecommuting is posited to enhance perceived autonomy and reduce work–life conflict, which should enhance job-related attitudes; but there is a fear that telecommuting damages work networks and career opportunities, hindering relationships in the social domain. In the following section, we will explore some of the benefits of telecommuting and walk through potential pitfalls (which are summarized in Table 3.3). It is not the intent of this chapter to determine whether telecommuting is *good or bad* for individuals and organizations, but rather to consider the realm of potential advantages and disadvantages of telework with the increasing use of ICTs.

3.2.1 Why Telecommute?

Following the lead of Kurland and Bailey (1999), we consider the benefits of telecommuting for society, for the organization, and for the individual.

3.2.1.1 Society

At the broadest level, telecommuting is good for society because it helps organizations support green initiatives and corporate social responsibility standards. Telecommuting has been credited as a potential way to slow global warming, by reducing commuters on the road, office energy, office construction, urban heating, business travel, and even paper usage (Global Workplace Analytics 2013). In the United States alone, it is estimated that the commuting workforce consumes 67 billion gallons of fuel annually. Telecommuting can reduce this by two billion while reducing vehicle miles traveled by 35 billion (Green 2013). Telecommuting lowers traffic congestion, auto accidents, and parking issues, especially in major cities (e.g., Kurland and Bailey 1999; Pearce 2009). Likewise, telework can reduce the pressure on transportation infrastructure, with reports that half-time telework alone can reduce road wear and tear by 112 billion miles a year in the United States (Global Workplace Analytics 2013).

Besides the daily commute, ICTs make it possible for employees to collaborate around the globe, reducing the added pollution and burden associated with business travel. It is also possible that decentralizing the workforce is useful for disaster preparedness. Three quarters of teleworkers believe they could continue to work in the face of a disaster, such as 9/11, compared with just above a quarter of non-teleworkers (Global Workplace Analytics 2013).

Telecommuting is also beneficial to society as it can better accommodate persons with disabilities (Anderson et al. 2001; Baker et al. 2006b). By creating a barrier-free workplace that removes space and time constraints, individuals with significant impairment can be given the opportunity to make a valuable contribution to society. Telecommuting also provides improved opportunities for balancing work with dependent-care responsibilities (e.g., Illegems and Verbeke 2004), which can be argued as good for society as a whole.

3.2.1.2 Organizations

Perhaps the most obvious benefit of telecommuting for organizations is the reduction in costs and increased profits. For instance, telework reduces overhead and real estate costs for most organizations (e.g., AT&T 1997), as well as lowers operating costs (Baker et al. 2006a, b). Furthermore, organizations can substantially profit from implementing telecommuting programs via increased productivity and retention and decreased number of sick days and absenteeism (e.g., Kurland and Bailey 1999). AT&T reported a $65 million increase in productivity and a net gain of $100 million when considering real estate savings from implementing telecommuting. Researchers have also reported a number of positive organizational outcomes resulting from telecommuting, such as increases in performance and organizational commitment and decreases in turnover intentions (e.g., Gajendran and Harrison 2007; Golden 2006).

In addition, without any geographic restrictions, telecommuting permits more flexibility in staffing of employees by providing a wider talent pool (Kurland and Bailey 1999). In many occupations, there is a shortage of skilled workers, and telework aids in the recruitment and retention of top talent while reducing staff redundancy (e.g., Abdel-Wahab 2007; Illegems and Verbeke 2004). Not only are organizations able to hire talented employees from around the globe, but offering telecommuting options is important because many prospective employees view telecommuting and flexible hours as an important workplace benefit. For instance, over 70 % of survey employees say the ability to telecommute is somewhat extremely important in choosing their next job (Global Workplace Analytics 2013).

3.2.1.3 Individual

Most research has focused on the implications of telecommuting for the individual. Reducing travel time and costs have been implicated as major benefits of telecommuting for employees (e.g., Kurland and Bailey 1999). Employees can save money on fuel, maintenance, parking, clothes, dependent care, and by living in locations where cost of living is lower. Also, the time and energy required to commute to work can be reallocated to workplace tasks when employees telecommute, benefiting both employees and employers.

Additionally, telecommuting allows employees more control over how and when work is completed. When individuals perceive more autonomy over their work, they tend to be more satisfied, less stressed, and have higher performance and creativity than when they are controlled (e.g., Deci and Ryan 2000). Given the rise in dual-income households and the number of working adults with both child- and elder-care responsibilities, flexible work arrangements may be more important than ever before. A number of studies support this, citing a positive relationship between telecommuting and perceptions of autonomy (e.g., Gajendran and Harrison 2007; Hornung and Glaser 2009; Illegems and Verbeke 2004; Kurland and Bailey 1999). Thus, it is no surprise that autonomy has been identified as one of the primary reasons for why telecommuting is desired by employees.

A number of studies have also demonstrated that telecommuting is related to increased job satisfaction and decreased stress and work–family conflict. For instance, Gajendran and Harrison's (2007) meta-analysis reported a positive relationship between telecommuting and job satisfaction and negative relationships between telecommuting and work–family conflict and telecommuting and stress. This is consistent with other reports indicating that telecommuting reduces stress, work–family conflict (e.g., Lautsch et al. 2009; Nicklin et al. 2009), and risks to physical health (e.g., Lundberg and Lindfors 2002). However, employees should be cautious that while telecommuting may lead to a reduction in work-to-family conflict, it may lead to an increase in family-to-work conflict.

3.2.2 *Why Not Telecommute?*

While telecommuting is associated with a number of positive outcomes, there are certain challenges faced by organizations and individuals that should be considered. For instance, as previously mentioned, telecommuting may be extremely beneficial for working parents trying to balance competing demands. Yet, removing the formal structure of the workplace may make it difficult to create boundaries around work and home life. Therefore, any organization or individual considering adopting telecommuting should not enter into the arrangement blindly and should carefully consider the following concerns.

3.2.2.1 Organizational Challenges

Many organizations are reluctant to embrace telecommuting because of additional start-up costs and extra expenditures associated with implementing and maintaining telework arrangements (e.g., Baker et al. 2006a, b; Illegems and Verbeke 2004), although additional telework costs are frequently offset by increased savings and productivity. Teleworkers require a variety of ICTs such as computers, software, cell phones, printers, fax machines, cameras, and other communication software (e.g., subscriptions to virtual meeting technology). It was estimated by the U.S. General Service Administration (GSA) that the average first-year cost per teleworker was $1,000 in 2006, which is likely higher today (Global Workplace Analytics 2013). Another very practical concern raised in the literature is over potential security breaches and the protection of company materials (e.g., Abdel-Wahab 2007; Pearce 2009). However, security training can help minimize such issues.

One of the most common concerns cited in the literature from an organizational perspective is management's fear of losing control over employee behavior (e.g., Kurland and Bailey 1999). With employees at a distance, managers usually cannot directly observe employees during the workday. While most employers indicate trusting their employees, there is still a preference for being able to physically observe what workers are actually doing (Global Workplace Analytics 2013). By not having direct in-person contact with subordinates, management may have difficulties with performance monitoring, performance management, schedule maintenance, and work coordination (e.g., Kurland and Bailey 1999). This could potentially lead to additional work for supervisors, as managers may have to adjust work assignments, meetings, and performance reviews to accommodate teleworkers (Olson 1988). However, the Boston College Center for Work and Family (2000) reports that 75 % of managers experienced no differences in workload.

Finally, it should be noted that while most studies show that telecommuting leads to higher levels of productivity in organizations, this finding is not universal. Some research has actually reported a decrease in productivity associated with telework arrangements (Duxbury and Higgins 2002; Hamilton 2002; Hartman et al. 1991).

Thus, the impetus is on organizations to ensure that telecommuting is appropriate for a given task in a given set of circumstances.

3.2.2.2 Individual Challenges

The most commonly cited concern individuals report is fear of social and professional isolation (e.g., Crandall and Gao 2005; Kurland and Bailey 1999). Teleworkers miss out on three different types of developmental activities while working outside the conventional office space: interpersonal networking, informal learning that enhances work-related skills, and mentoring from colleagues and supervisors. Being away from the office may create a lack of visibility, and teleworkers fear that being out of site may limit opportunities for promotion, rewards, and positive performance reviews (Cooper and Kurland 2002). Even if managers initiate consistent personnel policies and establish a culture of strong communication, it is possible that teleworkers miss out on informal interactions that occur in the workplace. For instance, while it is entirely possible for all employees (teleworkers and non-teleworkers) to be included in a meeting, teleworkers may miss out on spontaneous conversations that happen while walking into the meeting or after the meeting is over. This reduces the amount of information sharing for teleworkers. Teleworkers may also miss out on learning that cannot be scheduled, and it is often easier to receive explanations in person rather than by telephone or email. This can potentially have implications for promotion, formal and informal training, and other opportunities (e.g., Duxbury et al. 1998; Illegems and Verbeke 2004).

Further, teleworkers often lose opportunities to develop social relationships with colleagues and to interact with new employees when working outside of the office (e.g., Bloom et al. 2013; Illegems and Verbeke 2004; Pearce 2009). Spontaneous conversation, humor, and frustrations frequently create bonds between employees, and are often missed from telecommuting (Kurland and Bailey 1999). Social interaction and perceptions of relatedness are important for job satisfaction and overall psychological well-being (e.g., Deci and Ryan 2000). Thus, it is no surprise that there are scattered reports of lowered job satisfaction (e.g., Golden 2006, 2007; Golden et al. 2008), employee loyalty, and organizational commitment (Illegems and Verbeke 2004; Kurland and Bailey 1999) among some teleworkers.

While telecommuting has been credited in the literature for aiding in balancing work and life, some reports indicate that telework actually leads to *more* issues with work–life balance. This is likely because additional family demands result from fewer boundaries between work and home life (Igbraria and Guimares 1999; Kurland and Bailey 1999). While mobile technology makes it easier to accommodate work and family, there are increased expectations from both domains; thus, individuals may end up working *more* (Towers, et al. 2006). As cited previously, Golden et al. (2006) found that the more extensively individuals telecommute, the more that family interferes with work, resulting in greater perceptions of family-to-work conflict. Telework has also been associated with increased exhaustion associated with higher work–family conflict (Golden 2012) and decreased partner's overall satisfaction with life (Vittersø et al. 2003). Especially for those who engage in home-based telework, teleworkers may lose the restorative function of *being at home*, thus leading to negative outcomes (Hartig et al. 2007).

3.3 *When* to Telecommute?

A theme we continue to weave throughout this chapter is that there are varying degrees of telework. Although telecommuting continues to rise in prevalence, it should not be fostered indiscriminately because telework is not for every person, job, task, or organization. Instead, any telework arrangement should be driven by the preference of the individuals involved and the nature of the work to be performed. We discuss below several important person- and work-based considerations in deploying any telework program, but we do believe that at the crux of the matter is the job itself. A list of when telecommuting arrangements are expected to be most successful is provided in Table 3.4.

Table 3.4 Guidelines when to telecommute

Person-oriented factors	Work-oriented factors
Telework is suited for individuals who: Are trustworthy, dependable, and honest Have a strong performance record Can manage time and workload Have technological proficiency Have clear and consistent communication skills Have high self-management skills and self-discipline Have the desire and flexibility to work independently Have low social needs Have high autonomy needs Are results oriented Are good problem solvers Have demonstrated the ability to follow company policy and procedures Have a supportive family and home environment	A moderate amount of telecommuting may be most effective. When extensive telework is needed, ensure there are opportunities for socialization, mentorship, and information communication. If working from home, managers should be clear about expectations during the work day (e.g., extent of flexibility), and employees should be clear with family members regarding work boundaries. When possible, we believe flexible work schedules and autonomous work environments are beneficial, but within reason. We urge managers to use caution when tasks are highly interdependent. Additional training and communication technologies will be needed to ensure effective knowledge transfer and task completion. Managers must ensure that employees have the ICTs needed for the type of work required. Managers are largely responsible for creating a supportive culture surrounding telework. This includes educating teleworks and non-teleworkers about the benefits of telecommuting and ensuring transparency when it comes to norms and expectations.

3.3.1 *Person-Oriented Factors*

3.3.1.1 Demographics

One school of thought has suggested that individuals with certain demographic factors would be more likely to successfully telecommute. While this assumption may have been true at one point in history (e.g., the "working mother"), newer data suggests that telecommuting (at least in the United States) is not primarily driven by fixed demographics. For example, telework is utilized by both men (56 %) and women (44 %) in substantially similar proportions (World at Work 2011).[2]

3.3.1.2 Work–Life Balance

When entering into a telework arrangement, it is important for both the individual and the organization to consider family needs. Teleworkers experience higher levels of family-to-work conflict (e.g., Golden et al. 2006), as the home environment's demands are noticeably more salient. However, if the reduction in work-to-family conflict outweighs this, there may be an increase in productivity and decrease in employee stress.

Even when individuals express the preference to telecommute, the decision to assign telework requires that the demands and resources in the telework location (usually home) can be balanced with the demands and resources from work. If there are constant distractions from family while working at home, this will ultimately lead to reduced performance, satisfaction, and overall well-being. It is beneficial to telecommuters when supervisors require work–family separation while telecommuting, and this will ultimately result in less work–family conflict (Lautsch et al. 2009). Thus, we argue that telecommuting may be most effective when individuals can create boundaries between work and life. Developing a daily routine is advised for helping to define and maintain those boundaries, as well as establishing a beginning and end to the workday. It is also essential to have conversations with family members about interruptions (Hamilton 2002).

3.3.1.3 Social Needs

It is important to consider the employees' social needs and interpersonal relationships with colleagues and family members. Employees must consider how well they can work without social and professional interactions in the workplace. However, the recent rise of social network technologies such as Facebook and LinkedIn may challenge this view. Social networks enable employees to experience connectedness

[2] Research also suggests that both men and women experience some overlap between work and family when working from home; however, men experience more spatial overlap, and women experience more mental overlap (Hartig et al. 2007).

with both work and nonwork peers remotely, satisfying the need to feel connected. Some have blamed social network sites such as Facebook for presenteeism and loss of productivity. Yet, it is important to consider that the time spent on social networking may be a worthwhile investment if it is less time than would be spent socializing face to face. Further, the potential benefits of collaborating/socializing remotely with peers may foster communities of practice and informal learning that actually boosts productivity. This is especially important when considering the sophistication of ICTs for teleworkers.

3.3.1.4 Personological Fit

Although certain employees may naturally request telework, it is often up to managers to identify which individuals are suited for remote work. These decisions tend to be based on the manager's best judgment, rather than a formally validated selection tool. It is entirely possible that a senior employee does not have what it takes to be a successful telecommuter, while a newer employee may be a good fit for such arrangement. This can then potentially lead to issues of jealousy and fairness among employees (e.g., Cooper and Kurland 2002; Kurland and Bailey 1999). Thus, managers should use caution when determining who should telecommute. Pamela La Gioia, head of Telework Recruiting, suggests that managers must consider if individuals who want to telecommute are (1) self-starters, (2) very organized, (3) results-oriented, (4) comfortable with new technology, and (5) can push back when other life demands interfere with work (Fisher 2014). Teleworkers must feel comfortable making decisions without input from others, and it is also essential that these employees do not require constant supervision or opportunities for socialization. In sum, despite challenges in identifying individual suitability for telework, several characteristics of successful telecommuters have surfaced in the literature.[3]

3.3.2 Work-Oriented Factors

Factors surrounding the job itself and the work context are extremely important considerations for determining when to telecommute. We suggest that the nature of the task(s) to be performed can be examined in light of the six facets of telework proposed in Table 3.2: proportion, location, schedule, collaboration, synchrony, and autonomy.

[3] See also West and Anderson (2005), Abdel-Wahab (2007), O'Neil et al. (2009), and Fisher (2014).

3.3.2.1 Proportion

Perhaps one of the most commonly discussed features of telework effectiveness is the *amount* of time employees spend teleworking. As discussed, there is evidence that telecommuting and job satisfaction are positively related; however, telecommuting effectiveness may be best at *moderate* amounts. Research suggests that job satisfaction is curvilinearly related to the amount of time spent telecommuting (an "upside U relationship"; Golden and Veiga 2005; Virick et al. 2010). Therefore, job satisfaction initially increases with telecommuting, though satisfaction eventually declines with the highest amounts of telecommuting. Especially for creative tasks, such as new product development, it is best when there is a balance between virtual and face-to-face interaction (Coenen and Kok 2014). Managers are responsible for helping to create this balance and setting standards for the amount of telecommuting that should be done. Through establishing fixed goals with employees and constructing usage policies, a moderate amount of telecommuting can be maintained.

3.3.2.2 Location

The location of the telework creates varying levels of opportunity and challenge for organizational members. Kurland and Bailey (1999) provided a comprehensive summary of the advantages and challenges for society, organizations, and employees of four different locations of telework: home-based, satellite offices, neighborhood work centers, and mobile work. Our analysis closely parallels the work of Kurland and Baily, with a few minor modifications. As can be seen in Tables 3.5 and 3.6, telework locations share common advantages and challenges for individuals and organizations, but others are unique to the location. For instance, home-based telework introduces a number of additional concerns such as work–family balance and at-home distractions that are not problematic within the other locations, yet home-based telework is also credited for promoting work–life balance and saving time, money, and stress that might not be possible in other contexts. Therefore, it is important to examine the costs and benefits of telework location within a broader scope, considering the other telework factors. For example, mobile work may create some sense of professional and social isolation for individuals on a full-time basis, but this need not be the case if mobile work is on a part-time or as-needed basis. The appropriateness of the location is also dependent on the other telework considerations of schedule flexibility, synchrony, autonomy, and collaboration.

3.3.2.3 Schedule

While autonomy in general is an important consideration for telecommuters, schedule flexibility is of particular importance. In the beginning of this review, we cautioned readers to not use flexi-workers and teleworkers synonymously because they are indeed different. A teleworker works outside of the confines of the traditional

Table 3.5 Advantages of telecommuting locations[a]

	Home based work	Satellite offices	Neighbourhood work centers	Mobile work
Advantages for organizations				
Saves money	X			X
Greater productivity	X	X	X	X
Lower absenteeism	X			X
Better morale	X	X	X	
Fewer office interruptions	X			
Reduced overhead	X			
Wider talent pool	X	X	X	
Lower turnover	X	X	X	
Regulation compliance	X	X	X	
Customer proximity		X	X	X
Reduces unnecessary meetings	X	X	X	X
Advantages for individuals				
Less commuting time	X	X	X	X
Cost savings	X	X	X	X
Less stress	X	X	X	X
No need for relocation	X	X	X	X
More autonomy	X		X	
Schedule flexibility	X			
Fewer workplace distractions	X			
Absence of office politics	X		X	X
Work/life balance	X	X	X	X
Enhanced job satisfaction	X	X	X	X
Comfortable work environment	X			
Opportunities for disabled individuals	X			

[a]Tables 3.2 and 3.3 are modeled closely from Kurland and Bailey (1999)

office environment, but the flexibility of when the work is conducted can vary. For instance, a stock broker may work from home but is bound to his desk when the market is open, between the hours of 9 am and 4 pm, and this is the same for his in-office counterparts, whereas someone in insurance sales, whether a teleworker or not, may be able to modify his schedule as needed, sometimes working 8 am–4 pm, 9 am–5 pm, or 10 am–6 pm.

In general, research demonstrates that flexible work schedules are positively related to job satisfaction and employee productivity and negatively related to absenteeism, stress, and burnout (Baltes et al. 1999; Grzywacz et al. 2008). Specific to telecommuters, Hill et al. (2010) found in a global sample of over 24,000 respondents that benefits of working at home were enhanced when combined with schedule flexibility. In fact, schedule flexibility was a stronger predictor of work–life conflict than working at home. Golden (2012) also found a negative relationship between nontraditional telework (extent of telework conducted during nontraditional

Table 3.6 Challenges for telecommuting locations

	Home based work	Satellite offices	Neighbourhood work centers	Mobile work
Challenges for organizations				
Performance monitoring	X	X	X	X
Performance measurement	X	X	X	X
Managerial control	X	X	X	X
Mentoring	X	X	X	X
Fairness issues	X	X	X	
Synergy	X		X	X
Informal interaction	X		X	X
Organizational & Virtual culture	X	X	X	X
Organizational loyalty	X		X	X
Schedule maintenance	X		X	X
Work coordination	X		X	X
Communication	X			X
Internal customers	X	X	X	
Expenses and technology	X			X
Security issues	X		X	X
Challenges for individuals				
Social isolation	X		X	X
Professional isolation	X	X	X	X
Organizational culture	X		X	X
Reduced office influence	X	X	X	X
Work/family balance	X			
Informational interaction	X			
Home environment	X			
Longer hours	X			
Access to resources	X	X	X	X
Focusing on work	X			
Technological savvy	X			X

business hours) and time-based and strain-based family-to-work conflict. Thus, it is possible that schedule flexibility offsets some of the concerns for telecommuters regarding family interference with work. However, we recognize that the availability and success of flexible schedules is dependent on the type of work that is conducted.

3.3.2.4 Collaboration

Regardless of the factors previously discussed (time, flexibility, and location), certain features of the job have the capacity to make telework more or less successful. For instance, some jobs are simply not feasible for teleworkers and require physical collocation. If an employee must be physically present to complete a job function, then telework becomes less viable; for example, manufacturing, surgery, and farming all require the employee to be in physical proximity to a product or tool, obviating the possibility of telework.

Furthermore, jobs where employees can do some or all of their work alone and require little collaboration may be appropriate for telecommuting (e.g., Abdel-Wahab 2007). Task interdependence has been cited as an important predictor of telecommuter satisfaction (Golden and Veiga 2005) and productivity (Turetken et al. 2011). It seems that when tasks are highly interdependent, individuals are less satisfied and productive. This calls into question the suitability of telecommuting for tasks that require a high degree of interdependence.

When tasks are interdependent, the performance and outcome of one task is affected by, or needs interaction with, the performance and outcome of other tasks. For example, project management and event planning require a high degree of task interdependence because every individual component of the project is reliant on every other component, whereas something like IT support may require less task interdependence. While telecommuting may certainly be *easier* when task interdependence is low and the task is not already digitally mediated, this is not to say that telecommuting is *impossible* when task interdependence is high. However, "the greater the interdependence between tasks, the greater the amount of communication and coordination effort required, the greater the chance of breakdown and the greater the likelihood of loss of control" (Kumar et al. 2009, p. 644). Thus, it is important to recognize that when tasks are extremely interdependent, additional communication, collaboration, and control will be needed, and richer communication media will be essential for successful telecommuting. This highlights the importance of the six considerations of telecommuting that we proposed in Table 3.2. While it may be possible for tasks that are highly interdependent to be successfully completed remotely, managers should use discretion when determining proportion, location, and flexibility of telework arrangements under these circumstances. Furthermore, more sophisticated ICTs are needed when work requires extensive collaboration.

3.3.2.5 Synchrony

From a technical perspective, teleworkers must have the necessary ICTs to be effective outside the office. However, this will depend largely on the degree to which employees must work in unison (concurrently, at the same time) or serially (subsequent to one another, or "taking turns"). In our experience, most work does not strictly require real-time collaboration; instead, work is frequently completed by one person, passed off to another, and then volleyed back and forth or on to the next party. There is a clear parallel for synchrony in traditional work environments: work that is synchronous (concurrent) likely occurs around a table or in a meeting, whereas work that is asynchronous (serial) likely occurs at a single desk.

Thus, the major consideration is the extent to which work necessitates a virtual "meeting around a table" to work with other employees in real time. There are many technologies that enable this. This may include, but is not limited to, high-bandwidth virtual private networks, content-sharing capability, instant messaging, and online conference capability (e.g., Pearce 2009). The technical conditions for telework should correspond to the same technical conditions available for conventional work (e.g., Fetzner 2003). Initial technology testing, training sessions, supervised work periods, and effective communication between the telecommuter and office are effective techniques to ensure technology comprehension and proper utilization.

3.3.2.6 Autonomy

As previously mentioned, schedule flexibility is an important consideration for teleworkers, but *how* and *when* the work is completed in general is an significant factor for successful telecommuting arrangements. For instance, someone in sales who has an autonomous work environment may not only choose when she works but also how she addresses her clients (e.g., order, style, frequency, tone, etc.), whereas someone in a more controlled environment may have specific instructions on how and when to interact with clients (e.g., scripts, schedules, and restrictions). Across a variety of contexts, researchers have demonstrated the importance of autonomously-directed behavior (e.g., Weinstein et al. 2012). Thus, we expect the telecommuting environment to be no exception; autonomous behavior, when possible, should be associated with greater telecommuting success.

Research appears to support this assertion. Autonomy has been associated with higher job satisfaction, quality of life, and job performance, as well as lower turnover intentions, depression, and work–family conflict (Golden et al. 2006; Hornung and Glaser 2009; Kossek et al. 2006). Thus, telecommuting arrangements that provide some flexibility, autonomy, or job control seem to be the most effective. But again, we urge readers to consider this in light of the other important considerations addressed.

3.4 *How* to Successfully Telecommute?

Telework requires both organizations and employees to make accommodations to the way work is done and to accommodate changes in others. Consistent with other reviewed literature, we suggest that telework arrangements can be navigated successfully by fully addressing each of the following seven critical factors. This list, the seven "Cs" of successful telework, has been inductively derived as a result of our extensive research and applied experience. A summary of our recommendations for successful telework arrangements is provided in Table 3.7.

#1: Collocation of Labor

Unsurprisingly, the most important consideration for telework is the extent to which labor must be collocated. Some tasks require complete collocation, that two

Table 3.7 Recommendations for successful telework arrangements – The 7 C's

	Considerations
1. Collocation of labor	Determine what job *functions* lend themselves to telework
	Part-time telework arrangements seem to be most popular
	Asynchronous tasks are usually candidates for telework
2. Comfort with ICT	Use only the level of technology needed. A personal computer, internet access, and a phone are typically all that is required
	All stakeholders should be comfortable with the ICT: managers, coworkers, customers, etc.
3. Conflicts & compliments with work	Investments to set up a home or mobile office will likely pay for themselves in increased productivity
	Ensure that teleworkers' increased flexibility is not taken advantage of
4. Cohesion, support, trust	Enable employees to virtually connect with one another using social networks, such as Facebook or LinkedIn
	Ensure teleworkers have multiple contacts in the company
	Ensure there is a contact that the teleworker can voice any concerns or complaints to
5. Calendars, schedules, & structure	Utilize a shared calendar that shows when individuals are busy or available
	Provide only the structure that is absolutely necessary. Hours "on" should only be mandated if driven by a business or workflow need.
	Train managers on how to coordinate/manage teleworkers
6. Clear objectives	Hours "on" should be explicit, not assumed
	Performance criteria should be clear
	Consider using an online project planner, such as Basecamp
	Make clear the benefits of telework to all involved parties
7. Climate & culture	Ensure that all employees support any telework assignment
	Make clear the norms surrounding communication (e.g., e-mail reply, phone availability, instant messenger availability)
	Make clear the business case for telework to all stakeholders

or more workers be in the presence of each other or of some technology. Most manufacturing assembly tasks require individuals to physically operate machinery and handle raw materials, which clearly obviates the possibility of telework. Other tasks require little or no physical collocation. Many jobs in information technology (IT) enable employees to work from wherever they have access to a computer and Internet connection.

In the examples above, it is clear whether telework is appropriate. However, the examples above are somewhat misleading because the critical determinant of whether to telecommute happens not at the broadest *job* level but at the narrower *job function* level. In manufacturing assembly–type jobs, all job functions have to be collocated, but that is not the case with the vast majority of jobs. Instead, some job functions will be more appropriate for telework, while others less so. In the example of the IT employee above, job functions such as programming and customer service likely lend themselves to telework because physical collocation is not a necessary condition of performing the functions. However, if the employee were also responsible for server maintenance or physical network upgrades to a particular location, those particular job functions would NOT lend themselves to telework.

Thus, the extent to which job functions require workers to be physically collocated (either with each other or with a physical location) will have a strong impact on whether, when, and how individuals can telecommute. We suggest that organizations consider telework opportunities for any of the job functions that do not necessitate physical collocation. For example, a manufacturing technician may need to be in a shop to assemble a particular product; however, if part of the job also involves putting together architectural drawings, determining worker schedules, or auditing paperwork, these tasks should be considered candidates for telework. When having these discussions, it is also important to consider how telework will impact any project teams of which the potential teleworker is a member (Feldman and Gainey 1997).

We also suggest that telework need not be an all-or-nothing arrangement (Bailey and Kurland 2002). Studies show that most individuals who work from an office prefer to have the option to work several days a week from home, but would still like to maintain face time. The norms for this will continue to change faster than research can keep up. Nevertheless, it is likely that hybrid programs will continue to grow in popularity and that a balance of telework and face-to-face work will be situation specific (Coenen and Kok 2014).

#2: Comfort with Communication and Coordination Technology.

Frequent, clear communications and the structure that supports them provide the foundation to telework (Pearlson and Saunders 2001). Thus, being comfortable with the technology needed to effectively communicate and coordinate is another critical factor in considering telework arrangements. We have intentionally avoided any in-depth discussion of particular ICT because the technology changes so rapidly. It is becoming increasingly clear that mastery of technology for remote coordination is a necessary condition for telework.

It is tempting to consider only the teleworker's level of tech savvy, but this could be a mistake. It has been suggested by some that managers who oversee teleworkers must be familiar with the technology needed to understand their teleworker's daily pace (Ting 1997). We go beyond this: managers must be MORE comfortable with the technology than their teleworkers because managers often serve as the interface between office personnel and remote personnel. In this role, managers may have to orient non-teleworkers to the habits and workflow of teleworkers.

Regardless of the technology used, there must be a space for knowledge management (Coenen and Kok 2014). Individuals must be able to identify, preserve, and share the insights and knowledge they gain from their daily activities. They must also be able to store and retrieve communications that relate to project work and responsibilities. This will often be intertwined with communities of practice and social functions (Taskin and Bridoux 2010). Teleworkers must have the resources and support to interact and build a base of knowledge that fosters their own development and the organization's mission. It has been suggested three factors determine knowledge transfer in a telework environment (Taskin and Bridoux 2010): communication (how people exchange information), frequency (how often they communicate), and human resource management principles (the extent to which the organization presents needed resources).

We suggest that technology for the sake of technology is to be avoided. Instead, only the technology that is needed should be adopted. For example, if periodic discussions surrounding a project suffice, it may be counterproductive to require web conferences or videoconferencing. Employees should also have a hand in the technology that is used, as it will be their responsibility to become familiar with it. This is advisable because they will be more likely to adopt it if they have an interest or stake in the decision.

#3: Conflicts and Complements with Nonwork

One challenge to telework workflow is the interference of nonwork events. If employees are working from their home or from a public space (e.g., coffee spots), there are more distractions and less supervision. This makes it easier for the employee workflow to ebb. One way organizations can counter this fall back is by providing the resources employees need to set up a home office. Covering the cost of office furniture, technology, and supplies enables individuals to establish a base of operations, much like in a traditional office. Further, providing these supplies sets up an informal expectation that individuals will not always be working from subprime locations (e.g., bed, bathroom, outdoors). Managers may also suggest that a particular room be dedicated to the home office, as those who do so report less spillover from nonwork life (Hartig et al. 2007). It is important to keep in mind that greater autonomy is often (but not always) key to mitigating nonwork interference (Golden 2007).

On the other hand, many factors of the nonwork environment can actually foster productivity. A home-based office cuts out many productivity reducers that have been a hallmark of traditional offices for generations. Teleworkers can begin work earlier, as they lack a commute. They can work with fewer interruptions from coworkers. They may also be more readily available at flexible hours when business decisions are critical, such as early morning. In addition, family emergencies that would normally curtail an entire day of productivity can be mitigated by teleworkers (Major et al. 2008); by being onsite or being able to work on the move, teleworkers can recoup the losses that traditional commuters might not.

There are a host of additional nonwork benefits to telework. For example, telework can be used as an incentive. The number of days employees prefer to telework is double what they typically do (Major, et al. 2008). Thus, the opportunity to telework (or telework more) may provide a low-cost incentive to boost productivity and secure top talent. However, ensure that the telework arrangements are in line with the greater organizational vision and goals, otherwise the incentive may quickly disappear (Illegems and Verbeke 2004). We suggest that organizations make resources available to teleworkers to navigate work/non-work balance. It may be intrusive to mandate certain types of training. However, providing material that dispels stereotypes surrounding work–life balance, informs about expectations, and links resources may help new teleworkers adjust (Major et al. 2008).

#4: Cohesion, Support, and Trust

While being away from the physical base of operations, support and trust are critical success factors for telework (Kowalski and Swanson 2005). If the work environment is perceived as supportive by telecommuters, their telecommuting satisfaction will be enhanced (Hartman et al. 1991). In addition, when employees trust their managers, they have better reactions to telecommuting (Baker et al. 2006a). In part, cohesion, support, and trust can be fostered through formal means. Prior to beginning telework, managers should create a common understanding among all employees concerning the telework arrangements. Maruyama and Tietze (2012) recommend briefing events, workshops, and the sharing of documentation in order to lessen any anxieties from coworkers and supervisors. It is also important to convey to all employees the vision surrounding telework and the positive potential for telework to be successful (Fetzner 2003).

Cohesion, support, and trust are also built informally. Supervisors should keep informal lines of communication open because it improves outcomes such as identification with the organization and trust (Timmerman and Scott 2006). Supervisors should ensure their subordinates have more than one contact, especially for critical tasks. Multiple, informal communications that happen frequently can boost helping behaviors, feedback, and reduce role overload (Lautsch et al. 2009). Given the importance of effective leader communication and relationship-oriented behaviors in telework environments (Ting 1997), it is advisable for managers to regularly work to improve their communication skills.

Social interaction with coworkers is also important to maintain because informal workplace relationships breed coworker liking, commitment, and job satisfaction (Fay and Kline 2011). Research has shown that employees who feel connected to others and perceived as competent and valued have higher levels of performance (Cerasoli and Nicklin 2015). These relationships may not develop as readily when employees are not physically collocated. An extensive body of research shows that teams that experience a higher sense of cohesion, or belongingness and positive regards, well-being, and performance soar. In addition, social interaction among employees is often important for informal learning (Cerasoli et al. 2015) and interpersonal networking initiatives (Dahlstrom 2013). Social interaction is also important because frequent socialization helps break down cognitive and interpersonal biases that often hinder effective group telework (Walther et al. 2005). This is all the more important for teleworkers in high-intensity jobs (Thatcher and Zhu 2006). Managers should encourage, but not mandate, opportunities for interaction (Fay and Kline 2011), such that supervisors should use an information-sharing approach with telecommuters rather than a tight monitoring approach (e.g., Lautsch et al. 2009).

#5: Calendars, Schedules, and Structure

As managers, it is often challenging to relinquish control, especially when it comes to scheduling. Yet, research has shown it is often beneficial to allow employees to set their own schedules. For example, employees who have more control over their work schedule have less nonwork conflict, greater job satisfaction, and higher well-being (Moen et al. 2008).

Provided deadlines are met in a timely fashion, we recommend supervisors allow employees to self-regulate their schedules in a way that works with other employees of the organization. Part of the need for telework is that employees can better meet their own individual needs and preferences while upholding work obligations (Golden 2012). Periodic fixed teleconferences are a good idea, provided they occur only as frequently as updates are needed. These can also help managers keep appraised of their teleworker's progress and activities (Hartman et al. 1991). Having calls too frequently may encourage employees to "make up" material for the call, while having them too infrequently may force calls to take too long.

The level of structure provided to the employee will also depend on the task and the industry (Dahlstrom 2013). For example, public-sector employees may be used to more structure in the workplace, and thereby in telework more may be appropriate. Similarly, flexibility may be productive for creativity-type tasks but not so for more routine ones (Dutcher 2012).

Further, no two telework arrangements are identical because each teleworker has unique needs and resources. Thus, there is a need to recognize there are different types of remote work (Morganson et al 2010). We suggest managers be given flexibility in running telework programs because a "one-size-fits-all" approach is often suboptimal (Kurland and Bailey 1999). For example, working parents may telecommute to accommodate school hours, while working students may telework to accommodate coursework hours; it is likely the same arrangement would not suffice for both.

Managers may also need to develop new skill sets surrounding coordination of teleworkers (Lautsch et al. 2009). Teleworkers in multiple time zones/countries and with multiple competing obligations require a different set of management skills than do conventional workers (Kurland and Bailey 1999). This includes factors such as understanding travel times, coordinating with multiple time zones, patience with communication lag, understanding of different cultural norms for communications and work, and even familiarity with multiple languages. Supervisors should be attuned to all these issues, beyond those of workers in multiple flexible arrangements (Lautsch et al. 2009).

#6: Clear Objectives

Organizations should make work and business expectations/objectives clear to the employee (Pearlson and Saunders 2001). Some employees work well with a great deal of ambiguity, while others do not. This is not to say that organizations must spell out every task that an individual is to perform. Instead, we suggest the organization be clear about expectations from the job function level up. Thus, a clear vision should be articulated that includes accompanying mottos and symbols. Subordinate to the vision, there should be very general goals for the organization to attain. Then, there should be some link between the individual's job functions and these goals.

The standards for evaluating performance should also be clear (Hartman et al. 1991), although they need not be overly formal. As others have, we recommend performance management by outputs rather than inputs (Kurland and Bailey 1999). Provided employees meet their objectives or goals by ethical means in a timely fashion and without disturbing the workflow of others, employees should be left to their own devices to attain their goals. This has the added benefit of incentivizing employees to work more efficiently. Importantly, supervisors should make a concerted effort to provide feedback to teleworkers (Virick et al. 2010). In some cases, it may be as simple as a verbal "everything is looking good." Or, it may be a more formal, objective process. Either way, feedback is critical.

Organizations should also make clear the expectations of the telework program (Abdel-Wahab 2007). All employees, not just those teleworking, should be made aware of who will be teleworking and how they will do so (Kurland and Bailey 1999). This helps clarify cross-role expectations and break down biases and group polarization effects that naturally occur between two distinctly different groups (Cooper and Kurland 2002). Specifically, it has been suggested that interdependent teams decide upon (a) the appropriate use of collaboration technology, (b) the need to be clear in written communication, and (c) how responsive members must be (Thatcher and Bagger 2011).

Of course, telework programs require a substantial degree of preparation. It may be a good idea to pilot a telework program first so that potential pitfalls can be discovered and removed prior to the full program deployment (Illegems and Verbeke 2004). After this, training should be made available to orient both teleworkers and non-teleworkers to the program. Finally, the benefits of the telework program should be made clear to both the telework employee and others at all levels in the organization. A marketing strategy that shows how telework is beneficial to others in the organization may increase acceptance of the program and desire for others to telecommute (Anderson et al. 2001).

#7: Climate and Culture

Finally, organizations should periodically assess the climate of the workplace. For both the teleworker and non-teleworker employees, there is a great deal of autonomy, initiative, and patience required. Telework requires, and will flourish in, a climate of commitment and trust (Martínez-Sánchez et al. 2008). These types of tasks require a great deal of buy-in from all stakeholders (Kurland and Bailey 1999), and as such, the climate must be periodically assessed (informally or formally).

If employees need to be available to one another on a moment's notice, then it should be understood that employees will answer the phone during business hours. Or, it may be the case that e-mails need timely responses, and thus the expectation is that e-mails will be monitored and returned quickly. In a traditional workplace environment, norms (the unspoken rules for behavior) develop somewhat quickly, given frequent casual conversations and face-to-face discussions. However, these are naturally less frequent in a telework situation.

One way to develop these norms is to simply give them more time. When the pace or urgency of work is only occasionally high, periodic phone calls and e-mails will help the individual gradually learn unspoken expectations. However, when higher frequency and urgency coordination is necessary, it may be a good idea to make unspoken expectations explicit. Another way to develop these norms is through formal orientations, posters, handbooks, and conversations (Thatcher and Bagger 2011). While these may not be extensive, they are recommended to have some presence for reference purposes at the very least.

3.5 Conclusion and Future Directions

As technology continues to advance and new devices are introduced into society, it is important to consider what this means for the telecommuting workforce. Telecommuting once meant lugging files back and forth from the office, but now most companies have paperless documentation methods. Employees can now conduct their meetings without ever leaving their doorstep. High-quality technology permits teleworkers to replicate a company's website and resources from home, and enables teleworkers to stay up to date, access files, and effectively communicate with coworkers (Greer and Payne 2014). As companies continue to introduce new measures of communication, it is important to note its impact on the telecommuter.

Security issues are likely to shape the future of telework. According to a 2012 survey, over 90 % of organizations experienced a loss of either confidential or sensitive resources in the past year (Ponemon Institute 2012). This leakage could be significantly reduced or eliminated by IT security training, a process that two-thirds of telecommuters in the United States did not receive in 2011 (Staples). Each time a person accesses sensitive information from a Wi-Fi hotspot or unsecure wireless connection, that individual is risking the safety of that data. A proper training would instill telecommuters with the confidence and skillset to protect the company's critical data, disable file sharing and automatic connections, and successfully hide information from hackers.

In addition, new technologies that capitalize on multiple modalities are also likely to drive telework arrangements. Overall, usage of multiple electronic devices (e.g., smartphones, smartwatches, fitness wearables) is at an all-time high, as one would expect with the growing amount of accessible devices on the market. For example, as of 2013, 58 % of surveyed U.S. employees would willingly use wearable technology to aid job performance (and 12 % would actually feel disadvantaged if their coworker had wearable technology; Kelton 2012). Laptops, smartphones, and tablets are all being used alongside the traditional desktop because working on-the-go no longer restricts the worker to his or her home. Teleworkers are feeling more comfortable with several devices because networks have become increasingly mobile friendly. With the appropriate job circumstances and technical training, telework environments will continue to become more commonplace and favorable.

References

Abdel-Wahab A (2007) Employees' attitudes towards telecommuting. An empirical investigation in the Egyptian governorate of Dakahlia. Behav Inform Technol 26:367–375. doi:10.1080/01449290500535426

Anderson J, Bricout JC, West MD (2001) Telecommuting: meeting the needs of businesses and employees with disabilities. J Vocat Rehabil 16:97–104

AT&T (1997) The 1997 EH&S report. Retrieved from http://www.business.att.com/ehs/annual_reports/ehs_report/report97/common/l.html

Bailey DE, Kurland NB (2002) A review of telework research: findings, new directions and lessons for the study of modern work. J Organ Behav 23:383–400. doi:10.1002/job.144
Baker E, Avery G, Crawford J (2006a) Home alone: the role of technology in telecommuting. Inf Resour Manag J 19:1–22
Baker PA, Moon NW, Ward AC (2006b) Virtual exclusion and telework: barriers and opportunities of technocentric workplace accommodation policy. Work J Prev Assess Rehabil 27:421–430
Baltes BB, Briggs TE, Huff JW, Wright JA, Neuman GA (1999) Flexible and compressed workweek schedules: a meta-analysis of their effects on work-related criteria. J Appl Psychol 84:496–513
Bloom N, Liang J, Roberts J, Ying ZJ (2013) Does working from home work? Evidence from a Chinese experiment (Working paper no. 18871). Retrieved from The National Bureau of Economic Research website: http://www.nber.org/papers/w18871
Boston College Center for Work & Family (2000) Measuring the impact of workplace flexibility. Retrieved October 9, 2014 from http://www.bc.edu/content/dam/files/centers/cwf/research/pdf/flexexecsumm.pdf
Bricout JC (2004) Using telework to enhance return to work outcomes for individuals with spinal cord injuries. Neurorehabilitation 19:147–159
Cerasoli CP, Nicklin JM (2015) Psychological need satisfaction under self-determination theory predicts performance: A meta-analysis. Manuscript under revision
Cerasoli CP, Alliger GM, Donsbach JS, Mathieu JE, Tannenbaum SI (2015) Informal learning and its antecedents: an integrative and meta-analytic review. Manuscript under review
Coenen M, Kok RW (2014) Workplace flexibility and new product development performance: the role of telework and flexible work schedules. Eur Manag J. Advance e-pub ahead of print. doi:10.1016/j.emj.2013.12.003
Cooper CD, Kurland NB (2002) Telecommuting, professional isolation and employee development in public and private organizations. J Organ Behav 23:511–532. doi:10.1002/job.145
Crandall WR, Gao L (2005) An update on telecommuting: review and prospects for emerging issues. SAM Adv Manag J 70:30–37
Dahlstrom TR (2013) Telecommuting and leadership style. Public Pers Manag 42:438–451. doi:10.1177/0091026013495731
Deci EL, Ryan RM (2000) The 'what' and 'why' of goal pursuits: human needs and the self-determination of behavior. Psychol Inq 11:227–268
Dutcher E (2012) The effects of telecommuting on productivity: an experimental examination. The role of dull and creative tasks. J Econ Behav Organ 84:355–363. doi:10.1016/j.jebo.2012.04.009
Duxbury L, Higgins CA (2002) Telework: a primer for the millennium. In: Cooper C (ed) The new world of work. Sage, London
Duxbury LE, Higgins CA, Neufeld D (1998) Telework and the balance between work and family: is telework part of the problem or part of the solution? In: Igbaria M, Tan M (eds) The virtual workplace. Idea Group Publishing, Hershey, pp 218–255
Fay MJ, Kline SL (2011) Coworker relationships and informal communication in high-intensity telecommuting. J Appl Commun Res 39:144–163. doi:10.1080/00909882.2011.556136
Fay MJ, Kline SL (2012) The influence of informal communication on organizational identification and commitment in the context of high-intensity telecommuting. South Commun J 77:61–76. doi:10.1080/1041794x.2011.582921
Feldman DC, Gainey TW (1997) Patterns of telecommuting and their consequences: framing the research agenda. Hum Resour Manag Rev 7:369–388. doi:10.1016/S1053-4822(97)90025-5
Fetzner M (2003) Viability of telework at PROCEMPA. Cyberpsychol Behav 6:15–30. doi:10.1089/109493103321167938
Fisher A (2014) What it takes to telecommute, or manage people who do. CNN Money. Retrieved from http://www.management.fortune.cnn.com/tag/telecommuting/
Gajendran RS, Harrison DA (2007) The good, the bad, and the unknown about telecommuting: meta-analysis of psychological mediators and individual consequences. J Appl Psychol 92:1524–1541. doi:10.1037/0021-9010.92.6.1524

Garrett R, Danziger JN (2007) Which telework? Defining and testing a taxonomy of technology-mediated work at a distance. Soc Sci Comput Rev 25:27–47. doi:10.1177/0894439306293819

Gibson J, Blackwell CW, Dominicis P, Demerath N (2002) Telecommuting in the 21st century: benefits, issues, and a leadership model which will work. J Leadersh Stud 8:75–86. doi:10.1177/107179190200800407

Global Workplace Analytics (2013) Latest telecommuting statistics. Retrieved from http://www.globalworkplaceanalytics.com/telecommuting-statistics

Golden TD (2006) Avoiding depletion in virtual work: telework and the intervening impact of work exhaustion on commitment and turnover intentions. J Vocat Behav 69:176–187. doi:10.1016/j.jvb.2006.02.003

Golden T (2007) Co-workers who telework and the impact on those in the office: understanding the implications of virtual work for co-worker satisfaction and turnover intentions. Human Relat 60:1641–1667. doi:10.1177/0018726707084303Golden

Golden TD (2012) Altering the effects of work and family conflict on exhaustion: telework during traditional and nontraditional work hours. J Bus Psychol 27:255–269. doi:10.1007/s10869-011-9247-0

Golden TD, Fromen A (2011) Does it matter where your manager works? Comparing managerial work mode (traditional, telework, virtual) across subordinate work experiences and outcomes. Human Relat 64:1451–1475. doi:10.1177/0018726711418387

Golden TD, Veiga JF (2005) The impact of extent of telecommuting on job satisfaction: resolving inconsistent findings. J Manag 31:301–318. doi:10.1177/0149206304271768

Golden TD, Veiga JF, Simsek Z (2006) Telecommuting's differential impact on work-family conflict: is there no place like home? J Appl Psychol 91:1340–1350. doi:10.1037/0021-9010.91.6.1340

Golden TD, Veiga JF, Dino RN (2008) The impact of professional isolation on teleworker job performance and turnover intentions: does time spent teleworking, interaction face-to-face, or having access to communication-enhancing technology matter? J Appl Psychol 93:1412–1421

Green L (2013) Telecommuting: good for the planet and your business. Living Green Magazine. Retrieved from livinggreenmag.com/2013/05/23/green-business/telecommuting-good-for-the-planet-and-your-business/

Greer TW, Payne SC (2014) Overcoming telework challenges: outcomes of successful telework strategies. Psychol Manager J 17:87–111. doi:10.1037/mgr0000014

Grzywacz JG, Carlson DS, Shulkin S (2008) Schedule flexibility and stress: linking formal flexible arrangements and perceived flexibility to employee health. Community Work Family 11:199–214

Hamilton E (2002) Bringing work home: advantages and challenges of telecommuting. Publication by the Boston College Center for Work and Family, Chestnut Hill

Hartig T, Kylin C, Johansson G (2007) The telework tradeoff: stress mitigation vs. constrained restoration. Appl Psychol Int Rev 56:231–253. doi:10.1111/j.1464-0597.2006.00252.x

Hartman RI, Stoner CR, Arora R (1991) An investigation of selected variables affecting telecommuting productivity and satisfaction. J Bus Psychol 6:207–225. doi:10.1007/BF01126709

Hill EJ, Erickson JJ, Holmes EK, Ferris M (2010) Workplace flexibility, work hours, and work-life conflict: finding an extra day or two. J Fam Psychol 24:349–358. doi:10.1037/a0019282

Hornung S, Glaser J (2009) Home-based telecommuting and quality of life: further evidence on an employee-oriented human resource practice. Psychol Rep 104:395–402. doi:10.2466/PR0.104.2.395-402

Igbraria M, Guimares T (1999) Exploring differences in employee turnover intentions and its determinants among telecommuters and non-telecommuters. J Manag Inf Syst 16:147–164

Illegems V, Verbeke A (2004) Telework: what does it mean for management? Long Range Plan Int J Strateg Manag 37:319–334. doi:10.1016/j.lrp.2004.03.004

Kelton (2012) The state of workplace productivity report. Retrieved from http://www.cornerstoneondemand.com/sites/default/files/research/csod-rs-state-of-workplace-productivity-report.pdf

Koh C, Allen TD, Zafar N (2013) Dissecting reasons for not telecommuting: are nonusers a homogenous group? Psychol Manager J 16:243–260. doi:10.1037/mgr0000008

Kossek E, Lautsch BA, Eaton SC (2006) Telecommuting, control, and boundary management: correlates of policy use and practice, job control, and work-family effectiveness. J Vocat Behav 68:347–367. doi:10.1016/j.jvb.2005.07.002

Kowalski KB, Swanson JA (2005) Critical success factors in developing teleworking programs. Benchmarking 12(3):236–250

Kumar K, van Fenema PC, Von Glinow MA (2009) Offshoring and the global distribution of work: implications for task interdependence theory and practice. J Int Bus Stud 40:642–667

Kurland NB, Bailey DE (1999) Telework: the advantages and challenges of working here, there, anywhere, and anytime. Organ Dyn 28:53–68. doi:10.1016/S0090-2616(00)80016-9

Lautsch BA, Kossek E, Eaton SC (2009) Supervisory approaches and paradoxes in managing telecommuting implementation. Human Relat 62:795–827. doi:10.1177/0018726709104543

Lundberg U, Lindfors P (2002) Psychophysiological reactions to telework in female and male white-collar workers. J Occup Health Psychol 7:354–364. doi:10.1037/1076-8998.7.4.354

Major DA, Verive JM, Joice W (2008) Telework as a dependent care solution: examining current practice to improve telework management strategies. Psychol Manager J 11:65–91. doi:10.1080/10887150801967134

Mariani M (2000) Exploring the telecommuting paradox. Assoc Comput Mach Commun ACM 42:29–30

Martínez-Sánchez A, Pérez-Pérez M, Vela-Jiménez M, de-Luis-Carnicer P (2008) Telework adoption, change management, and firm performance. J Organ Chang Manag 21:7–31. doi:10.1108/09534810810847011

Maruyama T, Tietze S (2012) From anxiety to assurance: concerns and outcomes of telework. Pers Rev 41:450–469. doi:10.1108/00483481211229375

Moen P, Kelly EL, Huang Q (2008) Work, family, and life-course fit: does control over work time matter? J Vocat Behav 73:414–425

Morganson VJ, Major DA, Oborn KL, Verive JM, Heelan MP (2010) Comparing telework locations and traditional work arrangements: differences in work-life balance support, job satisfaction, and inclusion. J Manag Psychol 25:578–595. doi:10.1108/02683941011056941

Nicklin JM, Mayfield CO, Caputo PM, Arboleda MA, Cosentino RE, Lee M, Melinsky KA, Sackett AL, Roch SG (2009) Telecommuting and organizational attitudes and outcomes: a meta-analysis. Pravara Manag Rev 8:2–16

Nilles JM (1975) Telecommunications and organizational decentralization. IEEE Trans Commun COM-23(10):1142–1147

O'Neil TA, Hambley LA, Greidanus NS, MacDonnell R, Kline TJB (2009) Predicting teleworker success: an exploration of personality, motivational, situational, and job characteristics. N Technol Work Employ 24:144–162

Olson MH (1988) Organizational barriers to telecommuting. In: Korte WB, Robinson S, Steinle WJ (eds) Telework: present situation and future development of a new form of work organization. North-Holland, Amsterdam, pp 77–100

Pearce J (2009) Successful corporate telecommuting with technology considerations for late adopters. Organ Dyn 38:16–25. doi:10.1016/j.orgdyn.2008.10.002

Pearlson K, Saunders C (2001) There's no place like home: managing telecommuting paradoxes. Acad Manag Exec 15:117–128

Peters P, den Dulk L (2003) Cross cultural differences in managers' support for home-based telework: a theoretical elaboration. Int J Cross Cult Manag 3:329–346. doi:10.1177/1470595803003003005

Peters P, Tijdens KG, Wetzels C (2004) Employees' opportunities, preferences, and practices in telecommuting adoption. Inf Manag 41:469–482

Ponemon Institute (2012) 2012 confidential documents at risk study. Ponemon Institute Research Report. Retrieved from http://www.ciosummits.com/media/pdf/solution_spotlight/Ponemon%20White%20Paper%20FINAL.pdf

Reaney P (2012) About one in five workers worldwide telecommute: poll. Retrieved October 9, 2014 from http://www.reuters.com/article/2012/01/24/us-telecommuting/idUSTRE80N1IL20120124

Robert Half Singapore (2012) Singapore employers embrace flexible work arrangements. Retrieved October 9 2014 from http://www.roberthalf.com.sg/id/PR-03447/singapore-employers-embrace-flexible-work
Society for Human Resource Management (2013) SHRM workplace forecast: the top workplace trends according to HR professionals. Retrieved October 9, 2014 from http://www.shrm.org/research/futureworkplacetrends/documents/13-0146%20workplace_forecast_full_fnl.pdf
Standen P, Daniels K, Lamond D (1999) The home as a workplace: work–family interaction and psychological well-being in telework. J Occup Health Psychol 4:368–381. doi:10.1037/1076-8998.4.4.368
Staples (2011) There's no place like a home office: Staples survey shows telecommuters are happier and healthier, with 25% less stress when working from home. Retrieved October 9, 2014 from http://staplesadvantage.newshq.businesswire.com/press-release/staples-technology-solutions/theres-no-place-home-office-staples-survey-shows-telecomm
Taskin L, Bridoux F (2010) Telework: a challenge to knowledge transfer in organizations. Int J Human Res Manag 21:2503–2520. doi:10.1080/09585192.2010.516600
Taskin L, Devos V (2005) Paradoxes from the individualization of human resource management: the case of telework. J Bus Ethics 62:13–24
Thatcher SB, Bagger J (2011) Working in pajamas: telecommuting, unfairness sources, and unfairness perceptions. Negot Confl Manag Res 4:248–276. doi:10.1111/j.1750-4716.2011.00082.x
Thatcher SB, Zhu X (2006) Changing identities in a changing workplace: identification, identity enactment, self-verification, and telecommuting. Acad Manag Rev 31:1076–1088. doi:10.2307/20159267
Timmerman E, Scott C (2006) Virtually working: communicative and structural predictors of media use and key outcomes in virtual work teams. Commun Monogr 73:108–136
Ting Y (1997) Determinants of job satisfaction of federal government employees. Public Pers Manag 26:313–334
Tkaczyk C (2013). Marissa Mayer breaks her silence on Yahoo's telecommuting policy. Retrieved October 8, 2014 from http://fortune.com/2013/04/19/marissa-mayer-breaks-her-silence-on-yahoos-telecommuting-policy/
Towers I et al (2006) Time thieves and space invaders: technology, work and the organization. J Organ Chang Manag Space Time Organ Chang 19:593–618
Tugend A (2014) It's unclearly defined, but telecommuting is fast on the rise. The New York Times, B6
Turetken O, Jain A, Quesenberry B, Ngwenyama O (2011) An empirical investigation of the impact of individual and work characteristics. Prof Commun 54:56–67
Virick M, DaSilva N, Arrington K (2010) Moderators of the curvilinear relation between extent of telecommuting and job and life satisfaction: the role of performance outcome orientation and worker type. Human Relat 63:137–154. doi:10.1177/0018726709349198
Vittersø J, Akselsen S, Evjemo B, Julsrud T, Yttri B, Bergvik S (2003) Impacts of home-based telework on quality of life for employees and their partners. Quantitative and qualitative results from a European survey. J Happiness Stud 4:201–233. doi:10.1023/A:1024490621548
Walther JB, Loh T, Granka L (2005) Let me count the ways: the interchange of verbal and nonverbal cues in computer-mediated and face-to-face affinity. J Lang Soc Psychol 24:36–65
Weinstein N, Przybylski AK, Ryan RM (2012) The index of autonomous functioning: development of a scale of human autonomy. J Res Pers 46:397–413
West MD, Anderson J (2005) Telework and employees with disabilities: accommodation and funding options. J Vocat Rehabil 23:115–122
WorldatWork (2011) Telework 2011. Retrieved October 9, 2014 from http://www.worldatwork.org/waw/adimLink?id=53034

Chapter 4
Drivers and Consequences in Transforming Work Practices

Jungwoo Lee

Abstract As information revolution progresses at unprecedented pace, it has been predicted that the current paradigm of work established by industrial technology will be changing taking advantage of capabilities provided by information and communication technologies (ICT). Telecommuting is one of the most cited examples and flexible time another one, brought up to our attention more than decades ago. With the rapid insurgence of smart devices connected to the Internet, the world imagined is now becoming reality. The working paradigm is undergoing tremendous changes as evidenced by proliferating new theories in different areas of business management. Though the work transformation has been expected and envisioned for a while, the world is facing serious challenges in identifying and adapting to the novel characteristics of new ways of working, along with unanticipated side effects.

In this study, a systematic literature review of academic studies was conducted in order to identify constructs involved in realizing this new way of working incurred by ICT. Using keyword search related to work transformation such as telecommuting and flextime, total 913 research articles were selected from academic databases. Initial content analysis of these 913 articles revealed 372 variables related to work transformation; 13 sessions of focus group by different panels of experts were conducted reviewing real meanings and context of these constructs, removing duplicates and grouping similar variables. As a result, total of 37 variables were finalized as critically related to the work transformation; 16 were found to be at the individual level, 15 at the organizational level, and 6 at the society level. These variables are framed into a series of relational diagrams depicting possible drivers and consequences of transforming work practices. Suggestions are made for the use of these frameworks, and implications are discussed with limitations.

Keywords Work transformation • New ways of working • Telecommuting • Flexible work • Alternative work • Smart work • Working smarter • Systematic literature review • Information and communication technologies

J. Lee (✉)
Center for Work Science, Yonsei University, Seoul, Korea, Republic of (South Korea)
e-mail: jlee@yonsei.ac.kr

J. Lee (ed.), *The Impact of ICT on Work*, DOI 10.1007/978-981-287-612-6_4

4.1 Introduction

Firms have been striving to figure out how to increase the productivity, lower the labor cost, and subsequently increase the underlying efficiency of business operations. Task optimization and scheduling has been the primary goal of industrialized manufacturing and service firms. Advent of the scientific management at the beginning of the last century demands the analyses and synthesis of work practices, targeting to improve economic efficiency, especially labor productivity, by optimizing tasks as well as workplace designs. Keywords of scientific management include analysis, synthesis, rationality, empiricism, efficiency, elimination of waste, standardization, best practices, mass production, and systemization of knowledge. Scientific management principles are geared toward optimizing tasks by treating humans as part of business processes.

Mass production paradigm requires humans to come to work 5 days a week and 8 h a day. But emerging information and knowledge economy with capabilities provided by information and communication technology and changing nature of work allows a range of possibility. Information and communication technology (ICT) begins to undermine this practice of industrialized work, if not the principles, of scientific management. Evidences of the fundamental changes in the nature of work and business operations are abundant in research and practice: process innovation, employee empowerment, knowledge sharing, human-centered management, etc. Many routine jobs are computerized and automated. Today, most sought-after role models are successful inventors, surgeons, lawyers, investment bankers, and software engineers who are compensated for the quality of what they produce, not the quantity. The same is true for talented service providers, such as rainmakers bringing in clients, dealmakers winning transactions, top marketers, and consultants advising and persuading their clients.

How different is your work life today, compared to what it was 40 years ago, or 30, 20, or even 10 years ago? Clearly, mobile devices including phones, tablets, and computers are in every pocket, briefcase, and backpack, but what else has changed and why? In today's world, the shape and structure of work have changed. Work is now more cognitively complex, team based, demanding social skills, requiring technological competence, pressed by time, and extensively mobile. We are also working for organizations that are very different. Today's organizations are leaner and more agile with less hierarchical structure, less authoritative, and continually reorganizing.

People are proposing different views on organizational processes and tasks, other than the ones devised for industrial mass production systems in which humans are considered as part of business processes involving machines. These changes are fundamental because it demands to alter the fundamental perspectives that each individual maintains about tasks, job, and furthermore life itself. It is worth exploring the changing nature of organizations and work, the drivers behind the changes, and the consequences for workers and the workplace.

Scholars around the world have made observations concerning how ICT affects business, work, organization, culture, and life. With the advancement of ICT technology, particularly with the sudden popularity of mobile smart devices in recent years, the concept of "smart work" is being surfaced. Smart work refers to the work format that defies time and space using ICT and is expected to bring significant changes to individual workers, organizations, and their societies. Smart work in some sense accommodates the changing nature of work in coming information- and knowledge-based society. In this sense, the change of how people work not only affects a particular organization or its productivity but also the advancement of individual workers and their families, as well as their ways of life.

In the industrialization paradigm, we might only have to work hard as we were told as part of business processes, whereas this era of ICT demands us to overcome the physical limitation of time and space and work smart in a creative way to survive and sustain competitiveness. For example, the outcomes and achievements of knowledge work such as creating new business models would not be measurable in the same way as that of manual tasks in manufacturing factory floors. Today, we work at home or in other convenient settings using a variety of highly advanced computing and communication tools. The word "smart" seems to have a different meaning in this information society, though we have been using this word for a long time. The fusion of smart technology, human emotions, and creativity-oriented values into humans, systems, or processes has enabled us to solve difficult social issues in a "smarter" manner and to create a society where everyone could be happier.

However, despite that most studies on the impact of ICT on work presuppose the changing nature of work, few academic studies directly addressed this issue. Previous studies were conducted with specific foci on specific aspects, such as flexible working, home office, remote offices, telework, gamification, job crafting, etc. This fragmented way of studies may limit our views in understanding and investigating the phenomenon of "new ways of working due to ICT." As the new ways of working would be related to a lot of social and institutional issues as the work is the basis of the lives of our society, a larger picture of what is happening would be required. In this regard, in this study, a systematic literature review is conducted across these different areas of studies finding out the variables identified and used by researchers involved in studying the new ways of working.

4.2 Background

4.2.1 *Working "Smarter": New Ways of Working*

Recently, the term "smart work" has been used in practice as a neologism coined to describe a fusion of the present ICT development and working systems that have been proposed for the improvement of productivity and quality of life, like telecommuting, remote working, and flexible working, by major IT vendors and public services. For example, the concepts of smart work which are used by the Korean government are as follows:

- Smart work represents a flexible working system that allows everyone to work free from time and place constraints using ICT on a network (National Information Society Agency, November 2010).

- Smart work is a future-oriented work environment concept that allows people to work in a convenient and efficient manner anytime anywhere by breaking from the conventional concept of office (Council on National ICT Strategies Report to the President, July 2010).
- Smart work is a work-environment concept that helps enhance business efficiency by allowing people to work in a convenient and smart way anytime anywhere without being constrained by time and place ("Smart Work Activation Plan," Korea Communications Commission, January 2011).

In examining the definition of smart work, it is found that smart work is not commonly accepted yet and rather used broadly covering different terms found in previous studies. Telework in the United States, the United Kingdom, and Japan and flexible work in EU countries were being used in a similar sense, already for a while.

- "Telework" in the United States: The Telework Enhancement Act of 2010 defines "telework (or teleworking) as a work flexibility arrangement under which an employee (i.e., teleworker) performs his/her duties and responsibilities and other authorized activities from a newly approved worksite other than his/her traditional workplace."
- "Telework" in the United Kingdom: The Labour Force Survey by the Office of National Statistics defines teleworkers as "people who do some paid or unpaid work at their own home using both a phone and a computer." They include
  - People who mainly work from home in their main job—teleworkers and homeworkers
  - People who work in various locations but use their home as a base—home-based teleworkers
  - People who do not usually work at home or use their home as a base but did work at home at least one day in the reference period—occasional teleworkers
- "Telework" in Japan: The Ministry of Land, Infrastructure, Transport and Tourism defines telework as "a method of working in a flexible manner by using information and communication technologies without being constrained by time and place."
- "Flexible work" in the European Union: When carrying out an Establishment Survey on Working Time and Work-Life Balance (ESWT) for flexible working conditions in its member states, the European Union (EU) classifies flexible workers in terms of working time flexibility, overtime work, part-time work, etc.

4.2.2 Dimensions of New Ways of Working

On close inspection of these definitions with other related materials, four dimensions can be identified as defining the work transformation due to ICT that may be influenced by the use of ICT. First of all, the technology is the one that actually triggered these transformations; ICT itself would be a critical dimension in new ways of working. Depending upon the capabilities provided by ICT, the shape and

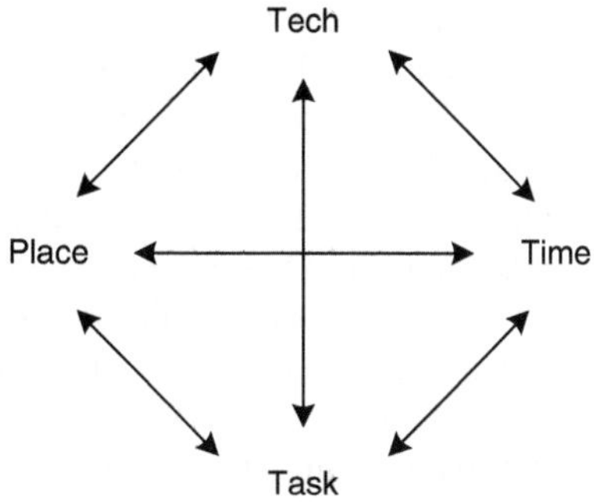

Fig. 4.1 Dimensions of new way of work

form of work might become different. Email and groupware, for example, allows people to communicate asynchronously in different locations. Also, these technologies enable us to work anywhere anytime with data storage and communication capabilities—cloud. You can access databases and keep working on the project during the night at home via Internet communication lines. Henceforth, time and place of work can be defined and regulated differently from the ones in the industrialized settings. In this regard, time and space are the other two dimensions that need to be dealt with in dealing with the new ways of working. At the same time, the nature of tasks may change with the use of ICT. For example, computing power may easily subsume the part of routine tasks such as calculation and verification. Secretarial tasks today usually do not include letter typing, which used to be the primary responsibility of a secretary in old times.

- Time (working time flexibility): a variety of work hour adjustments
- Place (workplace flexibility): a variety of feasible worksites and mobility
- Technology (use of ICT): available computing power and communication capabilities
- Task (knowledge intensity): knowledgification, projectification, and virtualization (Fig. 4.1)

4.3 Research Method: Systematic Literature Review

Over the last decades, there has been a substantial growth in the body of literature dealing with the impact of ICT on work and business process but in a fragmented manner scattered across different disciplines addressing a variety of perspectives, such as telecommuting, flexible time, home-based business, cowork, mobile work, process innovation, etc. Smart work mentioned above may sound like a neologism, but in fact the term has been used in different forms in relation to what ICT brings into the business and society in terms of productivity improvements, business efficiency, and quality of life. In the related fields, academic studies began long before dealing with the phenomena, not only to increase productivity but also to understand what is happening.

However, there is no consensus on how the work is actually changing in its nature, shape, and form. In response to this lack of consensus, a systematic review of related literature is conducted here. To integrate the fragmented pieces of research conducted across different domains and disciplines, related variables used in prior studies are collected and analyzed. For the first step, a computerized search was conducted using 15 different keywords using EBSCOHost search engine—alternative work, enterprise mobility, e-working, flexible work, flextime, home labor, home office, home-based business, home-based work, mobile office, telecommuting, telework, virtual office, working smart, and working smarter. A total of 913 articles surfaced containing these keywords.

4.4 Analysis

Content analysis of 913 collected articles was carried out by a panel of three experts, and a total of 372 variables seemed to be related to the changing nature of work due to ICT. Some variables are at the individual level such as attitudes, characteristics, and so on and some at the organizational level such as culture, structure, etc. In this regard, these variables can be largely grouped into three different levels: individual, organizational, and society.

4.4.1 Individual Level

Out of 372 variables identified, 145 belong to the individual level. Via a series of focus group activities, these 145 variables are refined and grouped into 16 categorical constructs related to the work transformation due to ICT at individual levels. Some seem to be preceding the transformation while some are related to the impact of transformation as presented in Fig. 4.2. Table 4.1 summarizes the variables and grouping constructs. Figure 4.2 also presents the proposed relationship among these 16 individual-level constructs.

At the individual level, three groups of variables are found to be preceding the transformation of work due to ICT: (1) individual characteristics, (2) accommodation, and (3) motivation. The individual characteristics include attitudes, independency, interpersonal skills, reliability, and self-direction levels while the accommodating factors include environmental condition of work and support from the family. Motivational factors include the personal controllability of time and individual situations and goals.

As for the critical transformation itself that may occur at the individual level, interesting and practical variables are found. Identified variables are creativity, decision latitude, decision flexibility, demand flexibility, informal flexibility, lateral communications, task expansion, timely communication, work intensification, etc. Importantly, it seems that creativity be increased as the result of work transforma-

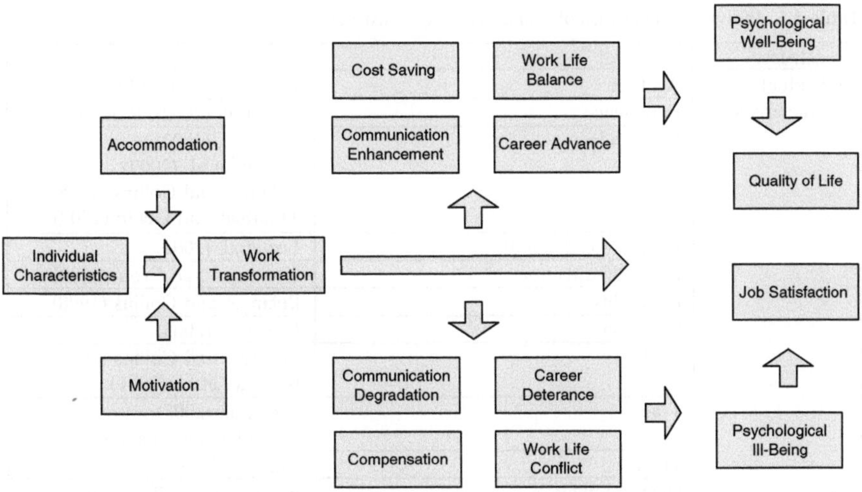

Fig. 4.2 Relational diagram for individual level

tion incurred by ICT (Schoemaker 2003; Ory et al. 2004) while decision latitude of workers increased after the transformation (Swanberg and Simmons 2008; Taskin and Devos 2005). In most cases, flexibility seems to be critically increased in terms of demand, informality, and decision-making with this ICT-related transformation of work (Kashefi 2007; Lee et al. 2002; Richman et al. 2008).

A series of focus groups identified two ultimate dependent variables: quality of life and job satisfaction. From the transformation of work toward the ultimate dependent, literature seems to have two divergent paths in reaching the ultimate outcome of work transformation—quality of life and job satisfaction. Path presented along the top consists of cost savings, communication enhancements, career advances, and work-life balance. These variables are mostly very positive. Saving costs, enhancing communications, advancing careers, and balancing work and life may lead to higher satisfaction and better quality of life. Compared to the positive connotation found in variables on the top part of the diagram, variables presented along the bottom contain somewhat negative connotations—compensation, communication degradation, career deterrence, and work-life conflict.

It should be noted here that there are studies that provide contradicting results about the impacts of transformed work at the individual level. Some studies find that it would be economically effective as the transformed work saves cost, while others argue that using it may increase the cost as it requires additional compensation, such as the equipment cost expensed at home for telework, etc. Also, there are studies that argue the new ways of work would make the communication smoother, while other studies point out that it would cause problems with communication as it reduces the chance of direct encounter between coworkers or with bosses.

When it comes to the dependent side, some argue that it can improve the workers' quality of life by increasing the psychological well-being as a result of well-balanced work and life, while others argue that it would create a work environment

Table 4.1 Individual level variables and grouping constructs

Constructs	Variables	References
Individual Characteristics	Attitude	Dex and Scheibl (2001)
	Experience	Lee et al. (2002), Reinsch (1997)
	Independency	Lee et al. (2002), O'Neill et al. (2009), Belanger and Collins (1998), Tremblay and Genin (2008)
	Interpersonally skilled	Lee et al. (2002)
	Low self-direction	Goodman and Crouter (2009)
	Reliability	Belanger and Collins (1998)
	Situation	Lee et al. (2000)
	Skill	Belanger and Collins (1998), Belanger et al. (2001)
	Trait	Lee et al. (2002), Tremblay and Genin (2008)
	Trust	Ralston (1989)
	Demographics	Blomme et al. (2010), Guelzow et al. (1991), Tremblay et al. (2006)
Accommodation	Physical requirements	Olson (1983)
	Supportive family/home environment	Beauregard (2011), Lyness and Kropf (2005)
	Like office environment	Tremblay and Genin (2008), Hardill and Green (2003)
Motivation	Control	Hohl (1996), Youngsoo and Sungkwon (2004), Swanberg et al. (2005), Grönlund (2007a)
	Individual objectives	Belanger and Collins (1998), Konradt et al. (2003)
Work transformation	Creativity	Schoemaker (2003), Ory et al. (2004)
	Decision latitude	Swanberg and Simmons (2008), Taskin and Devos (2005)
	Decision-making flexibility	Kashefi (2007)
	Demand flexibility	Lee et al. (2002)
	Informal flexibility	Richman et al. (2008)
	Lateral communication	Bosch-Sijtsema (2007)
	Task expansion	Bosch-Sijtsema (2007), Brandth and Kvande (2001), Molleman and Slomp (1999)
	Timely communication	Gittell (2000)
	Work intensification	Thom and Blum (1998)
Cost saving	Commute cost and time	Belanger and Collins (1998), Ralston (1989), Golembiewski and Proehl (1978), Mann and Holdsworth (2003)
	Financial benefit	Lee et al. (2000)
	Lower lunch and business clothing costs	Belanger and Collins (1998)
	Reduced travel time	Fish and Fish (2010), Hicks and Klimoski (1981)

(continued)

Table 4.1 (continued)

Constructs	Variables	References
Communication enhancement	Communication enhancement	Golembiewski and Proehl (1978)
	Informal communication	Fay and Kline (2011)
	Mutual respect	Gittell (2000)
Compensation	Benefit cut	Kashefi (2007)
	Pension cut	Pitt-Catsouphes et al. (2009), Branine (1999)
	Wage cut	Branine (1999), Moen et al. (2008), Weeden (2005)
Communication degradation	Problems in communication with colleagues	Leonardi et al. (2010), Wellman et al. (1996)
Work life balance	Family care	Mamaghani (2006), Shapiro et al. (2009a, b), Robinson (2005), Scandura and Lankau (1997), Andrews et al. (2004), Geurts et al. (2009)
	Life enhancement	Tremblay et al. (2006), Mann and Holdsworth (2003), Polach (2003)
	Marital equity	Guelzow et al. (1991), Andrews et al. (2004)
	Marital stress	Guelzow et al. (1991)
	Parental stress	Guelzow et al. (1991)
Work life conflict	Conflict	Blomme et al. (2010), Tremblay et al. (2006), Gajendran and Harrison (2007), Goleden et al. (2006), Damarin (2006), Grönlund (2007b), Wylie et al. (2010), Liu et al. (2011), Blair-Loy (2009)
	Spillover	Tremblay and Genin (2008), Golembiewski and Proehl (1978), Mann and Holdsworth (2003), Moen et al. (2008), Grönlund (2007b), Russell et al. (2009), Schieman and Glavin (2008), Hughes and Parkes (2007)
Career advance	Skill development	Eldridge and Nisar (2006)
	Career efficiencies	Brown et al. (2003)
	Career advancement	Barnett et al. (2004), Rogier and Padgett (2004)
	Continuity/Career development	Rogier and Padgett (2004), Johnson (2004)
	Need for achievement	O'Neill et al. (2009)
	Progress into top leadership positions	Shapiro et al. (2009a)
Career deterrence	Career impact	Branine (1999), Kelliher and Anderson (2008)
	Discouraged/negative career prospects	Rogier and Padgett (2004), Albion (2004)
	Losing come of the technical advances	Talukder (2003)

(continued)

Table 4.1 (continued)

Constructs	Variables	References
Psychological well-being	Benefits related to employees' health	Dex and Scheibl (2001), Pitt-Catsouphes et al. (2009)
	Less stress	Guelzow et al. (1991), Branine (1999)
	Reductions in physical and psychological symptoms of job strain	Beauregard (2011), Hughes and Parkes (2007), Albion (2004)
Psychological il-being	Stress	Konradt et al. (2003), Mann and Holdsworth (2003), Hughes and Parkes (2007), Raghuram and Wiesenfeld (2004)
	Loneliness	Mann and Holdsworth (2003)
	Lack of social interaction	Taskin and Devos (2005), O'Leary and Mortensen (2010)
	Sociability	O'Neill et al. (2009), Golden et al. (2008)
	Worry	Mann and Holdsworth (2003)
	Guilt	Mann and Holdsworth (2003)
	Irritability	Mann and Holdsworth (2003)
	Frustration	Mann and Holdsworth (2003)
Quality of life	Life enhancement	Branine (1999), Shapiro et al. (2009a)
	Quality of life	Tremblay et al. (2006), Atkinson and Hall (2009), Hall and Atkinson (2006)
Job satisfaction	Employee satisfaction	Richman et al. (2008), Manoochehri and Pinkerton (2003)
	High job satisfaction	Ralston (1989), Fay and Kline (2011)

where workers cannot concentrate on work due to the higher spillovers between work and life, increasing the interference of families destroying the balance between work and life that may lead to psychological ill-being. Some studies insist that new ways of work can help with individual careers as it freely adjusts the time and place of work to make it possible to add secondary jobs and participate in various professional projects, while other studies are concerned that it may have negative influences on individual careers due to the lack of interaction with supervisors to experience disadvantages in promotion.

There were studies that focused on examining the positive factors arguing that the stress of workers would be reduced and provide the mental stability to lead healthy lives leading to higher quality of life and job satisfaction, while other studies argued that it has a negative influence on the quality of life and job satisfaction as workers suffer from career deterrence and higher level of work–life conflict.

This kind of paradoxical duality in work transformation research might be natural as we do not have complete understanding of its characteristics and the nature of changes. It seems that, as the change is in progress, researchers are striving to figure

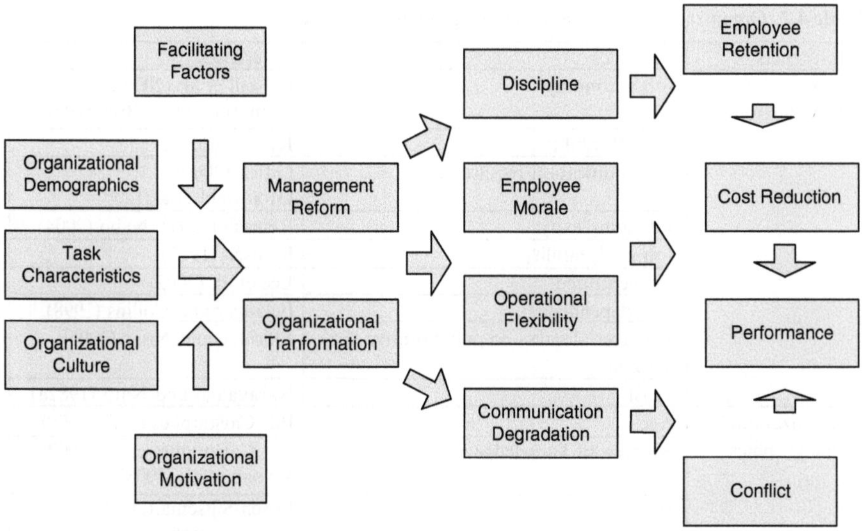

Fig. 4.3 Relational diagram of organizational level constructs

out the nature of changes and possibly the consequences. Further studies would be needed figuring out real impacts as well as appropriate designs of ICT channeling positives and suppressing negatives.

4.4.2 Organization Level

There were many studies that discussed the factors at the organizational level: 194 variables belong to the organizational level, and after the series of focus group refinements, these are grouped into 15 constructs. Figure 4.3 presents the relational diagram of constructs at the organizational level while Table 4.2 contains detailed variables and references.

Organizational-level antecedent factors appear to be similar to individual-level factors in terms of composition. It was analyzed that there are certain organizational characteristics, scale, and culture that can accept smart work successfully. It was analyzed that the jobs that are highly independent and autonomous and based on knowledge and information make it possible to accept smart work, and there was a number of studies that argued that the statistical characteristics of organizations, such as scale, age, and culture, serve as the variables that control the introduction or activation of smart work. Organizational facilities and motivation are also included in the antecedent factors similar to the accommodation and motivation of the individual level. These studies point out that it is the antecedent for the organization to build the infrastructure to execute smart work, and the smart work is executed by the demands of organization members or the motivations inside the organization to introduce smart work.

Table 4.2 Organizational level variables and grouping constructs

Constructs	Variables	References
Task characteristics	Job autonomy	O'Neill et al. (2009), Damarin (2006), Brey (1999)
	Task flexibility	Kashefi (2007)
	Communication requirements	Gittell (2000), Grosswald et al. (2001)
	Job complexity	Reinsch (1997), Nybø (2004)
	Job analyzability	Reinsch (1997)
	Concentrated	Lee et al. (2002)
	Interdependence	Belanger and Collins (1998)
	Managerial stress on collaborative working	Eldridge and Nisar (2006)
	Trust	Narayanan and Nath (1982a)
Organizational demographics	Age	Pitt-Catsouphes et al. (2009)
	Number of knowledge workers	Pitt-Catsouphes et al. (2009), Wilson et al. (2008)
	Size	Bosch-Sijtsema (2007), Pitt-Catsouphes et al. (2009), Wylie et al. (2010), Michie and Sheehan-Quinn (2001)
	Structure	Wylie et al. (2010)
Organizational Motivation	Accommodating employee demand	Swanberg and Simmons (2008), Dex and Scheibl (2001)
	Elaborating current culture and policy	Lee et al. (2000), Pitt-Catsouphes et al. (2009)
Organizational culture	Flexibility	Pitt-Catsouphes et al. (2009), Giannikis and Mihail (2011)
	Culture (Rituals, Norms)	Belanger et al. (2001), Beauregard (2011), Grosswald et al. (2001)
	Values	Lee et al. (2002)
Facilitating factors	Preceding cases	Lee et al. (2000, 2002)
Organization Transformation	Benefit of flextime	Ralston (1989)
	Casualization	Johnson (2004)
	Coordination	O'Leary and Mortensen (2010)
	Distancing	O'Reilly (1992)
	Flexibility	Thom and Blum (1998), O'Leary and Mortensen (2010)
	Formal program	Lee et al. (2000)
	Functional integration	Gittell (2000)
	Intensity of work	Lee et al. (2000), Russell et al. (2009)
	Justice	Kurland and Egan (1999)
	Lateral communication	Grosswald et al. (2001)
	Novel work schedule	Hammer and Barbera (1997)

(continued)

Table 4.2 (continued)

Constructs	Variables	References
	Org support	Lee et al. (2002), Richman et al. (2008), Beauregard (2011), Mann and Holdsworth (2003), Presser (1995)
	Policy	Lee et al. (2000)
	Procedural change	Taskin and Devos (2005), Lee et al. (2000), Brandth and Kvande (2001), Damarin (2006), Kurland and Egan (1999), Presser (1995), Narayanan and Nath (1982b)
	Quality of management supervision	Swanberg and Simmons (2008), Narayanan and Nath (1982b)
	Resource management	Ralston (1989)
	Work disintegration	Lee et al. (2000)
Management reform	Control	Gittell (2000)
	Supervision and Monitoring	Swanberg and Simmons (2008), Narayanan and Nath (1982b)
	Relationship quality	Reinsch (1997), Narayanan and Nath (1982b), Golden (2006)
Discipline	Absenteeism	Belanger and Collins (1998), Ralston (1989), Mann and Holdsworth (2003), Albion (2004)
Employee morale	Commitment	Lee et al. (2002), Dex and Scheibl (2001), Fay and Kline (2011), Branine (1999)
	Engagement	Richman et al. (2008)
	Participation	Johnson (2004)
	Employee morale	Belanger and Collins (1998), Golembiewski and Proehl (1978)
Operational flexibility	Contingent employment and Workforce flexibility	Mann and Holdsworth (2003), Wilson et al. (2008), Michie and Sheehan-Quinn (2001), O'Reilly (1992)
	Financial flexibility	Lee et al. (2000), Podnar and Golob (2010), Guerrier and Lockwood (1989)
	Functional flexibility	Kashefi (2007), O'Reilly (1992), Branine (2004)
	Process flexibility	Robinson (2005)
	Workload flexibility	Lee et al. (2000)
	Time flexibility	Scandura and Lankau (1997), Podnar and Golob (2010)
Communication degradation	Communication degradation	Branine (1999), Johnson (2004), Narayanan and Nath (1982b)
	Lack of informal support	Fay and Kline (2011), Branine (1999), Albion (2004)

(continued)

Table 4.2 (continued)

Constructs	Variables	References
Employee retention	Employee retention	Richman et al. (2008), Lee et al. (2000)
	Turnover intention	Blomme et al. (2010), Albion (2004), Cappelli and Neumark (2004)
	Shortage in skilled worker	Lee et al. (2002), Abdel-Wahab (2007)
Cost reduction	Cost	Belanger et al. (2001)
	Overhead	Belanger et al. (2001)
	Space	Mamaghani (2006)
	Employee turnover cost	Mamaghani (2006)
Conflict	Conflict between employee and management	Reinsch (1997), Branine (1999), Johnson (2004), Narayanan and Nath (1982b), Cascio and Shurygailo (2003)
	Conflict between teleworker and non-teleworker	Branine (1999), Johnson (2004), Narayanan and Nath (1982b), Lee et al. (2007), Whalley (2007)
	Lack of respect	Bogdanski and Setliff (2000)
	Continuity of care	Branine (1999)
	Communication problem	Johnson (2004)
	Downward communication	Narayanan and Nath (1982b)
	Employee assessment	Golembiewski and Proehl (1978), Albion (2004)
Performance	Corporate promotion	Lee et al. (2000)
	Diversity	Lee et al. (2000)
	Performance	Golden et al. (2008), Stavrou (2005)
	Productivity	Dex and Scheibl (2001), Ralston (1989)
	Profitability	Mamaghani (2006), MacEachen et al. (2008)
	Customer satisfaction	Alkadi et al. (2003)

When smart work is introduced, it motivates the organization to change or deform its management type or the organization itself. Smart work reduces the bureaucratic character or procedure of the organization and changes its task-processing procedure or organizational structure. A number of studies have been found that argue workers' direct demands, the pressure of labor and management, and/or the policy guides serve as the motivation to influence the introduction of smart work.

These antecedents of smart work ultimately influence the dependent variables that improve organizational performance and productivity. This study found that the change of organization with the introduction of smart work influences workers' satisfaction and increases workers' sacrifice to the organization to reduce transfer rate or absence rate. Smart work can also improve job performance and creativity, save the indirect cost to manage offices and operate office appliances, and save the costs related to real estate, especially office spaces and parking spaces. It was also found that workers can be hired flexibly according to the organization's circumstances to ensure flexibility of operation. On the other hand, it was analyzed that there is a number of negative factors, such as the conflicts between workers and managers caused by the lack of face-to-face communication between workers on smart work, the lowering loyalty to organizations, the loneliness of workers, and the inability to support the workers' work environment directly. In particular, this study determined that further studies should be conducted to address the managers' difficulty to evaluate the workers' work hours and dedication to evaluate their performance (Table 4.2).

4.4.3 Society Level

32 out of 372 variables belong to the society level. These 32 variables can be grouped into 6 constructs. Figure 4.4 shows the relational diagram of constructs at the society level while Table 4.3 presents details of references.

Previous literature showed that the development of information communication technology and devices are the antecedents leading smart work, and personal information protection and information security are mentioned as the important factors that should be considered in the social level when executing smart work. Preceded literature has mentioned that the introduction and activation of smart work have a positive influence to ensure employment security and gender equality and increase job opportunities for the disabled, seniors, and housewives and that it is a useful system that can reduce the use of transportation and safe parking space to save social costs and satisfy the low-carbon green growth policies. Preceded literature also argues that these factors make general social changes. The following figure structuralizes the relation of variable groups.

Considering the detailed variables in the social level, the development of infrastructural technology and the elements of environmental support that make smart

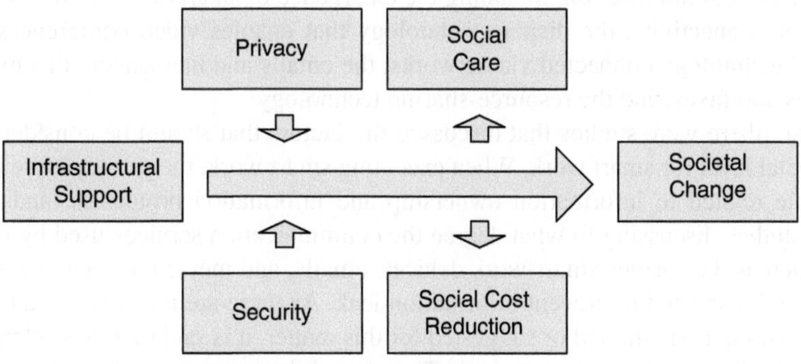

Fig. 4.4 Relational diagram of society level constructs

Table 4.3 Society level variables and grouping constructs

Constructs	Variables	References
Infrastructural support	Advance ICT	Gittell (2000), Grosswald et al. (2001), Wajcman et al. (2010)
	Environment	Belanger et al. (2001), Mamaghani (2006)
Privacy	Email monitoring or spot check	Voudouris (2004), Fay (1993), Munroe (2007)
	Information ownership	Abdel-Wahab (2007)
Security	Security	Munroe (2007)
Social care	Elder care	Pitt-Catsouphes et al. (2009), Michie and Sheehan-Quinn (2001)
	Employment stability	Kashefi (2007), Branine (1999); de Cuyper et al. (2009), Bratu (2009), Morgan and Allington (2002)
	Handicap care	Mamaghani (2006), Abdel-Wahab (2007)
	Sick care	Mamaghani (2006)
	Benefit the society	Manoochehri and Pinkerton (2003), Michie and Sheehan-Quinn (2001)
Social cost reduction	Pollution	Abdel-Wahab (2007)
	Traffic	Abdel-Wahab (2007)
Societal change	Freelance work	Hardill and Green (2003)
	Growing incidence of contingent employment	Wilson et al. (2008)

work possible composed the group of antecedents. Preceded studies mentioned the environmental element that incurs almost no cost of information exchange with the decreasing prices of computers and the spread of Internet connectivity. There were also studies that smart work was made possible by the development of technologies for smooth communication, including the emergence of smart devices, the wireless Internet connectivity, the display technology that enables video conferences, the virtual technology connected via networks, the emails and messengers that exceed phones and faxes, and the resource-sharing technology.

Also, there were studies that discussed the factors that should be considered in the social level for smart work. When executing smart work, the privacy issue is the variable related to information ownership and information protection, and there were studies discussing to what degree the communication services used by workers, such as the various smart-work devices, emails, and messengers, can be monitored and inspected to prevent information leak. As there are no clear standards or advanced methods studied or suggested for this matter, it is said that these elements influence the execution of smart work. Therefore, it is necessary to study the privacy issue.

There were studies that analyzed that security and information protection issues are the elements that influence the execution of smart work. It is also explained that smart work is used to work in a space outside the office and it is important to provide strict physical/technical security measures and that companies' introduction of smart work is influenced by the investment in security and concerns about information leak.

There are studies that argue that the influence of social interests and stability factors is strong when executing smart work. In other words, it is explained that these factors influence the activation of smart work because the smart work system that allows working from home or flexible work hours makes it possible for seniors and the people obliged to take care of children find jobs and old workers with know-how to continue working in the professional field. Also, workers who cannot physically go to work every day due to diseases can work without absence through smart work. Not only that, it is argued that the society generates profits overall as smart work allows stabilization of employment by increasing employment, creating jobs, and hiring the disabled.

The decrease in commuters instantly leads to the decrease in the use of transportation measures. This factor generates social benefits, such as economic benefits and decrease in environmental pollution, by decreasing traffic congestion. There was a study that argued that it generates economic effects by decreasing social costs.

This study also noticed some studies that argued smart work increases professional freelance jobs in various fields and promotes employment in various areas (Table 4.3).

4.5 Discussion

The changing nature of work due to the advanced and in-depth adoption of ICT is an important and critical phenomenon in the modern society. The new ways of work had been researched for decades under different terminologies such as telecommuting and flexible time schemes. In order to gain insights from previous related research, a systematic literature review has been conducted in order to reveal the related constructs and understand the basic nature and characteristics of these changes. From searches of academic databases, 913 related studies were selected. Total of 372 variables were identified from the literature as critically important in researching this changing nature of work phenomenon. Among the 372, 146 were at the individual level, 194 were at the organizational level, and 32 were at the society level. Subsequent focus group activities clustered 146 variables into 16 grouping constructs at the individual level, 194 into 15 at the organizational level, and 32 into 6 at the society level.

Also, close inspection of construct content reveals proposed relationships among these constructs: antecedents and consequences. As results, research frameworks are proposed and presented. This framework could be used for policy development as it suggests the constructs that could be monitored in the micro and macro levels about the changes being incurred by the use of ICT as it will proceed further deep down into the fabric of our society and business as technology advances.

Acknowledgments Preliminary results of this study had been presented at the 7th International Conference on Theory and Practice of Electronic Governance in Seoul, Korea, October 22–25, and the 1st International Workshop on the Changing Nature of Work due to ICT in Milan, Italy, December 15, 2013. This work was partially supported by the National Research Foundation of Korea Grant funded by the Korean Government (NRF-2012S1A3A2033474).

References

Abdel-Wahab AG (2007) Employees' attitudes towards telecommuting. An empirical investigation in the Egyptian Governorate of Dakahlia. Behav Inf Technol 26(5):367–375

Albion MJ (2004) A measure of attitudes towards flexible work options. Aust J Manag 29(2):275–294

Alkadi I, Alkadi G, Totaro M (2003) Effects of information technology on the business world. Hum Res Manag 22(3):99–103

Andrews AB et al (2004) Public perceptions about father involvement: results of a statewide household survey. J Fam Issues 25(5):603–633

Atkinson C, Hall L (2009) The role of gender in varying forms of flexible working. Gend Work Organ 16(6):650–666

Barnett RC et al (2004) Unintended consequences of job redesign. Community Work Fam 7(2):227–246

Beauregard TA (2011) Direct and indirect links between organizational work-home culture and employee well-being. Br J Manag 22(2):218–237

Belanger F, Collins RW (1998) Distributed work arrangements: a research framework. Inf Soc 14(2):137–152

Belanger F, Collins RW, Cheney PH (2001) Technology requirements and work group communication for telecommuters. Inf Syst Res 12(2):155–176

Blair-Loy M (2009) Work without end? Scheduling flexibility and work-to-family conflict among stockbrokers. Work Occup 36(4):279–317

Blomme RJ, Van Rheede A, Tromp DM (2010) Work-family conflict as a cause for turnover intentions in the hospitality industry. Tour Hosp Res 10(4):269–285

Bogdanski C, Setliff RJ (2000) Leaderless supervision: a response to Thomas. Hum Res Dev Q 11(2):197–201

Bosch-Sijtsema P (2007) The impact of individual expectations and expectation conflicts on virtual teams. Group Organ Manag 32(3):358–388

Brandth B, Kvande E (2001) Flexible work and flexible fathers. Work Employ Soc 15(2):251–267

Branine M (1999) Part-time work in the public health service of Denmark, France and the UK. Int J Hum Res Manage 10(3):411–428

Branine M (2004) Job sharing and equal opportunities under the new public management in local authorities. Int J Public Sect Manag 17(2):136–152

Bratu C (2009) Homework -- an Expression of Flexi-Security of Work Relations. Munca la domiciliu -- expresie a flexi-securităţii relaţiilor de muncă 61(4):81–91

Brey P (1999) Worker autonomy and the drama of digital networks in organizations. J Bus Ethics 22(1):15–25

Brown AJ, Swinyard W, Ogle J (2003) Women in academic medicine: a report of focus groups and questionnaires, with conjoint analysis. J Womens Health 12(10):999–1008

Cappelli P, Neumark D (2004) External churning and internal flexibility: evidence on the functional flexibility and core-periphery hypotheses. Ind Relat 43(1):148–182

Cascio WF, Shurygailo S (2003) E-Leadership and virtual teams. Organ Dyn 31(4):362–376
Damarin AK (2006) Rethinking occupational structure. Work Occup 33(4):429–463
de Cuyper N et al (2009) Organizations' use of temporary employment and a climate of job insecurity among Belgian and Spanish permanent workers. Econ Ind Democr 30(4):564–591
Dex S, Scheibl F (2001) Flexible and family-friendly working arrangements in UK-based SMEs: business cases. Br J Ind Relat 39(3):411–431
Eldridge D, Nisar TM (2006) The significance of employee skill in flexible work organizations. Int J Hum Res Manage 17(5):918–937
Fay SJ (1993) The rise and fall of tagging as a criminal justice measure in Britain. Int J Sociol Law 21(4):301–317
Fay MJ, Kline SL (2011) Coworker relationships and informal communication in high-intensity telecommuting. J Appl Commun Res 39(2):144–163
Fish LA, Fish LA (2010) Career expectations and perceptions of part-time MBA students. Coll Stud J 44(3):706–719
Gajendran RS, Harrison DA (2007) The good, the bad, and the unknown about telecommuting: meta-analysis of psychological mediators and individual consequences. J Appl Psychol 92(6):1524–1541
Geurts S et al (2009) Worktime demands and work-family interference: does worktime control buffer the adverse effects of high demands? J Bus Ethics 84:229–241
Giannikis SK, Mihail DM (2011) Flexible work arrangements in Greece: a study of employee perceptions. Int J Hum Res Manage 22(2):417–432
Gittell JH (2000) Organizing work to support relational co-ordination. Int J Hum Res Manage 11(3):517–539
Golden TD (2006) The role of relationships in understanding telecommuter satisfaction. J Organ Behav 27(3):319–340
Golden TD, Veiga JF, Dino RN (2008) The impact of professional isolation on teleworker job performance and turnover intentions: does time spent teleworking, interacting face-to-face, or having access to communication-enhancing technology matter? J Appl Psychol 93(6):1412–1421
Goleden TD, Veiga JF, Simsek Z (2006) Telecommuting's differential impact on work-family conflict: is there no place like home? J Appl Psychol 91(6):1340–1350
Golembiewski RT, Proehl CW Jr (1978) A survey of the empirical literature on flexible workhours: character and consequences of a major innovation. Acad Manage Rev 3(4):837–853
Goodman WB, Crouter AC (2009) Longitudinal associations between maternal work stress, negative work-family spillover, and depressive symptoms. Fam Relat 58(3):245–258
Grönlund A (2007a) Employee control in the era of flecibility: a stress buffer or a stress amplifier? Eur Soc 9(3):409–428
Grönlund A (2007b) More control, less conflict? Job demand–control, gender and work–family conflict. Gend Work Organ 14(5):476–497
Grosswald B, Ragland D, Fisher JM (2001) Critique of U.S. work/family programs and policies. J Progress Hum Serv 12(1):65–81
Guelzow MG, Bird GW, Koball EH (1991) An exploratory path analysis of the stress process for dual-career men and women. J Marriage Fam 53(1):151–164
Guerrier Y, Lockwood AJ (1989) Managing flexible working in hotels. Serv Ind J 9(3):406–419
Hall L, Atkinson C (2006) Improving working lives: flexible working and the role of employee control. Employ Relat 28(4):374–385
Hammer LB, Barbera KM (1997) Toward an integration of alternative work. Hum Res Plan 20(2):28–36
Hardill I, Green A (2003) Remote working—Altering the spatial contours of work and home in the new economy. N Technol Work Employ 18(3):212
Hicks WD, Klimoski RJ (1981) The impact of flextime on employee attitudes. Acad Manage J 24(2):333–341
Hohl KL (1996) The effects of flexible work arrangements. Nonprofit Manag Leadersh 7(1):69–86

Hughes EL, Parkes KR (2007) Work hours and well-being: the roles of work-time control and work-family interference. Work Stress 21(3):264–278
Johnson J (2004) Flexible working: changing the manager's role. Manag Decis 42(6):721–737
Kashefi M (2007) Work flexibility and its individual consequences. Can J Sociol 32(3):341–369
Kelliher C, Anderson D (2008) For better or for worse? An analysis of how flexible working practices influence employees' perceptions of job quality. Int J Hum Res Manage 19(3):419–431
Konradt U, Hertel G, Schmook R (2003) Quality of management by objectives, task-related stressors, and non-task-related stressors as predictors of stress and job satisfaction among teleworkers. Eur J Work Organ Psychol 12(1):61–79
Kurland NB, Egan TD (1999) Telecommuting: justice and control in the virtual organization. Organ Sci 10(4):500–513
Lee MD, MacDermid SM, Buck ML (2000) Organizational paradigms of reduced-load work: accomodation, elaboration, and transformation. Acad Manage J 43(6):1211–1226
Lee MD et al (2002) Contextual factors in the success of reduced-load work arrangements among managers and professionals. Hum Resour Manage 41(2):209–223
Lee H, Shin B, Higa K (2007) Telework vs. Central work: a comparative view of knowledge accessibility. Decis Support Syst 43(3):687–700
Leonardi PM, Treem JW, Jackson MH (2010) The connectivity paradox: using technology to both decrease and increase perceptions of distance in distributed work arrangements. J Appl Commun Res 38(1):85–105
Liu H et al (2011) Non-standard work schedules, work–family conflict and parental well-being: a comparison of married and cohabiting unions. Soc Sci Res 40(2):473–484
Lyness KS, Kropf MB (2005) The relationships of national gender equality and organizational support with work-family balance: a study of European managers. Hum Relat 58(1):33–60
MacEachen E, Polzer J, Clarke J (2008) "You are free to set your own hours": governing worker productivity and health through flexibility and resilience. Soc Sci Med 66(5):1019–1033
Mamaghani F (2006) Impact of information technology on the workforce of the future: an analysis. Int J Manag 23(4):845–850
Mann S, Holdsworth L (2003) The psychological impact of teleworking: stress, emotions and health. N Technol Work Employ 18(3):196
Manoochehri G, Pinkerton T (2003) Managing telecommuters: opportunities and challenges. Am Bus Rev 21(1):9–16
Michie J, Sheehan-Quinn M (2001) Labour market flexibility, human resource management and corporate performance. Br J Manag 12(4):287–306
Moen P, Kelly E, Huang R (2008) 'Fit' inside the work-family black box: an ecology of the life course, cycles of control reframing. J Occup Organ Psychol 81(3):411–433
Molleman E, Slomp J (1999) Functional flexibility and team performance. Int J Prod Res 37(8):1837–1858
Morgan P, Allington N (2002) Has the public sector retained its 'Model Employer' status? Public Money Manag 22(1):35–42
Munroe F (2007) Managing privacy and security compliance. J Health Care Compliance 9(1):69–85
Narayanan VK, Nath R (1982a) A field testing of some attitudinal and behavioral consequences of flexitime. J Appl Psychol 67(2):214–218
Narayanan VK, Nath R (1982b) Hierarchical level and the impact of flextime. Ind Rel 21(2):216–230
Nybø G (2004) Personnel development for dissolving jobs: towards a competency-based approach? Int J Hum Res Manage 15(3):549–564
O'Leary MB, Mortensen M (2010) Go (Con)figure: subgroups, imbalance, and isolates in geographically dispersed teams. Organ Sci 21(1):115–131
Olson MH (1983) Remote office work: changing work patterns in space and time. Commun ACM 26(3):182–187
O'Neill TA et al (2009) Predicting teleworker success: an exploration of personality, motivational, situational, and job characteristics. N Technol Work Employ 24(2):144–162

O'Reilly J (1992) Banking on flexibility: a comparison of the use of flexible employment strategies in the retail banking sector in Britain and France. Int J Hum Res Manage 3(1):35–58
Ory DT et al (2004) When is commuting desirable to the individual? Growth Chang 35(3):334–359
Pitt-Catsouphes M, Sano J, Matz-Costa C (2009) Unions' responsiveness to the aging of the workforce. J Workplace Behav Health 24(1/2):125–146
Podnar K, Golob U (2010) Friendly flexible working practices within the internal marketing framework: a service perspective. Serv Ind J 30(11):1773–1786
Polach J (2003) HRD's role in work-life integration issues: moving the workforce to a change in mindset. Hum Res Dev Int 6(1):57–68
Presser HB (1995) Job, family, and gender: determinants of nonstandard work schedules among employed Americans in 1991. Demography 32(4):577–598
Raghuram S, Wiesenfeld B (2004) Work-nonwork conflict and job stress among virtual workers. Hum Resour Manage 43(2/3):259–277
Ralston DA (1989) The benefits of flextime: real or imagined? J Organ Behav 10(4):369–373
Reinsch NL (1997) Relationships between telecommuting workers and their managers: an exploratory study. J Bus Commun 34(4):343–369
Richman AL et al (2008) The relationship of perceived flexibility, supportive work-life policies, and use of formal flexible arrangements and occasional flexibility to employee engagement and expected retention. Community Work Fam 11(2):183–197
Robinson W (2005) Ethical considerations in flexible work arrangements. Bus Soc Rev 110(2):213–224
Rogier SA, Padgett MY (2004) The impact of utilizing a flexible work schedule on the perceived career advancement potential of women. Hum Res Dev Q 15(1):89–106
Russell H, O'Connell PJ, McGinnity F (2009) The impact of flexible working arrangements on work–life conflict and work pressure in Ireland. Gend Work Organ 16(1):73–97
Scandura TA, Lankau MJ (1997) Relationships of gender, family responsibility and flexible work hours to organizational commitment and job satisfaction. J Organ Behav 18(4):377–391
Schieman S, Glavin P (2008) Trouble at the border? Gender, flexibility at work, and the work-home interface. Soc Probl 55(4):590–611
Schoemaker M (2003) Identity in flexible organizations: experiences in Dutch organizations. Creat Innov Manag 12(4):191–201
Shapiro M et al (2009a) Making sense of women as career self-agents: implications for human resource development. Hum Res Dev Q 20(4):477–501
Shapiro M, Blake-Beard S, O'Neill R (2009b) Canaries in the mine shaft: women signaling a new career model. People Strategy 32(3):52–59
Stavrou ET (2005) Flexible work bundles and organizational competitiveness: a cross-national study of the European work context. J Organ Behav 26(8):923–947
Swanberg JE, Simmons LA (2008) Quality jobs in the new millennium: incorporating flexible work options as a strategy to assist working families. Soc Ser Rev 82(1):119–147
Swanberg JE, Pitt-Catsouphes M, Drescher-Burke K (2005) A question of justice disparities in employees' access to flexible schedule arrangements. J Fam Issues 26(6):866–895
Talukder MDMI (2003) The perception of professionals and management personnel on the virtual organization. J Comput Inf Syst 43(3):92–99
Taskin L, Devos V (2005) Paradoxes from the individualization of human resource management: the case of telework. J Bus Ethics 62(1):13–24
Thom N, Blum A (1998) The structure of working hours in Swiss companies. Hum Res Manag J 8(3):77–84
Tremblay D-G, Genin É (2008) Permeability between work and non-work: the case of self-employed IT workers. Can J Commun 33(4):701–720
Tremblay D-G, Paquet R, Najem E (2006) Telework: a way to balance work and family or an increase in work–family conflict? Can J Commun 31(3):715–731
Voudouris I (2004) The use of flexible employment arrangements: some new evidence from Greek firms. Int J Hum Res Manage 15(1):131–146

Wajcman J et al (2010) Enacting virtual connections between work and home. J Sociol 46(3):257–275
Weeden KA (2005) Is there a flexiglass ceiling? Flexible work arrangements and wages in the United States. Soc Sci Res 34(2):454–482
Wellman B et al (1996) Computer networks as social networks: collaborative work, telework, and virtual community. Annu Rev Sociol 22(1):213–238
Whalley P (2007) Managing teleworkers and telecommuting strategies. Bus Ethics Q 17(1):163–172
Wilson K, Brown M, Cregan C (2008) Job quality and flexible practices: an investigation of employee perceptions. Int J Hum Res Manage 19(3):473–486
Wylie E et al (2010) What influences work-family conflict? The function of work support and working from home. Curr Psychol 29(2):104–120
Youngsoo J, Sungkwon W (2004) Flexible work breakdown structure for integrated cost and schedule control. J Constr Eng Manag 130(5):616–625

Part II
Practices and Cases: Phenomenological Analyses

Chapter 5
Future of Work and Work Skills in Knowledge-Intensive Services: Impact of New Media and Technologies

Rajendra K. Bandi and Vishal Shah

Abstract The increase in knowledge work combined with the popularity of new media and technologies is changing the nature of work. This has led to a need for and a rise in collaboration levels internally in an organization as well as the organization's ability to tap into and collaborate with its external ecosystem.

Through two case studies, we describe the changing nature of work and the kind of capabilities required for knowledge workers, managers, and organizations to be successful in this context. Social and Interpersonal Skills, Problem-Solving Skills, as well as the need for continuous learning emerge as essential requirements in this changing context. This also implies that the managers' role is changing from planning and coordination to functioning as enablers for their teams.

Keywords Work skills • Knowledge workers • Managerial role • New media

5.1 Introduction

Two significant trends are changing the nature of work and organizations today.

The increased rate of change in organizations has increased the complexity and ambiguity levels within even transactional processes, which traditionally were considered to be standardized. Nearly all work now requires significant analysis, judgment, and influence. Even roles that should be highly process driven spend a large portion of time handling exceptions or performing nonstandard work. This has resulted in almost everyone becoming a knowledge worker today!

R.K. Bandi (✉)
Indian Institute of Management Bangalore, Bengaluru, India
e-mail: rbandi@iimb.ernet.in

V. Shah
WIPRO Technologies, Bengaluru, India
e-mail: vishal.shah6@wipro.com

J. Lee (ed.), *The Impact of ICT on Work*, DOI 10.1007/978-981-287-612-6_5

Knowledge workers are defined, by Davenport, as "having high degrees of expertise, education, or experience, and the primary purpose of their jobs involves the creation, distribution, or application of knowledge" (Davenport 2005). A Knowledge-intensive work or service is characterized by high variety and complexity. They are delivered by highly qualified individuals and teams that operate in an environment of relatively high autonomy.

Further, the rise in popularity of new media and technologies like SMAC (Social, Mobile, Analytics, and Cloud) is also changing the way we live and work. Organizations are becoming flatter and more flexible and more connected to other organizations, in response to these new technologies. They are impacting every aspect of organizational structures and processes. Teams are becoming more distributed, placing ever more demands on employees and managers. Work is becoming more interconnected, across all corporate functions as well as with external partners, both domestic and international. New media and technologies are changing the way we live and work. Social media, mobile technology, big data, and automation are expected to have an impact on every aspect of our work and work life.

In this chapter, we examine some of these drivers that are likely to impact the nature of work. In particular, we focus on the area of "knowledge-intensive services." New media and technologies impact how teams that provide such services communicate, collaborate, and learn. They impact internal and external customer relations as well as engagement levels. Further as more millennials enter the workplace, their comfort levels with and preference for the new media and technologies is likely to accelerate these changes even more. We look at a few of the key trends that are impacting in organizations in this digital era.

5.2 The Increasing Need for Internal Collaboration

Knowledge work is highly collaborative. According to Davenport (2005), as knowledge workers are dispersed across the organizational structure and the globe, their work requires them to collaborate effectively with others in various functions, physical locations, time zones, and organizations.

The average employee today must collaborate with at least ten or more individuals within the organization just to accomplish his/her day-to-day work. Decisions are rarely made without consulting several individuals, which can sometimes slow down the process. Employees across the organization now share responsibility for cross-functional outcomes, increasing the prevalence of matrixed structures and cross-functional teams. For a majority of employees, the need to work within teams distributed across geographies is on the rise.

According to Ware and Grantham (2003), computing and communication technologies have transformed the traditional workplace into a virtual workspace. Technology allows employees to work flexibly and improve their work-life choices by working whenever and wherever they need. Tools and platforms like discussion forums, blogs, instant messaging (or chats), and wikis have also helped in the growth of distributed work processes and virtual teams. Virtual teams, however, need a reliable way to share schedules, documents, and artifacts, conduct meetings, and post updates. The choice of technologies for this includes videoconferencing, web conferencing, unified communications, mobile applications, commercial collaboration platforms, or custom-built ones similar to Facebook, LinkedIn, etc. For example, GitHub (https://github.com/), which started as a developers' collaboration platform, is now one of the largest collaboration spaces on the Internet.

5.3 The Emergence of Crowdsourcing or External Collaboration

Just as new technologies are increasing the need for internal collaboration, these technologies and social media platforms are also helping organizations reach outside their boundaries and tap into external resources. They are able to leverage on these external resources and in turn increase the scale and size of their operations. Work tasks are increasingly being accomplished through "crowdsourcing" techniques, in which software platforms enable Internet users to contribute to a project.

For example, several organizations are now hosting contests to elicit new ideas. Netflix, a provider of on-demand Internet streaming media, recently offered a prize of $1 million to anyone who could increase the accuracy of its movie recommendation system by 10 %. The toymaker Lego took a similar approach by hosting a website called the Lego Digital Designer. Through the website, Lego received many toy designs that they then proceeded to repackage and sell. Still other organizations are using online markets to identify talent, make predictions about the future, and generate new ideas and knowledge.

In the healthcare domain, organizations such as Curetogether (http://curetogether.com) and PatientsLikeMe (http://www.patientslikeme.com/) are allowing people to aggregate their personal health information to allow for clinical trials, connect with other people (patients), as well as use expertise available in public domain.

In fact, companies like elance.com and oDesk.com are very popular sites for "talent exchange" marketplaces. Freelancers register and bid for projects on these sites. Client companies that primarily work with freelancers need to have different systems as compared to one that has full-time employees.

In the next section, we describe two case studies which illustrate the above trends. The first case is that of a distributed support team that functions as one unit in the face of customer queries. This case highlights the increasing need for internal collaboration in providing knowledge-intensive services. The second case is that of the earliest marketplaces which involves what today is known as crowdsourcing.

5.4 TechHelp: A Distributed Technical Support Team: Case Study

5.4.1 Introduction

TechHelp is a remote technical support service provider team in Tech Portal.[1] Tech Portal is a web-based information portal that provides a wide range of services, ranging from news updates to online shopping. In the technology section of the portal, any visitor to the website can post a technical query and expect an email response for free. All the customer queries posted in this section are routed to TechHelp. Since this facility is free to all the portal visitors, the profile of customers who post queries on Portal varies from technology newbies to professional system administrators. Consequently, the queries posted on the site span across various technical domains and range from the simple to the very complex.

5.4.2 The Team

The TechHelp team is a distributed team providing round-the-clock support. Customer support executives report to team leaders who report to a support center manager responsible for the entire support center.

Most of the support personnel have a college degree and a technical diploma in computer applications. Basic Technical Support knowledge encompasses many domains, ranging from Operating Systems, Software, Hardware, and Networking. Over a period of time, support executives start specializing in different domains, based on their preferences and aptitude. However, this progression in knowledge levels is only possible within a band of technical domains. Team leaders and quality analysts are expected to have higher levels of technical expertise and customer support skills compared to support executives. Most team leaders and quality analysts in TechHelp had qualifications like the Microsoft Certified Professional (MCP) or Microsoft Certified Software Professional, apart from a basic technical degree.

5.4.3 Operations

All incoming customer queries are allocated to different support executives by team leaders, based on the query domains. An eCRM (Customer Relationship Management) application is used for assigning and routing the emails. When the support executive receives a query, she determines the appropriate response based on her domain knowledge and previous experience. While responding to the query, support executives also adhere to specified processes like using scripted opening

[1] Tech Portal is a pseudonym.

and closing statements, marking a copy of the response to the client Portal, including the original query in the response, and asking the customer for feedback. Team leaders check the responses for technical content and accuracy, spelling and language errors, and process adherence. To ensure that a seamless service is provided to the customer, support executives enter all the information and documents related to a specific case or query ID in a database called Case Tracker. This enables collaboration and information sharing across the team.

Queries are categorized into three levels based on their complexity. If the query is nonroutine or if the answer is not immediately evident to the support executive, she normally searches an internal company knowledge base for any information relevant to the query. If the knowledge base does not yield a satisfactory solution to the query, then she further searches the Internet for an appropriate solution. If further necessary, the support executive simulates the query on a computer system to find a solution. Support executives also frequently take the help of colleagues and seniors, in order to respond to the query. In a high-pressure situation, a backup team leader is appointed to share with the workload and maintain the quality of the response.

Support executives point out that providing technical support is more challenging in *remote technical support* than it is in a *face-to-face interaction* at the customer location. The lack of copresence with the customer introduces interpretive problems in the remote Technical Support situation. Firstly, the technical support person is dependent on the customer to get information about the customer's problem. Secondly, the support person must always consider the caller's level of understanding and the correctness of the customer's actions as part of the diagnosis. The successful completion of a call depends, therefore, on whether the support person can obtain and interpret the details of the problem the customer is facing. A support person thus needs to interpret the problem and the caller's understanding of the problem, which may be faulty. These interpretation difficulties are a constant feature of technical support work. See Fig. 5.1 for a conceptual model of the remote technical support interaction (adapted from Pentland 1995).

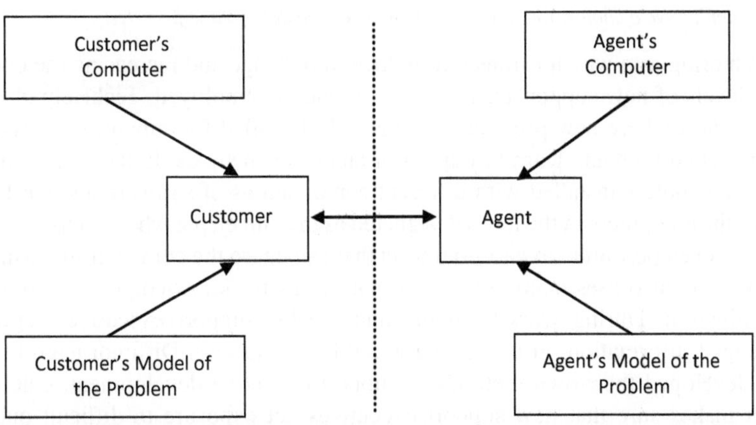

Fig. 5.1 The remote technical support interaction

Given the above interpretation difficulties, TechHelp has developed some basic guidelines for improving customer service in a remote support scenario. For instance, templates have been developed to standardize information collection about the problem situation when a query comes in. Support executives have also been explicitly instructed to read each query a number of times before drafting the response. Support executives have also been instructed to ask closed-ended questions to enable customers to send unambiguous replies.

5.4.4 Managing Knowledge

TechHelp has put in place different processes for managing learning and knowledge within the team. Employee training is the most preferred route for formal knowledge acquisition within the support team. Formal training is frequent and spans multiple areas.

All new support executives are trained on basic technical knowledge, client-specific knowledge, problem-solving skills, and customer service skills. The problem-solving skills training covers the entire query resolution process—information gathering and customer probing, root cause identification and analysis, Internet and knowledge base searching skills, and framing customer-friendly responses.

Once the new support executives are on the floor, training sessions are conducted in various formats. Refresher sessions are held through formal classroom sessions. Hardware training is conducted through practical hands-on sessions. Self-training is encouraged through training CDs. Customer queries belonging to new technical areas spur the support executives to regularly update themselves through the Internet, books, and computer-based tutorials. TechHelp also encourages employees to enroll in formal technical courses and sponsors such initiatives. As a result, many support executives have acquired certifications from Brainbench and Microsoft that are recognized in the industry. The need to keep oneself updated is important. One support executive emphasized the need for this:

You don't have a choice. You have to find the time to update yourself.

Mentoring as a way for transmitting tacit knowledge and increasing the competence levels of new support executives is frequently employed. TechHelp also has product labs where new products are regularly installed for support executives to tinker around with and learn through trial-and-error methods. In the lab, TechHelp has 15 computers installed with different combinations of software and hardware. One of the computers in the lab is designated as the guinea pig where support executives are even permitted to carry out tests that can cause the computer to crash.

The team also uses many other informal means for knowledge acquisition and dissemination. During working hours and breaks, support executives regularly exchanged information on interesting and difficult queries. Diffirent team leaders have developed their own methods to support executive development. One team leader makes sure that new support executives get exposure to difficult queries. Some support executives participate in various technology-related message boards and mailing lists on the Internet. One support executive even answered technical queries for a popular newspaper.

A corporate R&D team continuously scans information sources like the Internet and prepares troubleshooting notes on new products and applications. Research reports on new technologies and products are also prepared to help acquire new clients.

5.4.5 The Knowledge Management System

TechHelp has developed an in-house knowledge management system that supports its support executives in the query resolution process. The system's knowledge base consists of more than 13,000 unique queries. Compared to normal search engines, which throw up hundreds of results, the internal knowledge base saves valuable support executive time by displaying only four most relevant search results. While conducting the search, the system checks several tables and employed algorithms as well as weightage calculations to arrive at the four solutions. After reviewing the four solutions, the support executive can rate the usefulness of the solutions for the particular query. This feedback is used to dynamically reassign the weightages and improve the efficacy of the system's knowledge base.

5.4.6 Knowledge Retention Through Employee Retention

TechHelp's employee turnover was much below the industry average. Compared to industry standards, the compensation was on the higher side, which is an important factor. But what came out clearly in the interviews was that the support executives appreciated the work environment at TechHelp. For one, the organization encouraged acquisition of new skill sets, which was something the support executives valued. TechHelp's strong focus on technical support also reduced employee attrition rates since technical experts preferred working in such an environment as compared to an organization that had a broader focus on generic customer support. TechHelp also positioned itself as an organization specializing in generic technologies rather than in specific technology products. Since in India technical support executives compare themselves to software engineers, the company's vision fits very well with the employee aspirations.

Employees also appreciated the informal atmosphere and the approachability of management, and many said that they were not sure whether they would like working at other places as much as they did in TechHelp. TechHelp had a very informal culture. Support executives could listen to music while solving queries and even chat with friends on the Internet messengers. As long as a support executive was performing well, not too many questions were asked about other things. For instance, the support executives even played computer games sometimes to relax. One support executive actually complained that such an atmosphere made it difficult for him to concentrate at times, but this complaint was not very common.

5.5 TechChat: Crowdsourcing in the Technical Support Domain: A Case Study

5.5.1 Introduction

TechChat[2] is an Internet-based technical support portal that brings together seekers and providers of technical support. TechChat ties up with technology companies like Microsoft, Adobe, and Oracle for providing technical support to their customers. Technical support providers in turn tie up with TechChat and through TechChat provide technical support to the customers of the abovementioned organizations. TechChat gets a fee from technical support providers (for connecting with technical support seekers) as well as the vendor companies whose products are being supported on the portal.

Customers post their queries related to software applications and products on TechChat. Technical Support executives registered on the TechChat portal bid for the queries, and if their bid is selected, they get to offer solutions. If the query is resolved to the customers' satisfaction, then they are required to make a payment to the support executive. Initially, when customers posted queries, support executives registered on TechChat could quote their own prices and bid for queries. Later, TechChat fixed the prices as per the different query categories, varying from $20 to $180, depending on query complexity.

Support executives can belong to an organization or they can also be freelancing individuals. TechChat requires all support executives registered as technical support providers to have the appropriate qualifications and expertise. Customers can check the support executive's profile listed on the website before responding to a bid. Customers also rate the support executive on a scale of 1–5 after the interaction is complete. Support executives are required to maintain an average rating of four or more out of a maximum of five or they can get disqualified by TechChat for future queries.

The TechChat website has interactive chat and message board features. Customers and support executives can have a live chat with each other and can also leave messages and documents for each other. The application also has a *desktop sharing tool* that allows the technical support executives to log into the customers' systems and resolve the query directly. TechChat stores all interactions between customers and support executives, including the desktop sharing interactions, in order to have a record of the entire transaction.

5.5.2 Operations

All the registered support executives on TechChat try to bid for new queries as soon as possible, since the competition for these is intense. Support executives estimate their chances of resolving a query quickly and then place bids.

[2]TechChat is a pseudonym.

At the beginning of every chat session, customers are required to rate themselves as "beginners, intermediates, or experts." Support executives chat with the customer trying to understand the problem and simultaneously search relevant information sources, in order to provide the customer with a solution. If the customer is a novice or is unable to express the problem clearly, the support executive usually uses a desktop sharing facility which allows her to log into the customer's system.

For queries which seem more difficult, support executives place a bid after some quick considerations. Support executives try to find out if a similar request had been handled earlier or whether the additional information needed to solve the query can be easily obtained from the customer. Queries that seem very difficult or queries that have been left untouched for a long while on the website are only approached after the problem has been researched well. Support executives do not indiscriminately bid for queries because customers are likely to give support executives poor ratings if they are not satisfied with the query resolution process.

5.5.3 Knowledge Acquisition

The nature of knowledge acquisition processes can be illustrated through the manner in which a team of tech support executives started providing support for the Adobe range of products on TechChat. When the team initially considered providing support for Adobe products on the TechChat website, none of their support executives had any knowledge of this domain. None of the team members had even seen the software. However, purchasing the entire suite of Adobe products to train the support executives was considered expensive. So the support team purchased tutorials and books on Adobe products. A training program, which was a combination of self-study, exercises, and quizzes, was conducted for the support executives. Adobe queries from the TechChat site were used to conduct mock query resolution sessions through chat. The team discovered that many of the queries could be resolved simply by searching the publicly available knowledge base on the Adobe website. This training enabled the team to obtain the required certifications for registering at the TechChat site as Adobe experts. The support executives started bidding for queries and, during query resolution, used the desktop sharing tool to further familiarize themselves with the Adobe products. Over a period of time, they gradually developed the ability to solve more complex queries while maintaining the required customer satisfaction ratings.

5.6 Discussion and Implications of These Changes

In the following sections, we discuss the implications of the trends discussed in the earlier sections and further illustrated through these two cases. These are primarily around new Knowledge and Skills (individual and organizational) required in this changing context.

5.7 Social and Interpersonal Skills in Knowledge-Intensive Services

Communication media vary in the capacity to process rich information. Media Richness theory (Daft and Lengel 1986; Rice 1992) proposes that media differ in the ability to facilitate a common understanding and shared meaning among communicators. The theory asserts that four factors influence this: the ability of the medium to transmit multiple cues (e.g., vocal inflection, gestures), immediacy of feedback (media synchronicity), language variety, and the personal focus of the medium.

In remote interactions as media richness increases, attitudes can be gauged more easily through additional communication and interaction cues. The speed of response, intensity of the support executive's efforts, and even the tone of the support executives provided cues regarding support executive empathy. Hence, in both the case studies described earlier, formal norms for maintaining interactivity levels can be observed. Instructions for composing the query response and keeping the customer engaged and maintaining interactivity during query resolution had been specified. These norms were intended to ensure minimum quality standards for interactivity and engagement in the service delivery process.

In a distributed team, individuals need to develop strategies for engaging and motivating a dispersed group. Members of virtual teams need to become adept at finding environments that promote productivity and well-being. Online streams created by microblogging and social networking sites can serve as virtual water coolers, providing a sense of team spirit. For example, Yammer, which is a Facebook-like social media platform, can be used inside an organization for collaborative work. Collaborative platforms include features such as immediate feedback, clear objectives, and a staged series of challenges that can significantly drive participation and motivation.

The use of social media systems, however, also places greater focus on the importance of digital reputation management. Greater collaboration, both inside and outside the organization, will raise a variety of issues, from what can or cannot be shared with others to how individuals who make innovative contributions as knowledge connectors or brokers are identified and recognized.

5.8 Problem-Solving Skills in Knowledge-Intensive Services

We are on the threshold of a significant increase in the use of robots and automation in our workplaces. Smart machines, robots, and even smart pieces of code will increasingly enter our lives and replace humans. Machines can already do most of the work that bank clerks or tellers do. It seems likely now that in a relatively short period of time a great deal of the existing work will be automated and at the same time knowledge-based jobs will become more exception based. The problem-solving, judgment, and critical thinking components of the jobs will increase. Even the most basic jobs will begin to use information systems and become more knowledge intensive.

Solving a difficult problem demands good problem-solving skills. Getting the relevant details, identification of the cause, and developing a workable solution involves utilizing skills that deal with unstructured problems. As the exception-based and knowledge-based content of work increases, these skills become even more important, especially in the context of remote interaction with teams/individuals distributed over space and time. Some of the problem-solving behaviors that are becoming important are Cue Identification, Hypothesis Management, and Use of Heuristics in problem solving. These were observed in both the case studies described. We also observed the use of multiple databases, both internal as well as external, for problem resolution. Hence, information search and retrieval skills gain importance for problem resolution. Especially in a scenario where data is residing in numerous repositories and interaction tools today, the ability to locate and retrieve the right information in the right format is likely to be an important skill required.

5.9 The Need for Continuous Learning

In both the case studies described above (TechHelp and TechChat), we observe both informal and formal means of learning being used. The multiple media and occasions used for training, such as induction training, refresher training, product labs, use of self-learning content, and formal courses, all indicated the intense need for effective knowledge dissemination as well as knowledge retention. The knowledge base also played an important role in training new support executives and allowed them to become productive in a short period of time. Mentoring was another effective means of transferring tacit knowledge that formal training could not teach.

For a generation raised on multimedia and social networks, learning has become an interactive, collaborative experience. Operating manuals and study groups are fast being replaced by tablets, videos, apps, and online chats. Corporate learning professionals, in industries as diverse as insurance and food services, are recognizing the need to incorporate more social experiences into their learning programs. The medium of learning has started changing. Sites like Coursera and Udemy are providing opportunity for continuous learning. These are likely to go mainstream and get accepted by employers.

The starting point for social capabilities is increasing the visibility of expertise and by providing individuals with the opportunity to locate and connect with others who have needed skills and capabilities. This will mean that the social profile will become the symbol of expertise and reputation. Expertise will serve as an important form of recognition that can be explicitly recognized in social environments. In fact, the ideal worker in knowledge-intensive services will be "T shaped"— she would bring deep understanding of at least one field and have the capacity to converse in the language of a broader range of disciplines. Building this kind of a knowledge profile requires a sense of curiosity and a willingness to continue to learn, far beyond the years of formal education.

As extended life spans promote multiple careers and exposure to more industries and disciplines, it will be particularly important for workers to develop this T-shaped quality. But in a crowdsourcing-driven work environment driven by sequential, modular projects, it is not clear how workers will pick up the skills that they will need. In such a scenario, instead of companies investing a lot in employee training, employees themselves will have to take complete charge of their own learning and development.

5.10 Organizational Implications

Customer interaction protocols play an important role, as seen in both the cases, in delivering consistent service remotely. As the task knowledge intensity of the remote service increases, the need for information search and retrieval skills also increases, and therefore knowledge management systems and knowledge bases play a central role in the remote customer support services of today. In fact in many cases, the ability to retrieve correct information quickly at the right time may be more important than actual product or process knowledge. A customer support agent today needs to simultaneously have product expertise, problem-solving expertise, have good knowledge of the customer, and also be a good reference librarian. Product expertise alone will not suffice. Organizations need to recognize this, and accordingly, their training programs also need to cover all the different knowledge categories and need to employ multiple methodologies such as a classroom as well as hands-on training if agents are to deliver satisfactory performance. Agents also need to be trained on specific problem-solving skills as well as on customer interaction skills for controlling the interaction as well as to be able to handle irate customers. Organizations also need to factor the above characteristics in defining performance metrics and quality parameters (Shah and Bandi 2003).

5.11 The Managers' Changing Role

In the twentieth century, managers focused on planning and predictability. But in the new environment, managers must focus on how employees participate in informal communities of work or practice. Following fixed work plans and schedules is seen as less valuable than the ability to experiment and follow up. The central role of technology, then, might not be enforcing compliance but enabling participation.

In the digital era, managers now have to demonstrate a high degree of emotional intelligence and be able to relate to their employees. The new generation of employees joining the workforce expects organizations to be more open and transparent, and the current/emergent digital technologies help the organizations move in this direction. The explosion in user-generated media including the videos, blogs, and podcasts is demanding new media skills in the workplace. To lead effectively in a digital age, managers must operate outside their comfort zone, embrace new skills, exploit digital resources, and learn how best to channel them to continue driving their businesses toward success.

As stated at the beginning of the chapter, almost everyone is becoming a knowledge worker today, and work is increasingly becoming knowledge intensive and requires interactions with individuals at remote locations. Through two cases, we have described the changing nature of work and the kind of capabilities required for the knowledge workers, managers, and organizations to be successful in this context.

References

Daft RL, Lengel RH (1986) Organizational information requirements, media richness and structural design. Manage Sci 32(5):554–571

Davenport TH (2005) Thinking for a living: how to get better performances and results from knowledge workers. Harvard Business School Press, Boston

Pentland BT (1995) Read me what it says on your screen: the interpretative problem in technical service work. Technol Stud 2(1):50–79

Rice RE (1992) Task analyzability, use of new media, and effectiveness: a multi-site exploration of media richness. Organ Sci 3(4):475–500

Shah V, Bandi R (2003) Developing people capabilities in knowledge intensive remote services. Res Pract Hum Res Manage 11(1):55–64

Ware J, Grantham C (2003) The future of work: changing patterns of workforce management and their impact on the workplace. J Facil Manage 2(2):142–159

Chapter 6
Seeing Is Belonging: Remote Working, Identity and Staying Connected

Kristine Dery and Ella Hafermalz

Abstract This chapter examines how workers in a distributed environment use technologies to overcome the isolation and invisibility of virtual work. We examine the working lives of remote workers and show how they struggle with maintaining those 'informal' connections with the organisation that are typically associated with building a sense of belonging. Our findings identify new practices that engage technologies to maintain visual and social connections across the organisation. In this way, remote workers are establishing a sense of belonging and participation across the wider spectrum of organisational activities and opportunities. Insights into how technologies are used to build an identity and a presence in a largely virtual working environment are then used to generate a series of recommendations for the management of remote workers.

Keywords Remote working • Visibility • Organisational belonging • Communication technologies

6.1 Introduction

One of the more profound impacts of mobile and digital technologies has been the move away from the traditional tethers of co-located offices. Mobile connectivity, social media and cloud-based technologies are enabling new ways of designing work to meet a wide variety of personal and professional needs. However, while on the one hand the nirvana of a workplace that is no longer limited by temporal and spatial boundaries is alluring, on the other hand organisations are facing the challenge of maintaining a sense of organisational identity and belonging in an environment where employees are rarely co-located. This raises interesting questions

K. Dery (✉)
Center for Information Systems Research, MIT, Cambridge, MA, USA
e-mail: kdery@mit.edu

E. Hafermalz
Disciplines of Business Information Systems and Work and Organisational Studies, The University of Sydney Business School, The University of Sydney, Sydney, NSW, Australia
e-mail: ella.hafermalz@sydney.edu.au

J. Lee (ed.), *The Impact of ICT on Work*, DOI 10.1007/978-981-287-612-6_6

around the personal and organisational competencies required to effectively manage people when more remote working arrangements are in place.

This chapter begins with a brief overview of the current debates around the problems associated with remote working followed by a brief overview of our research project. We then use the work of Erving Goffman (1959) on identity to develop an understanding of how remote workers 'perform' their identity online by developing conversations, deploying visuals and building a virtual sense of self that enables a connection with the collective identity of the organisation. We argue that 'how you think your colleagues perceive you' was particularly important in remote working and that building and maintaining a consistent identity is challenging and requires a redefining of what it means to be 'visible'. We conclude by arguing that in order for remote workers to establish a sense of belonging, we need to focus on both the performance of identity and on creating a more visible organisational environment. New practices developed through the use of technology are critical to the effective management of remote workers.

6.2 Does Remote Working Work? An Ongoing Debate

There are differing views on whether distributed working models are effective. There is on the one side the argument that flexibility and mobility enable new ways of working with benefits for talent acquisition, new workplace design, global connectivity and other advantages that can be gained when time and space no longer constrain the design of work. However, on the other side, debates are surfacing that suggest that the lack of co-located engagement is detrimental to creativity and team dynamics. This debate surfaced more publicly in 2013, when CEO of *Yahoo!* Marissa Mayer recalled all her employees back to the office, citing the importance of corridors and water coolers in sparking creativity and collegiality.

The memo that was sent to staff read, 'We need to be one *Yahoo!* That starts with physically being together' (Keller 2013). New York Mayor Michael Bloomberg came out in support of Mayer, calling remote work 'one of the dumber ideas I've ever heard' (Daily Mail Reporter 2013). Richard Branson, founder of Virgin Group PLC, had a different perspective, deeming Mayer and Bloomberg's views a sign of 'old school thinking' and predicting that 'In 30 years' time, as technology moves forward even further, people are going to look back and wonder why offices ever existed' (Branson 2013). Adam Pisoni, co-founder of the Enterprise Social Networking platform Yammer, in his work on The Responsive Org, suggests that this debate arises out of the tensions created by traditional organisational forms trying to accommodate new ways of working (Responsive Org 2014).

Despite this debate raging on, we are still seeing a significant shift to more distributed working models, and it would seem that remote working is here to stay. Companies who want to extend their geographical reach without the need for expensive offices for their employees are increasingly looking to hire talent to work from home or other locations separate from a central office (Fried and Heinemeier Hansson 2013). In a recent report from Deloitte in their 'Building the Lucky Country' series, it is estimated that Australia, for example, stands to gain between $1.4 and $1.9 billion annually if just 10 % of employees were to work remotely for at least 50 % of the time (Deloitte 2012, p. 4). As a geographically large country, disparately populated and located a long way from major markets, technology will be critical to get access to the talent required to be innovative and productive. If the best person for the role lives on the other side of the country, or even on the other side of the world, they can still be hired and work productively for an organisation that may not even have physical headquarters.

The question therefore becomes not "does remote working work?" but rather "how do we manage remote workers more effectively?" We need to move away from the centre of the ring, where the punches are landing on the chins of the new versus the old ways of working, and illuminate the dark corner where issues such as identity and belonging are lurking. The corridors and the water coolers establish ways of seeing and understanding each other as more than just working cogs and build that sense of belonging (corporate engagement). Albert et al. (2000), Knippenberg and Schie (2000), and Kreiner and Ashforth (2004) are just some of the many academics who posit that workers with a strong sense of belonging or 'organisational identification' are more likely to contribute positively to the effectiveness of the organisation. As intimated by Branson, the ongoing development of technology is critical to remote working capabilities, and it is the new and individualised ways in which employees are using this technology to create a sense of identity and belonging that is significant in this ongoing debate.

For the purposes of this study, we have defined remote workers as knowledge workers who work for an organisation and do the majority of their work away from a central office (as distinct from a teleworker, who may work from home once or twice a week or when it is inconvenient to come in to the office). Remote workers may work from home or from cafes, the park or whatever location suits the task at hand while meeting their needs for connectivity (see Kolb et al. 2008). This kind of remote working is relatively new and is different from freelancing or being self-employed. Unlike freelancers and the self-employed, remote workers are typically salaried employees with long-term employment commitments. They work in teams, report to managers or may be managers themselves. As distinct from traditional working arrangements, the space in which work is performed is reframed. Remote workers are infrequently, if ever, co-located with other members of the organisation and rarely have a dedicated working space in the organisation. While the organisation may have a physical office where some staff regularly work, this is not the primary place of work for the remote worker. In a sense, they are defined by their absence from the traditional workplace with distance from other organisational members being the norm rather than the exception.

We were interested in what remote workers find difficult about this arrangement and how they are using technology in innovative ways to overcome those challenges. A theme that emerged from the research is the problems associated with being *invisible*. We found that remote workers and managers develop new ways of working together and that technology is used and adapted in a variety of ways to make the invisible visible in order to establish a sense of identity and belonging.

6.3 The Case Study

The findings in this chapter are from a pilot study which focused on an Australian organisation called Elevate (names and identifying features have been changed) as part of a wider study of remote working in Australia. Elevate employs approximately 100 people, with a focus on formulating and delivering educational workshops for a variety of ages. Elevate is a young organisation that has grown from a handful of employees (educators) to over 100 in the past 5 years, with the majority of employees under the age of 35. The educators deliver scripted workshops with convincing energy and enthusiasm, sometimes as many as six times in a day. Employees are often travelling to different locations, and while they see plenty of students and teachers, their interaction with the organisation they work for is largely virtual. Elevate have a small head office in Melbourne, with almost all of their staff working remotely. The majority of their employees work from their homes and on the road, full time. Teams stay in touch using their company-issued smartphones and laptops.

Our guiding research question was focused on understanding what the challenges were for these remote workers in staying connected and engaged with their organisation. To address this broad research question, we conducted in-depth semi-structured interviews and coupled this data with our existing knowledge of the organisation's operations from observations. Our interviews were conducted over the phone and in person and focused on the lived meaningful experience of the remote workers and their managers. This research approach is interpretivist, a research tradition that 'takes *human interpretation* as the starting point for developing knowledge about the social world' (Prasad 2005, p. 13).

The interviews were then transcribed and coded into themes. These thematic codes were then compared with relevant academic literature on identity to inform the analysis. The single-case study design is a result of the exploratory nature of this qualitative pilot study research, and the findings are not intended to be generalisable; however, we believe that the experiences and analysis included in this chapter are credible and to a certain extent 'transferable' (Guba and Lincoln 1989) in that they offer an initial insight into the lived world of remote workers – a topic that is relatively unexplored and which remains the focus of our ongoing research.

Through our semi-structured interviews with both remote workers and their managers, we gained a new perspective on how remote workers are overcoming the challenges of their unique position. We were interested in what remote workers find problematic about distributed work and how they were using technology in innovative ways to overcome those challenges. A major theme that emerged was the problem of being *invisible* and establishing an *identity.* In the following section, we examine a selection of interviews that illustrate some of these key findings.

6.4 Making Identity Visible

When Beth started working for Elevate in the mid-2000s, she was a part of a core team of facilitators who planned 'to change the world'. Her induction into her role as an educational life skills workshop facilitator involved living 'big brother style' with a group of colleagues in an apartment in Melbourne, Australia. Amongst this initial group were the company's founders. Together, they learned workshop scripts, received training in public speaking, marketed their brand new educational program and ate meals together in the early hours of the morning. This intensive experience was formative for Beth, and she went back to her home city (545 miles from the head office) with confidence in knowing that she belonged to a supportive and untiringly dedicated team. As the company grew, however, Beth began to feel less secure about her place in the organisation. She would hear names attached to faces she had never seen. When speaking about other founding members of the firm, she was confronted with question marks and blank stares. While Beth was in constant email and phone contact with her initial group of colleagues, the organisation itself was becoming something else, something that was difficult for her to grasp, and her confidence in her place within it began to destabilise.

While working remotely was an arrangement that she greatly valued, she began to experience the drawbacks of having little physical contact with her parent organisation. The growing number of new people, whom she had never met and had little 'sense of' was unsettling for Beth. More unsettling, however, was that these new employees had no sense of who *she* was. As a founding member of Elevate, Beth was accustomed to being a part of the organisation's narrative – she was aware of the mission, the heroes, the struggles and the accomplishments. But as the organisation grew nationally, the cohesive picture that she held of the organisation was less clear, and Beth's sense of identity within the organisation began to fade. This issue of invisibility and collective identity in an organisation is familiar to many – however, it seems to be amplified and negotiated in unique ways for remote workers. While this is the story of Elevate and some of its workers, many of the issues explored here and lessons learned are relevant to other organisations that are dealing with the transition to distributed work.

At the core of this issue for Beth, and for other remote workers we spoke with, is the problem of invisibility. Beth struggled to understand the organisation because she had not 'seen' its current members. She could not 'see' the head office in Melbourne, where decisions were being made. And, most frustratingly for Beth, she knew that her new colleagues had never seen her. What happens to our reputation and, as a consequence, our identity, when we are not visible to others? While it could be expected that an endorsement of Beth's work ethic and past dedication to the company would occasionally arise in conversation, there was no way for Beth to see or check in on this, or to review the nature and content of the message. When we consider that identity is a complex phenomenon that involves not only our version of our own story but also those stories told about us by others, it can be imagined that for the remote worker, who relies on electronic text and phone calls with a combination of close colleagues and near strangers, a sense of identity in relation to the company is constantly at risk.

A person's collective identity in an organization is based on what others know of them. Over time, we build a reputation, which is informed by our role in the organisation and what we do, as well as by how our past actions have been perceived by others. It is harder for the remote worker to influence or even know their own reputation. When Beth started at Elevate, she shared a collective experience with the founding team in Melbourne that cemented her reputation in the founding group.

When new members began to join Elevate, there was no way for these new employees to access that past experience, and as a remote worker, Beth's past became invisible. While one could expect stories of these 'early days' to be shared by senior members of the organisation, remote workers have little control over or knowledge of how their presence in the company is being represented to others, and as a consequence, their sense of identity is vulnerable.

The need for continuity of identity – to be known by others in the same way that we know ourselves – has long been a preoccupation of philosophers and scholars. Erik Erikson (1983) thought of a healthy identity as 'a multifaceted but ultimately coherent sense of self that is personally satisfying while at the same time being recognized and affirmed by the surrounding community' (Gardner and Davis 2013, p. 66). There is an inward-looking aspect to identity, which is concerned with knowing oneself, but it is also important that others know us in the way we would like to be known. Nietzsche (2007), for example, was concerned at feeling keenly misunderstood by his colleagues, famously declaring, 'Listen to me! for I am thus and thus. Do not, above all, confound me with what I am not!' This yearning for consistency of identity between how we think of ourselves and how we are perceived by others is associated with the importance of reputation, an ever-present concern in the business environment, as evidenced by the popularity of networks like LinkedIn.

Beth was concerned that how she thought of herself as a founding member of Elevate was no longer matching the view that new organisational members held of her. She described to us her experience of losing her sense of place in a growing company, and how this discontinuity left her feeling invisible and like she needed to rebuild her identity and reputation:

> I don't remember everyone, I can't see them, no one knows me, because, previously being a crucial part of the team, then everyone knows you and respects you and knows your work ethic, but with new people, you have to begin again, you have to go, this is who I am within this organisation, and rebuild your identity, because you lose that.

In the early stages of her role with Elevate, Beth felt like a 'crucial part of the team', and knew that everyone in the small organisation knew and respected her strong work ethic, an aspect of her self-image that is particularly important to her. Combined with the lack of physical and visual contact between herself and new members of Elevate, Beth felt that this important part of her identity was threatened by the growth of the organisation.

Beth's first full-time job was as a remote worker with Elevate, so she emphasised that perhaps this experience of losing your identity was a normal part of organisational change and growth. Certainly, all group dynamics involve constant identity shifts, and much research has been conducted looking at teams in the context of organisational change. What interests us as we explore the experiences of Beth and other remote workers is the issue of invisibility (when your colleagues 'can't see you' and you 'can't see them') that is added to the processes of creating and maintaining an organisational identity. We were interested to hear how over the years, as communication technologies have become more functional and accessible,

Beth and other remote workers have found ways around this problem of invisibility, by creating and using technological tools to enable remote workers and their colleagues to 'be seen'. The following section theorises how technologies relate to the way in which remote workers and other employees 'perform' their identities online in an ongoing struggle to become and remain visible.

6.5 Performing Identity Online

In his seminal work *The Presentation of Self in Everyday Life*, Erving Goffman (1959) employs the well-known metaphor of the stage to examine how everyday human interactions are negotiated in the manner of a performance. Expanding on this metaphor, Goffman outlines the difference between the *performer* and the *character* in a play. In essence, the performer is the person engaged in 'staging' the performance, while the character is the impression or image that the performer wishes to portray (Goffman 1959, p. 244). Here, Goffman explicates the subtle difference between who we are and who we communicate ourselves to be. Although Goffman is talking about interactions in everyday physical life, the analogy remains relevant and even illuminating in thinking about how remote workers perform their character in a more virtual communication environment.

Goffman explains that the aim of an interaction with another person is for the performance to resonate as natural – the character needs to be accepted by the audience so that they can suspend their disbelief and get engaged in the story. The successful 'staging' of a performance, in which the character is accepted by the audience as fairly much synonymous with the performer, depends on the success of the 'whole scene of his action':

> A correctly staged and performed scene leads the audience to impute a self to a performed character…The self, then, as a performed character, is not an organic thing that has a specific location, whose fundamental fate is to be born, to mature, and to die; it is a dramatic effect arising diffusely from a scene that is presented, and the characteristic issue, the crucial concern, is whether it will be credited or discredited. (Goffman 1959, pp. 244–245)

Goffman's notion of the self as a 'dramatic effect' and 'a performed character' is interesting in the context of technologically mediated interactions, and the metaphor of 'staging a scene' takes on a new complexity in the context of remote working. For a person working hundreds of miles away from their colleagues, the interactions that they have with those colleagues are primarily virtual, and the channels through which a credible impression can be made are limited, or they were at the time when Beth started at Elevate in late 2006.

In 2006, Facebook and LinkedIn were in their infancy in Australia, and these platforms certainly did not play a significant role in professional life for a young organisation like Elevate. Phone calls, text messages and email were the media through which remote workers at Elevate would sustain relationships and manage the impressions given to create and maintain a sense of self as part of a collective.

The 'scene' in Goffman's metaphor was being 'presented' through visually limited means of communication, and the capacity of these technologies to suitably present the self were, for Beth, inadequate. She not only struggled to see the other players of the scene (her colleagues), but the totality of the scene itself was unstable – what was this organisation that she was now a part of?

To get a better sense of who now made up Elevate as a company, Beth envisaged creating a platform not unlike Facebook or LinkedIn that could be used to display employee profiles. After several years of discussion, this platform was created in the form of an intranet that displayed a profile photo accompanied by brief information about the employee's role and involvement at Elevate. Beth describes thinking of these profiles as being a way to communicate past contributions within the organisation:

> We had little profiles of ourselves…because, if people don't know who you are they don't know what you've contributed to the program…and that was always a challenge, going – no one knows how much work and effort went in at the original time, and if there's no one having that conversation with these people, then you're just another person, that they don't know. Whereas, in my mind, it's a formative, crucial part of an original team identity that I have that other people don't have.

With the creation of profiles on a company intranet, the scene (as the organisation) and its characters (the organisation's employees) became visible to Beth for the first time since she was brought to Melbourne to meet her co-workers during the company's inception. While Beth laughs remembering how 'highly unusable' that first incarnation of the intranet was, it has led to the development of a far more sophisticated system that is operational today. Elevate's new intranet is now run on the Microsoft SharePoint platform, which connects with an Enterprise Social Network, Yammer. Together, these tools allow users to display their profiles, interact publicly and privately and show what they are working on. While such shared platforms are quite common in companies today, the example of Beth's request for a visual directory is indicative of a remote worker's need for visual displays of identity.

When thinking about the creation of online profiles for employees, Goffman's distinction between performer and character is again relevant. In a virtual world, it can be argued that the connection between the performer and the character is at greater risk of becoming tenuous. This also has implications for understanding trust in a virtual working environment. While traditional literature on trust in virtual environments focuses on how much one individual trusts another individual in an online environment, our research suggests that a less explored and yet important issue is the remote worker's perception of how much trust is being placed in their *performance of themselves* – how successfully is their character being performed? Beth can now use Yammer, group messaging applications, email, phone, text messages and other applications to make an impression of her character. But how well this performance 'comes off' is still harder to judge than in co-located settings. However, as we improve the capacity of technological tools to provide feedback in the form of likes, comments and other communications of emotion, and learn how to provide continuous feedback, the remote worker is becoming more included in and aware of the organisational scene.

6.6 Performers and Their Avatars

> Since the reality that the individual is concerned with is unperceivable at the moment, appearances must be relied upon in its stead. And, paradoxically, the more the individual is concerned with the reality that is not available to perception, the more must he concentrate his attention on appearances. (Goffman 1959, p. 242)

Goffman wrote about the performance of identity long before we began carrying powerful personal computers in our pockets. He posited that reality is unperceivable to the individual in the present moment, because of the complex interaction of performers and the characters they are performing. Goffman uses the metaphor of the stage where reality consists of every performer's intentions and motivations as expressed through the character they are playing, and it is therefore impossible to grasp the 'whole picture'while you are 'on stage' yourself. For example, most of us have experienced the misreading of a situation where we didn't have sufficient information to understand what was really going on. Rather than being frozen by this knowledge that information is incomplete, we rely on appearances – on what we can see. This makes it all the more important that we have some control over what we *show*.

When Beth first started at Elevate, there were very few means of *displaying* her identity to others in the organisation with whom she did not have an established relationship. Before intranets, social networks and smartphones made the display and sharing of identity-related images and impressions a common part of everyday organisational life, remote workers relied on limited information from which to construct their sense of organisational reality and had scant tools with which to take part in performing their own images and impressions on the organisational stage.

In Beth's case, the introduction of an intranet marked a new era at Elevate, in which employees who had never physically met could represent themselves to the organisation. They began to be able to perform their characters in more visible and nuanced ways. This capability has now evolved to include Yammer, video broadcasts, an extended intranet system based on SharePoint and several instant messaging applications used on smartphones. As well as using these digital tools for connecting on a daily basis, the company also continues to hold a bi-annual company-wide conference in Melbourne, in which all members of Elevate, whether they are based interstate or internationally, are flown to stay together in a hotel for several days during which they socialise, receive training, plan, problem- solve and reconnect.

Most of the year, however, is spent interacting virtually as an organisation. Each employee (remote workers especially) is engaged in the complex activity of performing their identity in the context of the organisation using communication technologies. There was a lot at stake in this performance – advancement and the associated increases in remuneration and responsibility depended on being noticed by the right people for the right reasons; reputations depended on communicating successes and attributes deemed desirable within the organisation; collegiate support rested on being perceived as a good team member; meaningful personal connections relied on being able to effectively communicate a consistent and amicable personality. For remote workers, the tools at their disposal for achieving these feats were, in most cases, a smartphone and a laptop and the myriad of applications that these devices afford.

While the remote workers who have more recently joined Elevate had the advantage of easy access to technologies such as smartphone applications that could be used to quickly and easily communicate images and text, they still grappled with the physical distance between the performer (the person working out of a distant location) and the character that appeared on screen. For example, Selma, who also lives and works remotely as a facilitator for Elevate, said that she sometimes forgot that she was a remote worker. The high level of social contact that she had in her role running workshops for students, and the constant messaging and phone calls shared between her teammates often created a sense of proximity that overrode the distributed nature of her work.

There were times, however, when the easy manner of relating to her colleagues facilitated by digital tools was interrupted by a realisation of distance:

> I definitely have that sense every now and then, that everyone's an avatar and so am I, in terms of my work team…we have a lot of contact every day, we're on [the smartphone messaging application] Kik all the time, and I think that's incredibly positive, and it's like 'what am I having for dinner' and 'oh my goodness this thing was annoying' and it's completely all the things you'd chat about if you were passing someone in an office together. Then other times I have this little moment where there's this sudden realisation that we're actually millions of miles away and they're in Perth and I'm in Sydney and we're only ever looking at each other's typed text and little picture.

While the miles are nearer hundreds than millions, the physical distance between Selma and her colleagues was clearly acutely felt, but only at certain moments. It seemed as if the work team was performing a scene in which the characters were co-located (i.e. they thought of themselves as being in the same place). Yet at times, a 'glitch' occurred in which this illusion was broken (i.e. the gap between performer and character became apparent) resulting in the realisation that 'everyone's an avatar' and thereby rendering the scene less authentic.

We asked Selma if she could identify what it was that prompted these glitches – that realisation or awareness of how, as she put it, 'we aren't physically in the same space', and she offered the following reflection:

> I'm trying to work out what kind of triggers the realisation in certain moments…I think if there's ever a minor misunderstanding between the team, which doesn't happen that much, or a little miscommunication. Then I'll suddenly be like oh, we're not in the same space…I think if someone does send – I mean this is kind of a weird one – but if someone does send a big picture of themselves, even if they're just kind of being silly…and it's that realisation that I only half recognised them because they'd had their hair dyed, or they'd lost weight or something like that.

Conflict in virtual teams is more detrimental to performance in distributed teams than it is to traditional or co-located teams (Hinds and Bailey 2003). As Selma has pointed out, however, conflict is not the only source of the glitch experience. The other times when she felt the impact of distance between her and her colleagues was when she found that someone's online persona was different in appearance to their current physical presence.

Selma's use of the word 'avatar' in introducing this problem of disconnect is relevant here, as the term has several connotations when interpreting the remote worker's experience in the context of Goffman's metaphor of the stage as outlined earlier. Today, an avatar is usually thought of as an icon or character that represents a person in a computer game or online environment. A related definition is that an avatar is the embodiment or manifestation of an idea or person – an avatar is often thought of as a simplified version of the original, but with the essence of what it represents intact. This bears similarities to Goffman's distinction between the performer and character in everyday life – your character is a version of you, but it needs 'work' to exist. Similarly, remote workers need to exert effort in creating and maintaining their avatars – the multi-faceted online impression of themselves that is performed through posts, messages, emails and updates.

Remote workers are, in many ways, pioneers in forging identities, reputations and relationships almost solely in the digital realm. Terence Cave's (1995, p. 116) essay on 'fictional identities' demonstrates how this question of where identity lies has in the past been explored in Science Fiction narratives, and remains ever relevant:

> Is the teleported person the same as the one who entered the teleporter? If my brain is transported to another body, am I still the same person? These narrative experiments are attempts to explore a duality or complexity which has always worried philosophers concerned with the identity of persons.

The question of who someone is has in philosophy long been debated in terms of mind/body, form/matter and, in the case of Goffman, performer/character. As can be gathered from Cave's hypothetical questions, emerging technologies mean the question of what identity is becomes at once more relevant and more complex. In a remote working environment, the duality of employee/avatar is an ongoing site of negotiation, and it is therefore important to consider how remote workers perform their own identity and how they experience the identity of their colleagues.

6.7 Collective Identity: Tethered to the Office

For the remote worker, the goal of making themselves known to others in the organisation is managed through ongoing identity work in a digital space. Daily contributions to online forums, group messaging platforms and even frequent video links with colleagues based in the head office are all strategies used by remote workers to forge relationships and stay connected on both a task and social level. These digital presentations of self are akin to those that happen in physical everyday situations; however, the dependence on technologically mediated communication requires the remote worker to constantly tend to these postings and portals in innovative ways to ensure that they are regularly 'seen' by colleagues who in turn validate their organisational membership.

An important aspect of identity depends on how we relate to others, and we often define ourselves based on our group membership (Tajfel 1982). Who *I* am in an organisation is tied up with who *you* are and, more importantly, who *we* are. In an organisational setting, the 'we' can refer alternately to a team unit, a project or geographical level, or to the organisation as a whole. The significance of this way of looking at identity is summarised by Cave (1995, p. 116):

> Our subjective sense of ourselves as individuals depends on our perception of individual others, and vice versa: this subject-object interdependence, or interpersonal perception of what it is to be an individual, again posits identity as an amalgam, joining what we are inclined to think of as essentially separate or different.

Cave is arguing that without another, it is difficult or even impossible to know oneself (see also Ricœur 1992). While we might think of ourselves as having an identity distinct from that of our colleagues, it is actually our relationship with those colleagues that gives us this sense of individuality. When working for an organisation, it can be said that we depend on each other for our sense of self.

Understanding identity as involving the stories that others tell *about* you is particularly salient in the context of remote working. As has been established, being visible in an organisational setting is an ongoing challenge for remote workers. In our research, it became clear that there was a great desire amongst remote workers to be connected with their colleagues and with the organisation – technically and socially (Dery et al. 2014). While official communications about tasks and objectives were important for everyday functioning, the people we spoke with emphasised the need for *informal* communication with colleagues. Being told when to finish a project or how to fill in a leave form were not the communications that remote workers felt were most important to their sense of connectedness to their colleagues and the organisation. Identity work was more likely to be carried out in forums created through what interviewees called informal modes of communication.

Because of the directed way in which email and phone calls operate, it would be considered strange in most organisations to phone an unacquainted person to ask solely about this colleague's private life, for example, what they were having for dinner, or whether they had any pets. Yet without these kinds of non-work or non-task related conversations, the nagging feeling of social isolation threatens to resurface. Without knowing their colleagues on this more personal level, and without regular opportunities to converse in social ways, a sense of self and belonging in relation to the organisation became diminished. The remote workers we spoke with were therefore finding new ways of having more frequent informal conversations, even with colleagues they had never met in person, by using communication technologies in innovative ways.

We found that these methods of communicating informally were mostly established by the remote workers themselves, rather than being installed by management. The remote workers we spoke with at Elevate, for example, were eager to have access to new ways of staying connected with their colleagues and visible in the organisation. When Beth first urged leaders at Elevate to develop an organisational intranet, she argued for the need for 'unstructured communication' in the organisation. She explained that this notion of unstructured communication was important because:

> It's that ability to not just talk about work at work. When you're a remote workforce you can't just have that body language that goes, I know who you are, I know what you contribute, I like you, you're a person, versus a voice out there somewhere, and I'd always had that from the beginning with my original team…so having an ability to have an unstructured like, "hey what colour is your hair" or "what, you've got a dog as well?" and getting to know people like you potentially could at an office space…and without a reason to communicate – if I'm not on a team call with a Blue team person, there's no reason for me to talk with them at work, so the only reason for me to talk with them would be in an unstructured way, to get to know them.

The important distinction here is between communication with a 'reason' versus exploratory communication that is circumstantial and spontaneous. Marissa Mayer drew attention to this form of communication when she said it was the 'water cooler' conversation that could not be recreated when employees worked from home (Guynn 2013). It was this form of unstructured communication that Mayer believed was important enough to require that her employees be co-located. The remote workers we spoke with certainly agreed that informal communication was important and more difficult given their physical distance from their colleagues; however, they have found ways to replicate and re-imagine the function of the water cooler in other ways, using technology. The aim of this type of conversation is to create the sense of 'we' that is associated with organisational belonging.

At Elevate, Beth asked for an intranet to be developed because she wanted a representation of herself and the work she had done and was doing to be visible to new members joining the organisation. Enterprise Social Networking platforms such as Yammer and Chatter are beginning to enable employees from all levels of the company to interact in an unstructured way around non-work related topics. Remote workers want to feel connected to the organisation and are finding ways such as these to make themselves seen and heard. While it is getting easier to become visible to one another, remote workers are often still struggling to be visible where it matters, at the centre of the action – the head office.

6.8 Head Office Syndrome: Visibility at the Core

Some organisations today operate entirely without a dedicated central office space. Although this may seem radical, it was only in fairly recent history that an 'office' referred to the physical site of mass work that we know today – 500 years ago, an office implied a position rather than a place (Haigh 2012, p. 12). As organisational structures and management styles have moved away from more hierarchical, classical models (Nelson 1980) and towards more team-based collaborative ways of organising, so too have office spaces shifted towards open-plan, flexible layouts, with prominent organisations trialling more innovative models such as activity-based working or Google's famous campus locations. What has remained constant, however, is the idea that an organisation will in most cases have a *hub* or a core base from which to operate. Often referred to as a head office, this is the site where most meetings are held, where the leaders of the organisation are to be found and often where activities are run that have the intention of bringing organisational members together in 'bonding' sessions and for collaboration.

Many organisations place a great financial and cultural emphasis on these spaces, and there is a strong history of management and organisational research into the effects of spatial arrangements on organisational culture and behaviour (Becker and Steele 1995; Gagliardi 1992; Haynes 2008; Kornberger and Clegg 2004; Steele 1981). Client floors are decorated with expensive artwork, and designers, architects and psychologists work together to determine which category and combination of furniture, lighting, seating arrangements and indoor plants will best stimulate productivity and lead to other organisational outcomes deemed desirable.

For companies like Google, Microsoft, Facebook and countless start-ups inspired by these technology giants, the head office is not just a place where work tasks are performed – they are imbued with a powerful mythology that draws top talent to apply to the firm, so that they too may work at the famous campus or CBD address. This mythology associated with the 'head office' challenges the remote worker's sense of organisational identity. When so much of the organisation's identity is invested in activities that take place in a designated building or set of buildings, it can be easy for a remote worker to feel 'left out' of what they imagine is happening at the centralised place of work.

At Elevate, Beth describes how, when she was working remotely, she assumed that everything that happened in their head office involved fun that she was missing out on. When she finally moved to head office to take a management position, she reflected on her time as a remote worker, when she would often think to herself,

> I really want to see the office, I wonder what they do in there, I literally thought people were just coming here, hanging out, having cupcakes all day, 'cause that was kind of my lifestyle and I assumed that everyone else was like that…but then now being here, there's no time, to do anything…but apparently that only happened about a year ago, so maybe it was cupcakes before then (laughs).

This mythology of the head office being a place of constant engagement and the cupcake metaphor for greater socialisation can be spurred on by the image that those working in the office try to portray. It is then fuelled by remote workers assuming that colleagues who are co-located are automatically more sociable and enjoying each other's company. As Beth herself discovered, however, a daily lived experience of an office does not always fulfil the image that such mythologies perpetuate.

Other remote workers who we interviewed talked about experiencing versions of what one remote worker called *head office syndrome*. In essence, 'head office syndrome' refers to the way in which decisions would be made in the head office without consultation with or consideration of remote workers. One hypothetical example of head office syndrome offered to us was a group of colleagues working together, and two of those colleagues happen to be co-located and discuss the project over lunch, thereby coming to a firm decision about an aspect of the project that is then shared with the rest of the team via email: 'Jerry and I have discussed it, and we've decided…' This practice was referred to as 'short-circuiting' and was pointed out as a source of frustration amongst remote workers.

A pertinent and related example is the issue of advancement within the organisation. At Elevate, it has until recently only been possible to act as a manager from the head office location. This is why Beth moved to Melbourne, leaving her extended family and friends behind, in order to take on a new position. Selma, as a more junior employee at Elevate, was aware of this dynamic, and it informed her thinking around career progression within the organisation:

> I know that there is actually a big part of me that wants to be at head office because it feels like it's the hub. So even though like I like a lot of elements of working remotely, I know that there's a part of me that if I think of a long-term career with Elevate – say if I think if I'm with the company in six years' time for example, the picture I have in my head is always me at head office in Melbourne…Because I think there's a bit of me that feels like that's still the core of – like that's still the heart of the company.

Selma's reflection has implications for thinking about how remote workers identify with the organisation. While she may be comfortable defining herself as a remote worker, she was nevertheless conscious of what she was remote *from* – that is, what she perceived to be the core or heart of the business – and she did not think that this distance was sustainable in light of her mid- to long-term career goals.

As technology systems improved within Elevate, however, the need to relocate for work was changing. With the introduction of new technologies and platforms, as well as new talent management practices, it became possible for remote workers to take on management roles outside of their head office. It also became easier for remote working employees at Elevate to maintain the kind of visibility in the head office that meant that they were considered for career advancement. Beth explains,

> Facilitators who want to be visible, can be. So we had a facilitator start on the Blue program in Perth, Owen, he, first day, he figured out how to use Yammer, it's intuitive but he's the first one who's actually done it, within one week of starting, to his first post on Yammer and then daily he would upload quotes, and then he'd be, like, hey this is what happened in my session today. So he now has people who know him, who may never have known him because he's chosen to become visible on Yammer and he's chosen to put something positive out there to the whole company…but it's definitely remote worker driven, and if they don't see it as an opportunity or they're not on there, still they're not visible.

As Beth pointed out, being visible in the head office and being considered for advancement did still depend on the remote worker's willingness and ability to be actively involved in performing their identity online. While there are more and more media for bridging the gap between the remote worker and the head office, the success of these still depends on the remote workers' skills in online identity management. This emphasis on skills cuts both ways. As remote working becomes more popular, both employees and employers are in need of new skills and practices to help them work effectively with one another at a distance.

6.9 Contributions and Recommendations for Practice

In this chapter, we have shown that organisations are increasingly hiring people to work remotely, and have explored how the way in which this practice 'works' is constantly evolving. One of the critical factors that determine the success of remote working structures is the creation of a sense of belonging. Our study shows a clear relationship between visibility and the performance of identity (see Fig. 6.1) in shaping the capabilities for those employees working remotely to establish a sense of belonging in the organisation.

We have shown how identity is played out through performance of online characters that can be thought of as avatars, through the creation and active management of online presence and through the building of virtual relationships based on familiarity created through visual, voice and text-based technologies. While we have shown that it can sometimes be isolating to work remotely from other colleagues, for the most part a constant stream of messages, pictures, video and Social Enterprise Networking feeds kept remote workers connected through a flow of formal and informal communications.

However, it was clear that performative identity was only possible for remote workers if the tools were firstly in place and secondly used in order to enable continuous and dynamic visibility. The ability to see each other, particularly if the

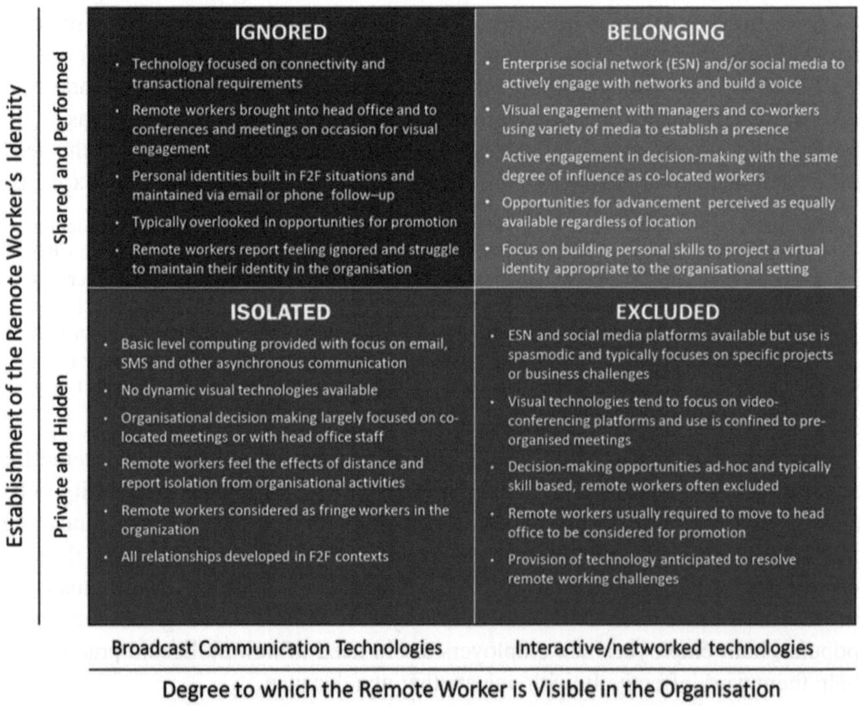

Fig. 6.1 Building a sense of organisational belonging for remote workers

seeing was in context, i.e. the office, made it easier to maintain a stable reputation and identity. Change, for example, in a colleagues' appearance or in the staffing of the organisation, could be particularly jarring for employees who place importance in fixed images (literal or figurative) of the organisation that inevitably change over time. Technology was extremely important in overcoming this kind of breakdown by developing the layers of connectivity required to build visibility to enable remote workers to both be seen and to see the wider context of their fellow workers.

Figure 6.1 is a useful tool from which to get a clearer picture of how this dynamic between performative identity creation and visibility plays out. The graphic aims to give a better understanding of how to build a sense of belonging and engagement from remote workers. Those who are struggling to establish visibility reported often feeling sidelined (ignored) or alone (isolated). By increasing access to technological platforms, it is possible to offer the capabilities for greater visibility from which to build some of the more informal practices associated with simply being together that engender a sense of belonging.

Remote workers also need capabilities in the building of a virtual identity that their co-workers can relate to. In other words, it is not enough just to be visible; employees must engage with each other and with the technologies in ways that make it possible to overcome distances and build meaningful relationships such that both remote workers and co-located workers have the same opportunities to add value. As research on remote working develops in tandem with new technologies and innovative use of established technologies, we believe there will be a better understanding of the needs of remote workers and that this improved understanding can lead to improved remote working and management practices.

We conclude by reiterating that there are many nuances surrounding remote working practices. Technologies are constantly evolving, and remote workers are finding ways to harness and develop various platforms that enable them to become more connected and visible – to ensure that their identity as part of the collective is known. We believe that as more and more organisations collaborate across temporal and geographical borders, the lessons we learn from further studying remote working practices can be illuminating in thinking about how work on all levels of the virtuality continuum can be conducted more effectively. Visibility in organisations is important to an employee's sense of identity, and while remote workers are finding ways of making themselves more visible, it is a collective undertaking that will only feature more prominently as work continues to become less about where we go and more about what we do, and who we are.

References

Albert S, Ashforth BE, Dutton JE (2000) Organizational identity and identification: charting new waters and building new bridges. Acad Manag Rev 25(1):13–17

Becker FD, Steele F (1995) Workplace by design: mapping the high-performance workscape. Jossey-Bass Publishers, San Francisco

Branson R (2013) One day offices will be a thing of the past. http://www.virgin.com/richard-branson/one-day-offices-will-be-a-thing-of-the-past

Cave T (1995) Fictional identities. In: Harris H (ed) Identity: essays based on Herbert Spencer lectures given in the University of Oxford. Clarendon, Oxford

Daily Mail Reporter (2013) Michael Bloomberg backs Marissa Mayer's ban saying that he's always thought working from home is 'one of the dumber ideas I've ever heard'. The Daily Mail UK, 27 February 2013. Retrieved from http://www.dailymail.co.uk/news/article-2286900/Michael-Bloomberg-backs-Marissa-Mayers-ban-saying-hes-thought-working-home-dumber-ideas-Ive-heard.html

Deloitte (2012) Digital disruption: short fuse, big bang? Building the lucky country: business imperatives for a prosperous Australia. Deloitte Touche Tohmatsu, Adelaide

Dery K, Kolb D, Maccormick J (2014) Working with connective flow: how smartphone use is evolving in practice. Eur J Inf Syst 23(5):558. doi:10.1057/ejis.2014.13

Erikson EH (1983) Identity: youth and crisis. Faber & Faber, London

Fried J, Heinemeier Hansson D (2013) Remote: office not required. Random House LLC, New York

Gagliardi P (1992) Symbols and artifacts: views of the corporate landscape. Aldine de Gruyter, New York

Gardner H, Davis K (2013) The app generation: how today's youth navigate identity, intimacy, and imagination in a digital world. Yale University Press, New Haven

Goffman E (1959) The presentation of self in everyday life. Anchor Books for Doubleday, New York

Guba EG, Lincoln YS (1989) Fourth generation evaluation. Sage Publications, Newbury Park

Guynn J (2013) Working moms wail at Yahoo. Chicago Tribune, 26 February 2013, pp 1–2.1. Retrieved from http://bit.ly/1uuJ8Pb

Haigh G (2012) The office: a hardworking history. Melbourne University Publishing, Carlton

Haynes BP (2008) The impact of office layout on productivity. J Facil Manag 6(3):189–201

Hinds PJ, Bailey DE (2003) Out of sight, out of sync: understanding conflict in distributed teams. Organ Sci 14(6):615–632. doi:10.1287/orsc.14.6.615.24872

Keller EG (2013) Yahoo CEO Marissa Mayer's work-from-home memo is from bygone era. The Guardian, 27 February 2013. Retrieved from http://www.theguardian.com/commentisfree/2013/feb/26/yahoo-ceo-marissa-mayer-memo-telecomute

Knippenberg D, Schie ECM (2000) Foci and correlates of organizational identification. J Occup Organ Psychol 73(2):137–147. doi:10.1348/096317900166949

Kolb DG, Collins PD, Lind EA (2008) Requisite connectivity. Organ Dyn 37(2):181–189. doi:10.1016/j.orgdyn.2008.02.004

Kornberger M, Clegg SR (2004) Bringing space back in: organizing the generative building. Organ Stud 25(7):1095–1114. doi:10.1177/0170840604046312

Kreiner GE, Ashforth BE (2004) Evidence toward an expanded model of organizational identification. J Organ Behav 25(1):1–27. doi:10.1002/job.234

Nelson D (1980) Frederick W. Taylor and the rise of scientific management. University of Wisconsin Press, Madison

Nietzsche F (2007) Ecce homo: how to become what you are. Oxford University Press, Oxford

Prasad P (2005) Crafting qualitative research: working in the postpositivist traditions. M.E. Sharpe, Armonk

Ricœur P (1992) Oneself as another. University of Chicago Press, Chicago

Steele F (1981) The sense of place. CBI Pub. Co., Boston

Tajfel H (1982) Social psychology of intergroup relations. Annu Rev Psychol 33(1):1–39. doi:10.1146/annurev.ps.33.020182.000245

Responsive Org (2014) Manifesto. Retrieved 10 July, 2014, from http://www.theresponsiveorg.com/

Chapter 7
Smart Workplace Technology Buzz

Siegfried Schallenmueller

Abstract During the last decade, technology at the workplace has changed. Real-time communication and collaboration capabilities such as video, instant messaging, presence management, and web sharing have been added to the workplace ecosystem as enterprises have started to introduce social media systems to shape a new way of knowledge management and employee communication and connectivity. Though the introduction of such workplace technology has often been driven from an executive level as part of a vision and optimization initiative with high expectations, adoption among the user community is varying from excitement to denial. The mentioned areas of technology are part of an open infrastructure, and in contrast to business applications (e.g., SAP), there is no dedicated business process guiding the adoption. The adoption is influenced both by technical features and the specific culture of the enterprise. Trust within teams and management actions has, among other factors, a strong impact on the outcome. Therefore, a multidimensional view on technology and organizational aspects, both on a group and an individual level, is needed to guide enterprises through the journey to a digital workplace. Within this chapter, we will present a framework capturing the various dimensions and discuss the application along a specific case. We will also suggest how to approach complex rollouts of workplace technology with a focus on real-time communication and collaboration in an enterprise and how a framework can support a structured way of implementation and community development fostering adoption.

Keywords Social collaboration technology • Digital workplace • Interdependence of technology and organizational change • Case study

---

S. Schallenmueller (✉)
Department of Information Systems / Interorganisational Systems,
University of Muenster, Muenster, Germany
e-mail: siegfried.schallenmueller@ercis.de

J. Lee (ed.), *The Impact of ICT on Work*, DOI 10.1007/978-981-287-612-6_7

7.1 Introduction

7.1.1 New Generations of Employees and Advanced Technical Capabilities Increase the Relevance of Workplace Technology

The relevance of technology in the workplace has changed over the last decade. Until recently, workplace technology still focused on supporting standard work routines such as spreadsheet calculations, word processing, or accessing documents on an intranet. However, a whole new set of technical capabilities evolved during the last 5 years. Specifically, the rise of social technologies for the enterprise as Yammer, copying the concepts of social tools as Facebook, added new possibilities for employees to connect and share information. Social technologies and unified communication and collaboration technologies enable new ways of working such as sharing knowledge or connecting employees across time and geography. A strong driver for the discussion around the workplace of the future is the change of behavior and expectations of employees. Meister and Willyerd (2010) outline in their book on the workplace 2020 that "… never a generation has entered the workplace using technologies so far ahead of those adopted by its employer." The rise of social media in an enterprise environment supporting knowledge management and team building and the adoption of privately used capabilities such as the use of Skype or Facetime into the professional life have set the ground for new ways of working (Fenwick et al. 2011). The dependence on communication practices based on using Facebook became obvious during an outage of Facebook in August 2014 when users were calling the police to get help (Iain 2014).

During previous years, the introduction of workplace technology at enterprise level was focused on unified communication and collaboration such as video conferencing, chat, and presence management. Document management systems and social media platforms have also been seen as second stream of workplace technology driven by another set of stakeholders in the enterprise. Initiated by both the user community and the vendors, the two technology areas are converging in the digital workplace. Vendors have started to provide technical platforms unifying synchronous and asynchronous communication and collaboration. Thus, they are delivering their interpretation of Facebook or Skype for the enterprise world. As corporate e-mail systems or directories have been extended to capture profile information from social media platforms such as LinkedIn, the new solutions become more and more integrated with the existing infrastructure.

This development goes along with the deployment of powerful but complex use cases with a strong focus on support of "Bring your own device/application strategies" versus traditional desktop and communication technology.

7.1.2 *Emergence of Social Collaboration Infrastructure (SCI): Workplace Technology as Information Infrastructure*

As outlined before, workplace technology has significantly developed over the last decade. A core part of it is Real-Time Communication (RTC). RTC has its roots both in the telecommunications and the groupware market. Consequently, RTC systems integrate groupware functionality with (IP-based) communications media.

The following table summarizes the building blocks of RTC (Table 7.1).

Although enterprise social media systems such as Jive, IBM Connections, and MS Sharepoint and RTC systems have originally developed in parallel, recent development shows RTC functionality and social media systems merging.

All major vendors of social media systems have created interfaces and integrations with key RTC capabilities such as presence management, chat, web conferencing, and video. We refer to this bundle of capabilities as social collaboration infrastructure (SCI). In this sense, SCI is an emerging set of multiple technologies becoming more and more interlinked, which can be used in a flexible way by individuals, teams, or an enterprise, even at an interenterprise level. In contrast to RTC, social technologies add asynchronous communication and collaboration capabilities

Table 7.1 Building blocks of RTC systems (Riemer and Frößler (2007, p. 209)

Concept	Description
Unified Communications (UC)	Various media and communication channels
	Media and device integration
	Rule-based configuration of message routing and call diversion
	Definition of preferred media
	Unified messaging portal
Presence information	Presence awareness of people, media classes, and devices
	Aggregation of presence information on group, role, and object level
	Active buddy list management
	Individualized and automatic signalling
Contextualization	Embedding and customizing of RTC features to organizational processes
	Integration with office software and enterprise applications
	Context specific buddy lists
	Mobile RTC with location-based services
eCollaboration	Audio and video conferences, web seminars
	Ad hoc application sharing
	Joint whiteboards and discussion forums
	Team calendars and contact management
	Document folders

to the workplace. Social technologies also drive a different way of connecting with peers, colleagues, and managers by reducing formal hierarchies. Additionally, the way knowledge and information is shared between employees, management, and organizations changes from a formal process as known from intranets to an informal user-driven process, following implicit rules and policies.

SCI spans a broad range of technical capabilities to engage with individuals and groups inside and outside the enterprise. However, a dilemma evolves in deploying SCI within enterprises since the interpretation of how to use the technical capabilities does not follow a clear process such as using a SAP form to enter bookings in a travel reservation system. SCI needs to be seen as an infrastructure which requires different approaches to foster introduction and adoption.

7.1.3 SCI as Infrastructure

We conceptualize SCI as an information infrastructure in line with Hanseth and Lyytinen's (2004) definition of an information infrastructure as "a shared, open heterogeneous and evolving socio-technical system consisting of a set of IT and their users, operations and design communities". They "…have the potential to transform how we work because the technology is built around improving relationships, not just heightening efficiencies." (Guinan et al. 2014).

Orlikowski and Iacono (1999, p. 358) also highlight that "technology is social, dynamic, and multiple". It is

- … meant to be social because their form, function, and operation reflect the interests, assumptions, values, objectives, resources, materials, and skills of their makers;
- … dynamic and provisional because new materials are invented, different features are developed, existing functions fail and are corrected, new standards are set, and users adapt the artefact for new and different uses;
- … finally multiple. It does not consist of a single thing but is typically a multiplicity of tools and a variety of different configurations of often fragile and fragmentary components.

The authors emphasize both the social and functional element of technology and underline the evolving interaction between technical capabilities and the users. Deploying a similar set of functional capabilities in an enterprise can result in very different ways of adoption and establishment of use practices depending on how users adapt the concrete set of features within their environment, cultural background, and enterprise culture. Therefore, a nuanced, well-grounded understanding of the users and existing work practices becomes even more important since for the first time four generations of employees with a broad variety of values, beliefs, expectations, and capabilities work together in the workplace (Meister and Willyerd 2010).

7.1.4 Importance of Understanding the User Community Profiles and Structure

Lou et al. (2000) emphasize the unique challenges of introducing collaboration systems: "... social, collaboration-oriented technologies pose some unique challenges in terms of jumpstarting use and acceptance. Unlike individual productivity tools such as word processors, spreadsheets, or online databases, the value of social technologies is only evident when the technology is used by a critical mass of people to collectively get work done."

Mobilizing a critical mass of people requires an understanding of the user dynamics in an enterprise, covering both user profiles and group structures, in order to build an implementation strategy fostering a rapid adoption among the employee community. For instance, identifying highly creative teams within a larger group of employees can help to create quick successes which then can be used as an example for the broader employee community.

The reality of deploying SCI appears to be different. A recent study by Ovum and Dimension Data produced alarming findings from a survey with 1,320 enterprises in 2013 (DimensionData 2013). Emphasizing the role of workplace technology, the study emphasizes that 78 % of the CIOs have developed a workplace strategy. Unfortunately, the involvement of the user community in building the strategy is quite low. Over 70 % of enterprises make a UCC investment based on recommendations of their global IT directors with emphasis on technical requirements and needs. Only 20 % of the companies integrated input on functional requirements from users. The study also reports on the relevance of user profiling, stating that only 38 % of the large enterprises out of the sample profiled their users. The research also reveals that 21 % believe their users all have the same requirements, and 13 % don't see the value in profiling.

In light of these findings, it should not be surprising that workplace strategies and the introduction of SCI primarily focus on technical roadmaps and capabilities rather than user needs.

7.1.5 Success Factors for Introducing SCI

We believe that a successful introduction of SCI requires an integrated view of a technical and organizational perspective. Furthermore, we hypothesize that the organizational and managerial framing, as well as the process of implementation, will impact the outcome significantly. The discussion on introduction of new SCI, as in the case provided here, is led by two questions:

1. How is the use of these technologies introduced and framed by management? For example, is it part of a broader organizational transformation or organization development initiative? Have strategic goals been articulated? What does managerial action and support to "make it happen" look like?

2. What is the response of the employees, individually and in groups? That is, if the technology has been framed as social or collaborative technology, how does it become embedded into the work routines, into ways of collaborating?

Considering SCI as an open information infrastructure, the appropriation by the individual users or a group may be very different depending on the company's culture, team structures, and cultural environment. Therefore, the understanding of the introduction and adoption of SCI requires the analysis both of the characteristics of the technology and the organizational context established by management actions and employee behavior.

Based on a framework developed by Vehring (2014) which provides an integrated view of technology characteristics, managerial actions, and employee actions on an individual and group level and extensions around this framework, we present methods to support the introduction of SCI. Also, we use the framework and extensions to reflect the actions of the company presented in the case.

7.2 Conceptual Framework for Designing the Introduction of SCI

The simultaneous consideration of multiple perspectives of introducing SCI requires systematic approaches for managers to understand interdependencies and design the rollout process appropriately. The following figure presents a framework by Vehring and Kramer (2012). It outlines the interdependencies between managerial and employees' actions and how they are related to technology characteristics.

The effects and interdependencies develop along four facilitating factors: (1) cultural fit, (2) space for appropriation, (3) voluntariness, and (4) network/group externalities as outlined by Vehring (2014) below.

1. Cultural fit

Technology might be experienced as being culturally charged. Management needs to be aware of the existing culture and of a possible fit or conflict between values ascribed to the new technology and values and practices of the organizational culture.

2. Space for appropriation

SCI provides an open information infrastructure, which can be employed by the users in multiple ways. In case of open infrastructures, management needs to accept that users need time for understanding benefits and establishing new working practices both on an individual and group level. Specific actions of the management such as coaching or technology stewarding, but also dedicated communication of best practices, can support the appropriation phase.

3. Voluntariness

Often driven by a management attitude but also legal restrictions, the voluntary use of technology can both facilitate and hinder adoption. Presence management as part of modern collaboration platforms is often a critical element. Even if individuals adopt presence management as part of their working practice, only the use on a group level can unlock the full potential of the collaboration platform. If voluntariness is a leading principle of the rollout, dedicated measures need to address the benefits on a group or corporate level.

4. Network/group externalities

SCI fosters collaboration and needs to be adopted by a critical mass of users to be of value. Specifically in case of voluntariness, the adoption needs to be fostered through various measures as coaches, community management, and extensive communication.

The four facilitating factors (ellipsoids) in the framework (Fig. 7.1) provide a structured approach for reflecting the various dimensions of introducing SCI in an enterprise context. It supports managers aiming for an integrated approach introducing SCI versus overemphasizing the technical aspects.

Cultural fit and voluntariness play a significant role. An enterprise needs to be well aware of its own culture before designing the introduction process and governance structure. Voluntariness can have very positive effects for adopting new

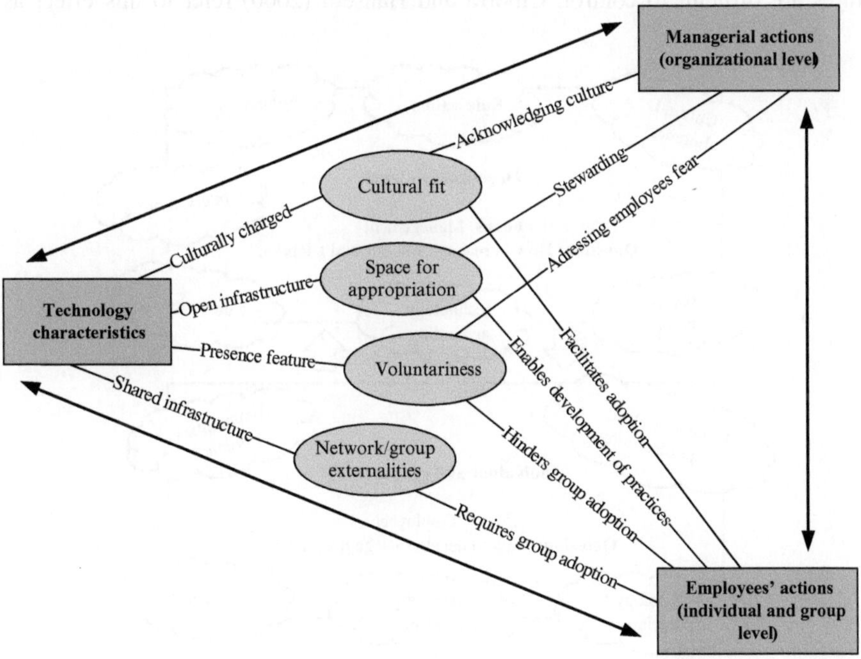

Fig. 7.1 Framework of socio-technical and multilevel dynamics (Vehring 2014, p. 63)

technologies, i.e., employees are used to having choices and can also shape interworking in other areas. It can cause uncertainty and negative effects in cases where employees are used to a strong set of rules and governance, not allowing space for individual practices.

Management also needs to understand the enterprise culture since the level of guidance and rule setting by the management needs to match culture of the employees. Here again, the level of rule setting in other areas of the enterprise is an indicator of whether the management sets tight rules on using the new technology vs. leaving room for experiments and development of individual practices.

The following figure details the dynamic interrelationship between managerial actions to facilitate rollout and adoption of technology referring to the right side of the framework in Fig. 7.1 on the one side and the employees' development of usage practices on the other side (Fig. 7.2).

7.2.1 *The Organizational Level: How to Manage Rollout and Adoption?*

While management often sets focus on control over business processes and technology by seeking for a strategic alignment of information infrastructure and business strategy, empirical examples have demonstrated that open information infrastructures are difficult to control. Ciborra and Hanseth (2000) refer to this effect as

Fig. 7.2 Theoretical concepts and constructs (Adopted from Vehring 2014, p. 17)

"technology drifting." Facing this issue of having no full control of open information infrastructures requires a different set of approaches in contrast to traditional management instruments like setting policies and instructing how to use specific technology (i.e., "Each employee needs to set his presence status according to his current task."). Metaphorical illustrations for such approaches focusing on guidance by the management versus instructing are cultivation or technology stewardship. Both cultivation and technology stewardship represent noninvasive activities from the management with different levels of intensity.

Ciborra and Hanseth (2000) position cultivation as interference with and support for a material that is in itself dynamic and possesses its own logic of growth. This concept differs fundamentally from the idea of rationally planning and designing a technical system. Rather, Saccol and Reinhard (2006) see the implementation of a new technology as a natural process which can be compared to cultivating a tree, where "there is no total control over its future shape and size, but it is possible to water it, fertilize it, prune the branches to adapt it to certain dimensions, or train it to grow in the right direction." In this sense, management acts as guide or instructor in the early phase of the introduction process, "seeding" the ground and observing the evolution.

Addressing the same type of issues, Wenger et al. (2009) introduces the metaphor/concept of stewardship as a more active and intense involvement of management. This concept is based on the idea of taking care of a community by helping to choose, configure, and use technologies to best suit its needs. According to Vehring (2014), the steward needs to understand their community well enough to be able to respond to its technology needs. Technology stewards also need to have enough awareness of technology developments to have a sense of what is available and possible. By combining community understanding and technology awareness, they should be able to help their communities make informed technology choices. Stewards shepherd their community through the process of adopting or rejecting the new technology. When a community changes technology, planning and facilitating the nontechnical aspects of the transition process is substantial. In the everyday use, stewards need to integrate the use of technology into the everyday practices of the community as it evolves.

Stewarding is a sensitive, highly interactive approach to guide users through the adoption process. The requirements for the role of a steward are high, therefore in some cases there might be no suitable managers available to fulfill the role. An alternate concept could be using dedicated user groups out of the user community as intermediary. In this case, managers can become stewards to this group, which then interacts with the broader user community.

For management, the challenge is to assess how applicable approaches such as cultivation and stewarding are. Here, access to the employees and understanding of the cultural background of the enterprise are key decision points.

Guinan et al. (2014) distinguish approaches of fostering the introduction of SCI based on different management styles and personalities. Their approaches can be seen as distinct instantiations of cultivation and stewarding. They state that "… some companies begin with a bottom-up strategy that relies on finding and enabling young experimenters to use social technologies to enhance their individual productivity while other companies start with a middle-out approach, finding and helping corporate entrepreneurs in middle management to use social media to improve collaboration on teams and projects. Finally, others use a top-down strategy, finding enlightened executives who are open to new technology and the potential of social technologies to strengthen their organizational culture."

The following table illustrates the characteristics of the approaches and can help academics to interpret the observations and managers to integrate this approach into their rollout design (Table 7.2).

7.2.2 *The Individual and Group Level: How to Develop Usage Practices?*

On this level, the change or establishing of existing or new communication repertories is a key area to monitor. Often, understanding existing routines is important when providing new ways of technology support. We have observed cases (Schallenmueller 2010) when the introduction of new SCI failed (i.e., video conferencing) because voice conferencing had become a dominant and highly accepted way of working. The whole enterprise was familiar with voice conferencing, and effective support had been provided in the past. Managing change in the communication repertoire requires a profound understanding of existing practices and an adjusted communication and consideration based on new technology to be introduced. Regulatory constraints, such as labor participation, regulation, or privacy laws further restrict the use of SCI.

While fostering communities of practice during rollout of new technology and allowing space for appropriation helps to let bottom-up usage grow, the identification and nomination of role models is critical for success. This requires a careful selection of enthusiasts and evangelists for convincing users and driving the gain of user mindshare helping to build a critical mass of users.

With the presented framework and extensions, we provide a conceptualization of the various perspectives of introducing SCI. The adoption of SCI does not follow a strict process but requires a careful design of various elements to drive success.

In the next section, we present a case on the introduction of SCI in an enterprise with 500 employees and use the presented framework and extensions for reflecting the actions of the enterprise.

7.3 Case Study

7.3.1 *Method*

The case analysis is based on semistructured interviews with the executive sponsors of the SCI project and members of the user experience team. This group of 12 employees acted as a continuous nontechnical interface with the user community

Table 7.2 Approaches for introducing social technology in the organization (Guinan et al. 2014, p. 346)

	Young experimenters bottom-up	Corporate entrepreneurs middle-out	Enlightened executive top-down
Advantages	Familiar with social technologies	Established networks across the organizations for effective diffusion	Have the status to engage others
	Less training required	Vast institutional knowledge to seed platforms with engaging content	Can be role models for the organization
	Helps build personal corporate relationships quickly	Control projects, so can quickly apply and show value	Can control rewards and incentive systems to jumpstart adoption
Challenges	Lack status and credibility to influence others to adopt	Still may not be able to convince less tech-savvy executives	Often lack technical expertise to see social technology value
	Smaller network, so hard to enable wide diffusion	May not control incentives for adoption	May not be a good fit for ROI-driven executives
		May lack bandwidth	
When to use	Newer, fast growing organizations	Middle managers have influence with project management	Patient executives willing to invest time and resources
	Flatter organizations	Large, dispersed organizations with many silos	Executives who have visibility and relationships with lower levels
	Transparent BYOD policy		Very competitive settings where time-to-market is critical
Ensuring success	Frame benefits in terms of personal effectiveness	Pick the right middle managers	Show how social technologies can create value
	Give time to experiment	Pick the right projects	Provide a personal guide
	Highlight their personal successes	Provide real-time training and support	Create a cross-functional steering committee

during the rollout and over the first 9 months of adoption. Case data were collected in early 2013 and revisited in mid 2014. After the presentation of the case, we will use the framework and approaches to link the methodology to the actions and findings provided by the case.

7.3.2 Background

We present the case of a systems integrator with 500 employees working nationwide in a major European country. For further reference, we will name the company "Eagle." The core business of Eagle is to provide technical services and solutions based on real-time communication technology to medium and large enterprises.

At the end of 2012, the management of Eagle took a decision to introduce SCI just after going through a phase of massive reorganization and restructuring. As a consequence, Eagle had reduced its workforce by 300 employees and changed the governance model from a regional setup into a fully centralized, functional organization with two core areas: sales, including presales, and services. The case information was collected from a series of interviews both with management stakeholders and employees. The semistructured interviews were conducted mid 2013 and focus group discussions led with the user experience team in March 2014. The user experience team is a dedicated group fostering the introduction process which will be described in the following case presentation.

The case of Eagle is characterized by two key aspects:

- Strong alignment of business goals with the planned introduction of SCI
- High awareness of management stakeholders on the sensitivity of adoption

SCI was seen as an important lever for achieving the business goals. Revenue and gross profit targets had to be accomplished with a massively reduced workforce and major changes in communication and organizational structures. By introducing a centralized organization, the need for collaboration across the country increased significantly. Employees who had never been in touch before suddenly had to start working together on proposals or bids while physically located in different cities or working from home. SCI was seen as a key lever for mastering the workload and making the new collaboration structures work.

Senior management was facing the challenge that an earlier introduction of SCI had limited success since, on the one hand, the regional setup had limited the effects and the scope had focused on real-time communication only. Therefore, senior management was sensitive to the adoption process and the interplay of users and technology.

The following section provides a summary of Eagle's situation in terms of the (1) cultural environment, (2) technical environment, and (3) key areas of organizational/process changes.

1. Cultural environment

Eagle's culture was built on a close interworking of regional teams. The company headquarters was focusing on a remote operation in the service area, controlling, and accounting. About 90 % of the operational tasks and decisions were performed within the regions including sales, consulting, and project management and system integration. Culturally, the employees were used to communicating and collaborating face to face in their regional offices, and information often was exchanged during lunch and a coffee break. Most of the employees have known each other for more than 10 years; therefore, collaboration was built on trust and an individual level of cooperation.

2. Technical environment

Due to the geographic proximity of resources and family-type culture, workplace technology played a minor role in the daily working routine. For collaboration with the headquarters, a telepresence system had been introduced in 2012 but was seen primarily for management and business review communication with a formal process to book sessions.

SCI was selectively put in place but not consistent across all employees or functions. Mostly technical people were using RTC technology from the key vendors of Eagle.

3. Key areas of change

With the full centralization of all functions within Eagle, key changes were needed to work with resources from other locations. This strongly affected Pre-Sales/Bid Management and Technical Experts. The daily routine of the sales unit did not change too much in terms of their client interfacing but in terms of the support structure they were used to working with.

For Presales and Bid Management and Technical Experts, the need to align and discuss customer situations and the joint creation of documents and proposals became a challenge across geography, which needed technical support.

Formerly, sales people did have assigned support resources in their region. Now, they needed to queue their request to a workflow system. While in the past people had understood each other working with the same client for ages, now the formal requirements to specify a request were raised to ensure any support engineer was able to help independent of location or previous involvement with a client.

7.4 The SCI Project

In this chapter, we will describe the project Eagle initiated in late 2012 in more detail and present the considerations of Eagle during the planning and implementation phase. We will focus on the role of the management since it assumed a significant role in shaping the outcome of the SCI project.

7.4.1 Technical Scope of the SCI Project

The technical scope of the project consisted of the deployment of SCI capabilities to all employees accessible within the company buildings and through mobile/home working infrastructure. With the new infrastructure, existing spot solutions were upgraded and harmonized with the new setup.

The following table shows the functionality provided to *all* employees (Table 7.3).

Part of the technical scope was also the tight integration of the core functionality with the users' desktop environment (e.g., MS Outlook plugins) and the usage of mobile apps for accessing conferencing or web sessions. Since the availability of a dedicated app for mobile phones was pushing the usage of new web conferencing capabilities, the need for entering codes and dial-in was replaced by an automated process. This process allowed the users to enter the conference just from their calendar and directly receive a call on their mobile or home office phone connecting the user to the conference.

7.4.2 Eagle's Management Perspective

The key challenge in the SCI project was to generate a critical mass of users across all departments. Specifically, users in back office functions or from the financial community had been used to working in the regional environment with very low technical support. With the new centralized setup, the organization had turned into a big virtual team where the command and adoption of the SCI was required for all users.

The management of Eagle was very much aware of this issue and therefore invested heavily in activities to make the adoption work. The next section outlines the managerial actions of Eagle's management.

The SCI project was announced at the end-of-year event 2012, which also marked the celebration of the successful turnaround of Eagle. Eagle had undertaken a massive restructuring and stabilized the business during this phase. After a long

Table 7.3 Technical scope of the SCI project

Software	Web based tools for screen sharing and multi party video conferencing for desktop and mobile devices
	Instant messaging and presence management
	Access to tele presence sessions through desktops and mobile devices
	Access to web based document management system with integrated workflows
	Sharepoint platform for document management, community support and internal networking (e.g. MyPage feature)
Hardware	High end HD web cam
	High end smartphone

period of negative results, the business had turned into a profitable business, and both from a mindset point of view and a structural point of view, Eagle was facing the beginning of a new chapter in its history.

The employees had gone through a phase of high pressure and workload, and the expectation that the announcements would come true were very high.

Senior management intended to position the SCI project as the beginning of a new era of workplace support and demonstration of Eagle's ability to make things happen. It should also give a strong signal to clients and key vendors that Eagle can master highly complex projects both technically and from a project management point of view.

Facing the described business challenges, the senior management of Eagle was trying to ensure maximum success of the project. Anticipation of the culture of Eagle and potential fears or concerns of the employees was a strong driver for management activities. Management of Eagle wanted to find the right balance between control and bottom-up development of the adoption. Eagle's management was very aware of being the critical transition point between technology on the one side and employees' new working practice on the other side.

7.4.3 Finding the Right Balance Between Control and Bottom-Up Development

Referring to Guinan et al.'s (2014) typology, Eagle decided to go for a combination of the "Corporate Entrepreneurs Middle-Out" and the "Enlightened Executive Top-Down" approach. The strong involvement of executive management allowed allocation of resources for the project. Reflecting the existing working practices and attempts of deploying new technology in the past, the senior management decided to involve a dedicated user experience team (UXT) next to the technical teams in the project. The UXT can be seen as a specific form of stewardship extending the reach of the management by having a dedicated team interacting with the community.

Part of the UXT were also middle managers out of the management team of the executive sponsor. They represented the majority of the employees, and the executive sponsor acted as a role model promoting the use of the SCI.

Voluntariness as one of the facilitating factors (ellipsoids) from the framework in Fig. 7.1 was the leading principle with the deployment of the workplace technology. Therefore, the work of the UXT was highly relevant to trigger and foster a self-adoption process driven by self-motivation, curiosity, and passion. This was mostly achieved through a regular and intense interaction of the UXT and the user community.

The UXT manager stated, "A shift from technology centric to people centric. In the triangle of technology, processes and people historically technology always came first. The restructuration brought a shift to put people first."

7.4.4 User-Driven Use Case Development

This shift resulted in an extensive definition of use case scenarios. These use cases were created with UXT members from various areas of the company. The use cases were developed with the relevant subcommunity. For example, bid management and proposal development became an important use case involving users nationwide. Here, the combination of MS Sharepoint with real-time collaboration tools, such as WebEx for document sharing and video, became highly relevant. Video added a new dimension to the use case especially during the initial phase of users working together across various locations. With the use case development, traditional work practices were discussed. Instead of sending multiple e-mails with attachments on bid and planning documents, the group switched to storing documents in a central web-based system and shared the same instance during meetings with the new tools.

Another use case centered around team meetings. While those had been mostly face to face in the old regional setup, the new collaboration tools supported virtual meetings with multiparty video capabilities. The use case included setting up these team meetings and aligning rules for virtual meetings including agenda setting. Here, the focus was on understanding the dynamics of virtual sessions compared to a face-to-face session and how practices from face-to-face sessions evolve in virtual sessions (as private vs. public chat or timekeeping).

The use cases were moderated by the UXT together with users across various departments. The UXT facilitated both training and sample runs of the use cases to understand issues and capturing information for ongoing communication on the SCI project.

The UXT consisted of 12 mostly nontechnical employees across all departments and locations and worked on use cases and support of working practices. The UXT also assumed responsibility for creating the training materials, webinars, and early acceptance testing. Right from the start of the activities, a pilot user community was nominated by management. This community of 50 employees was selected from all departments and was involved in the communication from the very beginning. Therefore, almost 10 % of the workforce became involved in the pilot rollout. Creating a community was another important mechanism to promote and collect feedback.

The following figure summarizes the various roles of the project organization (Fig. 7.3).

The design of the organizational setup was key to the project, and by the selection of specific users into the various role areas, the intent was to reduce barriers from the very beginning. The following table provides the reasoning for driving the organizational design of the project setup (Table 7.4).

7.4.5 Communication Strategy

The UXT moderated forums and communities on MS Sharepoint to promote best practices and collect feedback. The UXT discussions with the technical expert community generated suggestions and, even more importantly, provided immediate feedback to the user community, fostering an ongoing dialogue.

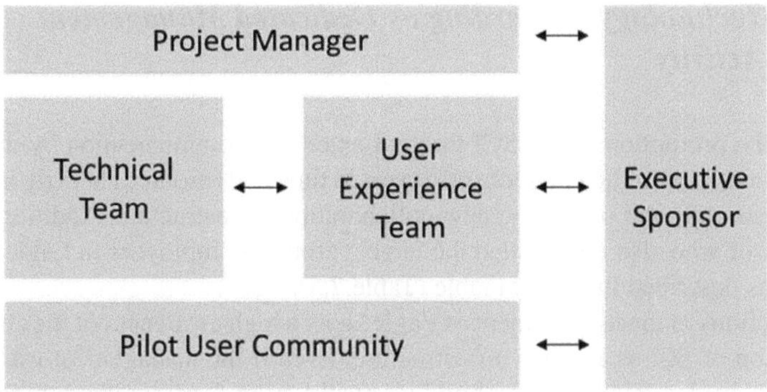

Fig. 7.3 Organizational set up of the workplace project

Table 7.4 Organizational design – roles, competencies, rationale

Role	Competencies and rationale
Executive sponsor	Represented the biggest group among the user community
	High affinity to the workplace technologies
	High need for communication and collaboration across the company and all locations
	Good communication/presentation skills as ambassador among the management team and the company
Project manager	Strong communication skills and both technical and user focus
	Technical skills are sufficient to anticipate issues and provide guidance to the two sub teams
Technical team	Lead: High technical skills across various vendors involved, no dedicated focus on one vendor
	Team: members with both technical and good communication skills, include sponsors of "competitive" tools and vendors to embrace discussion within the focus group
User experience team	Lead: low technical level, high communication skills and network within the company with various departments, user among users, no management role
	Team: low to medium technical level, members from all departments, including workers council and employees with a distinct working practice or vendor preference to anticipate discussions within the focus group
	Integration of middle manager
Pilot user community	Mix of users across all departments, multi-generational, capture cross department teams (e.g. controlling, sales, bid management in various locations) in order to capture realistic pilot scenarios – both on an individual and group level

Adopted from Wenger et al. (2009)

Wherever possible, small podcasts were produced to share feedback and best practices in an appealing way. There was a clear understanding from the very beginning that the distribution of tons of manuals would fail to reach the user community.

7.4.6 *Technology Stewarding as Dedicated Management Activity*

Next to the promotion of the SCI through extensive communication by the senior management, one of the key sponsors invested time and resources heavily into guiding his team into the use of the new collaboration infrastructure. Additionally, the key sponsor who also represented the largest group of employees in Eagle acted as steward as described in the next table (Table 7.5).

The actions of the management of Eagle show a high awareness of the challenges of adoption of SCI as an open infrastructure. Even if the management was not following an academic model, key building blocks from the framework presented in Fig. 7.1 and the extensions can be identified and observed. In the next section, we describe how the employees perceived the SCI and started acting on an individual level and group level.

7.4.7 *Employee Actions*

The SCI was deployed to *all* employees. On the one hand, this decision allowed high flexibility from whichever location an employee was able to work (office, home office, mobile); on the other hand, Eagle's management set a clear expectation by investing in advanced and costly infrastructure and devices independent of role and hierarchical level. Before outlining the activities of the employees, a short description of the rollout to the employees is provided.

Table 7.5 Executive sponsors stewarding activities

Activities	Description
Community understanding	Being in charge of the largest unit within Eagle, the steward was very familiar with the daily routines and processes.
Technology awareness	The steward himself had long-term experience in using SCI with a strong focus on video and virtual meetings. He was very skilled in the command of the collaboration platform.
Selection and installation	The steward actively shared his view on working practices with the new SCI and suggested various settings of use according to the meeting scenarios
Adoption and transition	The steward was very well aware of the different groups using technology before in the unit and issues which had occurred in the past. I would not use a comma here. If the sentence sounds awkward, you can write "…unit as well as issues which had…"
	He shared his positive and negative experiences openly with the team and motivated ongoing use of the collaboration platform
Everyday use	The steward made the new SCI both part of his daily work and of his team. He utilized the technology in every contact with his team and employees of the unit – also actively asking how the users perceived the use and sharing his own experience.

7.4.8 Rollout Procedure

The implementation took place within 4 months from January to April 2013. Before the rollout, an extensive test period had been performed by the UXT followed by an initial rollout to the pilot community. The feedback was used to tune the final rollout. The rollout was done location by location. This decision was taken to maximize the use of a local support employee who was recruited either from the UXT or pilot community. Prior to the rollout, webinars had been created, and a dedicated Sharepoint community was established to provide a single point of information.

Additionally, a continuous flow of information during 2 months before rollout was driven by the UXT, and eight webinars had been offered to prepare for readiness. The focus of the webinars had been the presentation of the overall tools set and basic training along major use cases such as discussing the creation of a bid.

Nevertheless, the project team was well aware that webinars, training, and a Sharepoint site would not be sufficient to make the rollout successful.

Therefore, the local coaches had an important role both providing face-to-face support and stimulating the users. They also had the task of actively approaching home office workers and salespeople, who were traveling most of the time and had lost touch with a brick-and-mortar location.

The actual rollout was done within *1* week in order to ensure consistent availability to most of the employees in a short time frame.

During the roll out and 2 weeks after, a dedicated remote support team took care of technical questions and handling issues.

7.4.9 Status 12 Months After Rollout

In terms of the adoption of various technology areas among the user communities, the following section provides an overview by key technology areas.

7.4.10 Instant Messaging

The instant messaging functionality was adopted quite consistently throughout the company. One reason was the partial deployment of an instant messaging (IM) system previous to the rollout, therefore the usage was known to 20 % of the employees, which acted as an accelerator.

IM is used for quick informal communication. One of the key use cases is knocking on someone's door or interrupting someone when he is shown as busy or on the phone. In the technical area, IM is used for supporting the management of onsite resources as part of a dedicated business process.

7.4.11 Web Conferencing

Web conferencing has become a broadly used functionality across all departments. It was very much driven by the geographic split of the resources. Apart from the accounting teams, which work mostly in one place, all other departments have adopted web conferencing as daily work practice. Access is highly integrated with MS Outlook.

The use of multiparty video conferencing as an element of the web conferencing system was popular during the first 3 months. Especially when people had never met before in the former setup, they were curious to get to know "face to face" by video. The drop of video usage was common across all departments. Only teams where "sponsors" were actively pushing video during web meetings kept usage on a higher level.

7.4.12 Video (Telepresence)

In this section, we focus on the telepresence-based video. While this had been a "privilege" of the management team in the past, the broad initiative on workplace technology accelerated a broader usage across departments and employees. Another enabler was the deployment of desktop clients for accessing the telepresence systems from home. In line with a rise of home office users after the rollout, the booking of the telepresence systems boosted by 75 %. Departments with regular management calls and strongly distributed locations made videoconferencing a standard practice within their meetings.

Usage of video in the senior management team also increased. About 30 % of regular board meetings were moving to video meetings, relaxing the need to be at the headquarters.

7.4.13 Presence Management

Presence Management turned out to be a difficult feature to adopt. Various policies have been established within individual teams. The status is coupled with the outlook scheduler, yet only 25 % of the employees use the presence status as a meaningful indicator of availability. The majority still picks up the phone or checks out the calendar of the party they want to contact.

7.4.14 Document Management

The availability of a web-based document repository was quickly adopted. The need was high, therefore turning from a regional to a central setup resulted in a high demand for easy access to documents (offers, contracts, documentation), which was key for working across regions.

7.4.15 Community Support

The community support functionality was quickly adopted within the technical teams familiar with technical forums. A broader use of community support functionality took time. The creation of communities on the SCI was driven by individuals. The sales management started to build communities for specific customers, and also the project management team used communities for documenting procedures and best practices.

7.4.16 "MyPage"

The MyPage function allowed each employee to share details of his background and interests. This function was used very rarely. The basic information was uploaded automatically as name, department, and phone number. Only 10 % percent of the employees extended their profile with additional information.

The effort of the UXT helped very much to drive a successful rollout. Specifically, the regular exchange with the user community and the use case development had the highest impact. The use community in every department and location knew someone to reach out to for support or simply discussing new working practices. Therefore, a continuous buzz on the SCI project could be maintained during the first months. After this strong effort, the adoption process was left to the user community. The UXT focused on selective user support and managing the SCI community site on MS Sharepoint.

7.5 Findings and Discussion

The key observation is that early adopters were those who had a real need which was met by the SCI. Driven by the high pressure of the reorganization, the group of employees working in a distributed environment had grown significantly.

Another smaller group was established by technical gurus who critically evaluated the new SCI in terms of added functionalities from the very beginning. They became "power users" driving the continuous development and improvement of the platform.

The impact of the management sponsor and the UXT became tangible when the time and resource effort of the UXT and the management sponsor slowed down. At this stage, the usage of the SCI focused on the core functionality.

Speed and success of the SCI project were highly important, given the transformation the enterprise had been facing.

Therefore, Eagle had decided to go for a top-down approach jumpstarting the adoption mixed with middle management involvement. The executive manager both represented the majority of the user community and had the power to assign resources to the project to ensure speed and focus. A good practice would have been driving the adoption by the middle management by gathering a broader community of evangelists with existing networks. In the specific case, the executive sponsor was aware of the technical implications and found a balance between ROI and operational benefits. The direct access to budget and resources was key to make the critical timeline happen.

Finally, from a *strategic point of view*, the availability of a consistent platform for all employees initially clearly created a high motivation and ability to demonstrate to clients and partners how innovative technology was empowering internal processes. Promoting the complex integration of multiple technologies in the partner community was very successful, and a lot of positive feedback was gathered to build future projects on.

From *a tactical point of view*, the availability of a consistent SCI turned out to be highly important to establish new communication routes among the employees. The new SCI had been adopted by those departments which had been affected most by the reduction of workforce and faced a nationwide need for interaction on an intra- and interteam level. Pressure from the daily operation created a massive pull of using SCI in these departments.

7.5.1 SCI Introduction Is a Balancing Act

The introduction of SCI appears as a balancing act between corporate requirements, technological affordances, and managerial and employee (inter)action. From our point of view, there is no one size fits all: different approaches may be successful depending on the corporate culture and the cautious "management" – monitoring, coaching, and stewarding mixed with prescribing where necessary – of the process.

7.5.2 Value of the Framework to Management and Enterprises

The framework provides a methodical foundation, which creates high value for managers facing the introduction of SCI. It helps managers to understand the various aspects beyond technology and can be used as checklist for discussion with internal stakeholders on budget and involvement in order to design the overall implementation. Understanding the framework takes the discussion around an enterprise workplace project far beyond a technical rollout and related user training. Taking the frameworks seriously requires spending efforts on user profiling, understanding the culture in the enterprise, and developing a strategy on adoption with the same effort as planning overcoming technical challenges.

The frameworks do not provide a recipe for the management but provide a systematic collection of ingredients to cook a meal fitting the specific enterprise. This process is the key value of the frameworks and will improve the quality and sustainability of the rollout and consequent adoption. Driving the process within an enterprise starting a workplace project or initiative requires a high level of openness of the decisions made and team members to the ideas and concepts. The application will likely require external experts or moderators to explain and train the use of the frameworks.

7.6 Contribution to Research

The research presented here summarizes a coherent set of related frameworks for understanding and guiding the introduction of workplace technology. Facing an increase both in complexity and variety of workplace projects, researchers need to continue to develop the understanding of the interdependences between the technology itself, activity of the management, and the inter-/intrateam level. Driven by a continuing education of users in the private life through new devices and increasingly more complex interactions through Facebook, WhatsApp, Skype, or Google Hangouts, the role of the individual becomes more relevant and needs further research as the impact on existing teams and established culture in the enterprise is concerned.

The frameworks support the understanding of *multilevel and dynamic concepts*, like culture and voluntariness, which played an important role during rollout and adoption of the case presented. Vehring (2014) outlines "…understanding technology as infrastructures and socio-technical systems has several implications for its organizational roll-out and adoption. As such technologies need to become embedded into social and organizational *practices* (technology-in-practices) adoption is not primarily about a task-technology-fit."

The research presented is a call for deepening the understanding of these interdependences along various industries and cultural environments. Further research needs to explore how interdependences can be quantified and compared to a pure qualitative approach. This would help to refine the frameworks and create more sensitive instruments for explaining and guiding effects. Still, there is a risk that research cases are too specific and findings cannot be generalized. Therefore, broadening the application of the frameworks along a broader case library will provide more clarity on the effects during rollout and post rollout phase.

References

Ciborra CU, Hanseth O (2000) From control to drift. The dynamics of corporate information infrastructures. Oxford University Press, Oxford, pp 2–11

DimensionData (2013) Strategic, user-driven, and managed: the future of unified communications and collaboration

Fenwick N, Leaver S, Paderni LS, Blackburn L (2011) Social business strategy—an empowered report: rethink your enterprise approach to social technology. Forrester Research, Cambridge

Guinan PJ, Parise S, Rollag P (2014) Jumpstarting the use of social technologies in your organization. Bus Horiz 57:337–347

Hanseth O, Lyytinen K (2004) Theorizing about the design of information infrastructures: design kernel theories and principles. Work Pap Inf Environ Sys Organ 4(4):207–241

Iain T (2014) Facebook goes down, people dial 911. Business Media. Retrieved August 3, 2014, from http://www.theregister.co.uk/2014/08/01/facebook_outage/

Lou H, Luo W, Strong D (2000) Perceived critical mass effect on groupware acceptance. Eur J Inf Syst 9(2):91–103

Meister JC, Willyerd K (2010) The 2020 workplace: how innovative companies attract, develop, and keep tomorrow's employees today. Harper Collins, New York

Orlikowski WJ, Iacono SC (1999) The truth is not out there: an enacted view of the "Digital Economy". In: Understanding the digital economy: data, tools, and research. MIT Press, Cambridge

Riemer K, Frößler F (2007) Introducing real-time collaboration systems: development of a conceptual scheme and research directions. Commun Assoc Inf Syst 20:204–225

Saccol AZ, Reinhard N (2006) The hospitality metaphor as a theoretical lens for understanding the ICT adoption process. J Inf Technol 2(3):154–164

Schallenmueller S (2010) Cross company comparison of the introduction and adoption of Real Time Collaboration Infrastructure (RTC). DIGIT 2010 proceedings. Paper 12

Vehring N (2014) Roll-out and adoption of corporate communication and collaboration platforms: exploring multilevel dynamics and management implications. Doctoral Dissertation, University of Muenster

Vehring N, Kramer M (2012) Exploring the dynamics of culture in the roll-out and adoption of eCollaboration technology: a case study comparison. Americas Conference on Information Systems (AMCIS), Muenster: Seattle

Wenger E, White N, Smith JD (2009) Digital habitats: stewarding technology for communities. CPsquare, Portland

Chapter 8
Gamification of Service Desk Work

Sue Conger

Abstract Gamification is an emerging science that seeks to redesign work processes to more fully resemble complex forms of play. This chapter examines gamification and Service Desk gamification to redesign the work of IT Service Desk workers.

Service Desks provide support for IT use in organizations and are one of the main entry points to the IT organization. As a result of their importance, Service Desks seek to provide high-quality services that provide both psychic and work satisfaction to employees. As important as Service Desk work is within an organization, the daily work can be stultifying and unsatisfactory to those who do it. This research seeks to redesign Service Desk jobs to gamify them through publication of communal quality metrics and rewards from use of game elements to increase work motivation.

Keywords Gamification • Service desk • Job motivation • Feedback

8.1 Introduction

Much routine work in business is boring and demotivating. As many as 52 % of employees are unengaged and another 19 % disengaged by their work (Goasduff and Pettey 2011). These high levels of disaffection reduce productivity and innovation, while promoting undesirable behaviors (Digital Leaders 2014). As complex forms of knowledge work become automated, the problems of previously interesting work becoming boring also increase (Davenport 2011). Service Desks that support IT use in companies are one example of a computer-mediated job environment that can be tedious and boring. They are the focus of this practical, applied research

S. Conger (✉)
Satish & Yasmin Gupta College of Business, University of Dallas, Irving, TX, USA

University of Canterbury, Christchurch, New Zealand

Rhodes University, Grahamstown, South Africa

University of South Africa, Pretoria, South Africa
e-mail: sconger@udallas.edu

J. Lee (ed.), *The Impact of ICT on Work*, DOI 10.1007/978-981-287-612-6_8

to apply gamification concepts to improve work quality and employee job satisfaction. The research questions are what game elements might be appropriate for a Service Desk and how might those game elements be applied to Service Desk work.

Service Desks are one example of a computer-mediated job environment that can be tedious and boring. Service Desks are the focus of this applied research to improve work quality and employee satisfaction through gamification. The research addresses the questions of what gamification elements might be applied to a Service Desk, what are contingencies for deciding which elements to use, and what are issues in applying gamification in a work setting? These are important issues because as gamification grows in importance, the potential to subvert natural, intrinsic motivation toward performance for rewards also grows. If this were to happen, overall performance would suffer, possibly irrevocably (Hamari et al. 2014; Muntean 2011). As a result, care must be taken to address the key issues in enhancing intrinsic motivation to obtain desired behaviors.

Many situations, both in work and school, already contain game elements. For instance, at school, students "quest" through courses to learn and progress to eventually fail or obtain a degree, a "badge" of success (O'Donovan 2012). Similarly, at work, we progress through tasks (quests) to meet goals and objectives (achievements) to succeed on performance reviews and obtain a higher salary or a different, improved job (rewards). Work "games" are not well defined or recognized and may also be demotivating with feedback coming only in the form of grades and performance reviews that occur annually rather than as behaviors occur (O'Donovan 2012). Plus, if management's job expectations do not match performance evaluation criteria, it is unlikely that the expectations will be fulfilled. In addition, job motivation and encouragement may be in short supply if a company is experiencing tough economic times or significant change and turmoil. By adding a few game elements to job tasks, they can become more motivating, providing instant feedback and, possibly, rewards, and can transform a mundane activity into one that is more enjoyable and pleasant to perform (O'Donovan 2012; Starbuck and Webster 1991; Webster 1988; Webster and Martocchio 1993).

Further, as Generation Y's digital natives enter the workforce, they expect to use technology that they have used their entire lives in the workplace. By age 21, the average person has spent about 2,500 h reading books but about 10,000 h playing computer games (de Boer et al. 2013). As a result, interesting, engaging interfaces, structured to provide work as a challenge, similar to a game, are expected (Digital Leaders 2014; O'Donovan 2012).

Gamification, or the "use of game design elements in non-game contexts" (Deterding et al. 2011a, p. 2), is viewed as a deterrent to work disaffection and a device that can engage Gen Y workers, who make up a large proportion of Service Desk staff. By making technology more interesting and by encouraging users to perform desired behaviors that solve real problems, gamification can exploit a human predisposition to play (Marczewski 2013). Key goals of gamification in business are to increase intrinsic employee motivation and productivity while eliciting desired behaviors in a noncoercive manner (Fogg 2002; Gartner 2011; Marczewski 2013; McCormick 2013; Muntean 2011).

Gamifying embeds game elements in a manner that increases the potential for work satisfaction and development of new skills related to the work. Common gamification elements are recognition in the form of badges, points, and rewards, narrative, challenges, user control, user decisions, and mastery development (Burke 2014; Marczewski 2013; McCormick 2013; Muntean 2011). In education, gamification has been shown to motivate students, improve learning efficiency, and enhance retention of learned material (Burke 2014; Blohm and Leimeister 2013). These outcomes appear to translate to work environments as well (Burke 2014).

This chapter develops concepts of gamification discussing its history, pitfalls, and application to a Service Desk work situation. The discussion is based on action research conducted by the author during 2013–2014 for several Service Desks and similar research to design gamified educational Internet assignments for students in rural and poor locales. The next section describes the development and use of gamification and identifies the range of possibilities for inclusion of game elements in a Service Desk environment.

8.2 Gamification

Successful computer games evidence their success through rapid growth of using populations. Even simple games, for instance, Angry Birds, developed over one billion users in 3 years (Scott-Mackay 2014). Weight Watchers automated "country challenges," thus pitting hundreds of thousands of rivals who develop loyalty to their countries and their compatriots while losing weight (Scott-Mackay 2014).

Gamification does *not* turn work into a game; rather, it injects game elements into work situations to make intrinsically boring or mundane work more interesting (Muntean 2011; Scott-Mackay 2014). Further, by applying a game context to serious problems, innovative solutions to global problems might be developed through the phenomenon of crowdstorming, that is, creating a game in which the solutions to problems are solved collectively by all player-participants (Scott-Mackay 2014).

Pre-2002, early research in the area of games focused on making both work and learning more enjoyable (e.g., Malone 1981, 1982; Webster 1988, 1989). Some research focused mainly on enhancement of early childhood education with some game elements for, as Plato said,

> "No compulsory learning can remain in the soul… In teaching children, train them by a kind of game, and you will be able to see more clearly the natural bent of each" (Plato *The Republic, Book* vii, as cited in Malone 1981, p. 333).

Even business applications of game concepts seek to improve innovativeness and foster a more enjoyable work environment by embedding elements of play in work (Gartner 2011; Malone and Lepper 1987; Martocchio and Webster 1992; McCormick 2013; Webster 1988; Webster and Martocchio 1993). These early authors incorporated other game elements, almost subconsciously, including feedback

(Martocchio and Webster 1992), competition (Starbuck and Webster 1991), and social interactions about the play (Starbuck and Webster 1991).

Most often, even though there might be positive work benefits, the early authors sought to elicit pleasure and enjoyment from the play or game elements, ideally resulting in a state of "flow" in which the individual loses track of time and place (Webster 1989; Starbuck and Webster 1991). Use of play elements was recommended only in situations where time was not an issue but concentration was, thus engineering design, librarian information searches, and other productive work that includes iterative periods of reflection and search would be candidates for gamification (Starbuck and Webster 1991).

More modern views of gamification can be attached to the coining of the word in 2002 (Marczewski 2013). Deterding et al. (2011b) are credited for the "official" definition of gamification although there was general recognition that gamification meant the use of game elements and not the creation of a game per se. Table 8.1 lists the game goals and outcomes expressed in research. The emphasis has shifted over the last two decades from learning-based outcomes (Fogg et al. 2002; Malone and Lepper 1987; Webster 1988) to business-based outcomes with the most commonly cited goals being increased task engagement, desired behaviors, and pleasure from work performance (Witt et al. 2011; Marczewski 2013; McCormick 2013; Muntean 2011; Simões et al. 2013). Marczewski (2013) argues that managers balk at the term "fun" as "un-work like" and focus exclusively on potential business outcomes that can affect revenues. There is little agreement that this is a complete list of outcomes,

Table 8.1 General game goals and outcomes

Game goals and outcomes	Reference works
Fun, pleasure	Malone and Lepper (1987), Martocchio and Webster (1992), McCormick (2013), and Webster (1988, 1989)
Increase altruism	Simões et al. (2013)
Increase brainstorming and alternatives development	McCormick (2013) and Starbuck and Webster (1991)
Increase company loyalty	Simões et al. (2013)
Increase competition	Simões et al. (2013)
Increase effectiveness of learning	Fogg (2002)
Increase efficiency of learning	Fogg (2002)
Increase information dissemination	McCormick (2013)
Increase motivation	Malone and Lepper (1987), Marczewski (2013), and McCormick (2013)
Increase productivity	Marczewski (2013)
Increase self-expression	Simões et al. (2013)
Increase skills, skill building	McCormick (2013)
Increase social capital	Bartle (2004) and Fitz-Walter et al. (2011)
Increase task engagement	Witt et al. (2011), Marczewski (2013), McCormick (2013), Muntean (2011), and Webster (1989)
Increased self-expression	Simões et al. (2013)
Obtain desired behaviors	Marczewski (2013), McCormick (2013), Muntean (2011), and Simões et al. (2013)

Table 8.2 General game elements

Game design elements	Reference works
Accuracy required	Kapp (2012)
Audio/video effects	Malone and Lepper (1987) and Webster (1988)
Behavioral expectations	Marczewski (2013) and Muntean (2011)
Challenge	deBoer et al. (2013) and Malone (1981, 1982)
Clear means of advancement	Muntean (2011)
Competition	Malone and Lepper (1987)
Competition visibility	deBoer et al. (2013) and Muntean (2011)
Drill down through data	Muntean (2011)
Feedback	Malone (1981), Muntean (2011), and Webster (1988, 1989)
Forms of accountability	Muntean (2011)
Goals, missions	Malone (1981, 1982), Malone and Lepper (1987), Muntean (2011), and Viola (2011)
Interesting context	Fogg (2009a) and Muntean (2011)
Motivation	Fogg (2009a) and Marczewski (2013)
Narrative that is progressively revealed difficulty as the 'game' proceeds	Malone and Lepper (1987), Malone and Lepper (198x), Muntean (2011), and Webster (1988)
Next steps, known outcome, clear process	Fogg (2009a), Muntean (2011), and Webster (1988)
Social engagement	Malone and Lepper (1987) and Marczewski (2013)
Time pressure, deadlines	Kapp (2012), Malone (1981), and Muntean (2011)
Trigger to desired outcome	Fogg (2009) and Muntean (2011)

and in fact, it appears that almost any outcome could be possible with the right gamification motivating (Fogg 2002; 2014).

Game design elements (See Table 8.2) describe an environment in which tasks are tied to goals and challenges, possibly with fostered competition among staff, with individual outcomes monitored and made public (deBoer et al. 2015; Malone 1981; Marczewski 2013; Muntean 2011). The purpose of any narrative would be to identify next steps in the process and essentially walk a person through the desired behaviors. All behaviors would invoke instant feedback to reinforce, and possibly reward, desired behavior, correct undesired behavior, impart time pressure as the task requires, or establish task accountability (Fogg 2009b; Malone 1982; Marczewski 2013; Muntean 2011). Other elements that may or may not apply are data drilldown of outcomes in an online dashboard, accuracy of work, and triggers for different types of work (Fogg 2009b; Kapp 2012; Muntean 2011).

Some research suggests that only positive feedback should be given (Martocchio and Webster 1992), but in business, that may not be effective, thus suggesting that positive feedback be shared and more public and that negative feedback be private and pointed toward the desired behavior. Wording can be significant. For instance, negative feedback such as "You failed to thank the client" could be modified as positive feedback "Always remember to thank the client." The second, positive, statement is more likely to elicit the desired behavior than the first (Malone 1982; Martocchio and Webster 1992).

Game elements set the stage for, and should be designed to encourage, the desired behaviors. Therefore, time should be spent matching goals with design elements to encourage or elicit a desired outcome and the method of attention and reward to be given to them. If gamification is successful, it should lead to more effective learning and motivation. In turn, increased motivation and learning should lead to higher-quality outputs or products and should lead to employees who are better able to react to new situations or tasks (Starbuck and Webster 1991; Webster and Martocchio 1993).

Rewards can take many forms, the most common of which are listed in Table 8.3. Achievement recognition seems universally recognized as a key element of feedback and can take many forms (Burke 2014; de Boer et al. 2013; Fitz-Walter, et al. 2011; Simões et al. 2013). For instance, achievement might recognize individual or group accomplishments, information sharing, some form of altruistic behavior, posting on a website or to a blog, or any other behavior. Further, learning of skills, attainment of some performance milestone, and fostering of further engagement may all be forms of achievement that are recognized (Burke 2014).

Other rewards such as progress bars, notifications and feedback, and leaderboards are all noninterruptive forms that motivate an individual to continue their work (Burke 2014). To many authors, the outcome "fun" is not the desired effect for work situations as it can easily cause players to lose sight of their work goals and replace them with game goals (Marczewski 2013; Schell 2012).

Table 8.4 lists different identity game elements, and Table 8.5 identifies various personality types associated with gamified environments. While there is little agreement on personality types, participating/nonparticipating, social/nonsocial, and intrinsic/extrinsic are common (Muntean 2011; O'Donovan 2012). The "killer" type carries over from actual online games but has also been identified with work gamification (Deterding 2011).

Table 8.3 Game player reward elements

Reward elements	Reference works
Achievements	deBoer et al. (2013), Fitz-Walter et al. (2011), and Simões et al. (2013)
Awards	Muntean (2011), Simões et al. (2013), and Viola (2011)
Badges	deBoer et al. (2013), Muntean (2011), Simões et al. (2013), and Viola (2011)
Classifications	Muntean (2011) and Viola (2011)
Gifting, charity	Muntean (2011), Simões et al. (2013), and Viola (2011)
Leader board	deBoer et al. (2011), Muntean (2011), and Simões et al. (2013)
Levels	Muntean (2011), Simões et al. (2013), and Viola (2011)
Notifications, feedback	Burke (2014), Muntean (2011), and Viola (2011)
Progress bars	deBoer et al. (2013)
Rewards	Burke (2014), Muntean (2011), and Viola (2011)
Virtual currency	deBoer et al. (2013)
Virtual/Real goods	Muntean (2011), Simões et al. (2013), and Viola (2011)

Table 8.4 Game player identity elements

Individual identify elements	Reference works
Avatar	Burke (2014) and Muntean (2011)
Name	Muntean (2011)
Named group	Muntean (2011) and Simões et al. (2013)
Personalizable profile	Burke (2014) and Muntean (2011)

Table 8.5 Game player personality elements

Personality type	Characteristics	Reference works
Achiever	Doing, completing, succeeding	Bartle (2004), Deterding (2011), Muntean (2011), and O'Donovan (2012)
Apathetic participant	Uninterested in participating	Digital Leader (2014)
Explorer, seeker	Engaging curiosity	Bartle (2004), Deterding (2011), Muntean (2011), and O'Donovan (2012)
Extrinsic personality	Being buffeted by fate	Muntean (2011) and Viola (2011)
Intrinsic personality	Managing self and actions	Muntean (2011) and Viola (2011)
Killer, conqueror	Defeating (killing) others, winning	Bartle (2004), Deterding (2011), Muntean (2011), and O'Donovan (2012)
Mastermind	Solving puzzles, making efficient decisions	O'Donovan (2012)
Money motivated	Working for pay	Alattar (2012)
Multi-motivations	Feelings of accomplishment, Obtaining public acclaim, Increasing social capital, etc.	Muntean (2011) and Viola (2011)
Non-money motivated	Working for feelings of accomplishment	Alattar (2012)
Socializer	Gaining trust, working in teams	Bartle (2004), Deterding (2011), Muntean (2011), and O'Donovan (2012)
Survivor	Escaping threats, mastering complex situations	O'Donovan (2012)

Muntean (2011) recommends that individuals be allowed to customize their game presence with a custom avatar, name, and profile (Table 8.4). Often, avatars or names can signal one's predisposition toward a given personality type (Table 8.5). If a predominance of one or two types exists, the environment can be oriented toward encouraging or redirecting behaviors as desired. If most of the personality types are present, the environment should be designed to appeal to all groups with effort spent on ensuring that each personality type is rewarded similarly for the same behaviors even though the behaviors might be triggered by different game stimuli (O'Donovan 2012).

To the extent that groups are required for the efforts, they should be encouraged to create a group name that distinguishes them from the other groups, their competition (Muntean 2011). Even if competition is not part of the context, grouping individuals causes them to perceive a competitive environment in which they will be compared to other groups. As a result, if social participation is the goal, high-performing groups should be recognized and encouraged and rated on their sociability and group achievements, such as cross-training or mentoring (Burke 2014; Schell 2012).

Personality types differ (Table 8.5) and should be attended to in both educational training and game element design (Muntean 2011). Thus, except for apathetic, extrinsic personalities, elements that contain achievements, searching, self-management, decisions, rewards, public leaderboards, teamwork, and complex ambiguous situations should be worked into the designed system (Alattar 2012; Bartle 2004; Deterding 2011; Muntean 2011; O'Donovan 2012; Viola 2011). To the extent that two or more personality-based job elements can be combined, they should appeal to two or more of the personality types. Groups that are disaffected – the apathetics and extrinsics – may not respond to any stimuli but might be persuaded to participate in the design effort and, thus, alter their outlooks sufficiently to behave as one of the other predominant types (Muntean 2011; Viola 2011).

The appeal of design and reward elements differs by personality type. Killers seek to destroy their competition and should be encouraged to behave as Conquerors who "best" their competition (Bartle 2004; O'Donovan 2012). O'Donovan (2012) found that Seekers most desire a visual narrative to drive their activities, while Masterminds prefer assessments and badges that indicate advancement, and Conquerors seek leaderboard postings of their achievements. Thus, each personality type needs clear ways to excel at work and be recognized for it, particularly in a cooperative environment.

O'Donovan's three main personality types – seeker, mastermind, and conqueror – are similar to those of programmers who fall into Myers-Briggs categories for intuitive-thinker (NT) and sensor-judge (SJ) classifications (2012). "NT types tend to visualize the completed solution to a problem, while SJ types tend to visualize the steps necessary to implement the solution" (Hardiman 1997, 10). These ways of thinking about problems and solutions should be incorporated into the gamified design to the extent possible as they are intrinsic to the type of troubleshooting performed on a Service Desk.

The last game characteristics are common metrics (Table 8.6). The metrics proposed by Rumburg and Zbikowski represent the seven best practices recommended through Help Desk International (HDI), a practitioner organization supporting Service and Service Desk professionals. The other metrics all relate to Internet use of some type. Neither Internet use nor page views nor time indicates success of a work gamification effort. For the Internet metrics, there is no empirical work found that justifies these metrics as a complete set, thus these can only be thought of as samples of participant use.

To summarize this section, gamification takes elements of games and applies them to work or learning situations. In the process of gamifying, first goals and objectives are defined. The goals are then matched to work elements that match game elements. The personality types of the individuals involved in the activity should be evaluated before design is completed and used to provide motivators and game elements that appeal to all of the requisite personality types. Then, the game/

Table 8.6 Game metrics

Game metrics	Reference works
First Call Resolution (FCR)	Rumburg and Zbikowski (n.d.)
Frequency of visit	Muntean (2011)
Multi-location access	Conger (2014)
Multi-media access used	Conger (2012) and deFreitas and Griffith (2008)
Page views	Muntean (2011)
Participation (Total or per visit)	Muntean (2011)
Time on site or page	Muntean (2011)
Total time per page	Muntean (2011)
Cost per contact	Rumburg and Zbikowski (n.d.)
Aggregate service desk performance	Rumburg and Zbikowski (n.d.)
Agent satisfaction	Rumburg and Zbikowski (n.d.)
First level resolution rate	Rumburg and Zbikowski (n.d.)
Agent utilization	Rumburg and Zbikowski (n.d.)
Customer satisfaction	Rumburg and Zbikowski (n.d.)

Table 8.7 Potential game problems

Gamification issues	Reference works
Anti-social	Muntean (2011) and Simões et al. (2013)
Does not suit purpose; ignores personality differences and needs	Muntean (2011) and O'Donovan (2012)
External rewards devalue internal rewards, rewards invokeundesiredmotivationor consequences	Hamari et al. (2014), Marczewski (2013), Muntean (2011), O'Donovan (2012), and Schell (2010, 2012)
Maturity does not support gamification	deBoer et al. (2013)
One-upmanship	Marczewski (2013)
Uses only monetizable components of games	Bogost (2011)
Uses only trivial, least important aspects of games	Bogost (2011)

work elements and related outcomes should be matched to how each will be recognized and/or rewarded in the designed environment. Finally, metrics that indicate usage, success (or failure) of the gamified elements, and actual outcomes and achievements of the individuals should be developed.

8.2.1 The Downside of Gamification

There are several nontrivial issues relating to gamification to be considered and mitigated during design of gamified work. The first entry in Table 8.7 – antisocial behavior – is the most serious and the easiest to deal with. To the extent that the activity is a social activity, social actions, social evaluations, and social rewards should be used (Muntean 2011; Simões et al. 2013). For instance, instead of individual contribution, team contribution and team efforts and outcomes can be the unit of evaluation and reward. If mentoring or information sharing, good citizenship, altruistic behaviors, or other social actions are expected during work fulfillment, they, too, should be evaluated and rewarded. For instance, for a Service Desk, populating a Known Errors Database, mentoring junior staff, and sharing solutions or techniques all might be occasions for recognition.

Conversely, if social actions are desired, then individual efforts might invoke behavioral change feedback (Webster 1989). For instance, if an individual does not share known information with a junior colleague as expected, they can be admonished, for instance, "[Name] might have benefited from your experience on [topic]." Similarly, if trust is required for information sharing to take place, outside of the gamified environment, trust-building exercises with role-playing to indicate situations for appropriate information sharing can facilitate the desired behaviors.

The issues of game elements that do not suit the purpose or ignore user personality differences are less simple. To the extent that goals and objectives are matched to work outcomes which are then expressed in terms of how they might appeal to multiple personality types, suitability should be relatively assured. But prototypes should be developed and tested with feedback from actual users to ensure "fit" of the game elements to the work design (Burke 2014; Marczewski 2013). If there is any doubt, the game elements should be omitted from any final effort.

Another serious issue is the potential devaluation of internal motivation or the subverting of motivation to focus solely on rewards (Hamari et al. 2014; Marczewski 2013; Muntean 2011; O'Donovan 2012; Schell 2010, 2012). Individuals have both hedonic and utilitarian outcomes they expect from any experience. To the extent that pleasure and fun supplant a need to excel at work, reward systems can negatively affect motivation in unintended ways. In addition, to the extent that being on a leaderboard is viewed as a main requirement for organizational advancement, the recognition and reward systems may be overdone (Hamari et al. 2014). Work can become a game of one-upmanship in which employees forget about work and seek to be higher in rankings than some peer (Marczewski 2013). In the extreme, Jesse Schell cites studies that show that "if you bribe someone to do something, they always come to hate that thing." (2012). The key, then, is to engage the desired group while not alienating the target group or other employees. Through gamification, the unengaged may be saved by making the work more interesting and engaging. The disengaged, who actively dislike their work, may be unaffected by game elements and may, in fact, need to be replaced. Also, research has shown that "engagement-, completion-, and performance-contingent rewards [can] undermine free-choice intrinsic motivation" (Marczewski 2013, 20). Therefore, care in designing reward systems needs to be taken into account, and the rewards need to be temporary, i.e., tied to attainment of mastery, creativity must also be rewarded in some way, or opting out after an opt-in should be allowed (Marczewski 2013). The negative effects of devaluing internal motivation or one-upmanship can be counteracted by voluntary participation, having strictly enforced rules, rewarding not just individual but also altruistic and group behaviors, altering the rewards along the "journey" from novice to expert at the target task, monitoring quality and quantity of work, and managing journeys with different rewards for different tasks (Marczewski 2013).

De Boer et al. (2013) argue that organizational and departmental maturity is required to derive the maximal gains from a gamified work environment. In an organization with no discernible processes, where individuals operate on their own ingenuity and there is no standardized, repeatable work performed, gamification will be wasted on this organization (de Boer et al. 2013). In addition, with uneven repeatability, staff pleasure and enjoyment may increase, but desired behaviors are unlikely to be evoked. As a result, de Boer et al. (2013) recommend standardized processes and an emphasis on business execution and innovation as the basis for any game element use in work settings. They further recommend that to achieve maximal profits from business gamification, an organization should be operating at the highest levels of maturity, with fully standardized processes across the organization, a level of excellence that would merit ISO 9000, or similar, certification. While there is no empirical justification for these observations, de Boer et al. (2013) are likely correct that immature organizations are unlikely to benefit significantly from gamification efforts. Thus, organizational maturity should be considered and evaluated before any gamification decisions are taken.

Bogost (2011) raises several issues about gamification in that he believes the *quest*, the creative, ambiguous, exploratory narrative aspects of games, is ignored to use only monetizable or trivial game components such as badges, leaderboards, and so on. To some extent, this is a legitimate argument in that each work environment has its own expected outcomes and products. As a result, the narrative necessarily must follow the expected process flow with known inputs and known, expected outcomes. This does not imply that there is no room for creativity or exploration, only that they will be necessarily constrained by the work being performed. This seems a reasonable trade-off if the organization can benefit in other ways from gamification.

To summarize, poorly designed gamification elements can destroy any positive affect toward work (Marczewski 2013; Muntean 2011). Disregard for social needs can shift behaviors away from desired team efforts (Simões et al. 2013). Too few rewards might not appeal to the requisite variety of personality needs, while too many rewards might undermine intrinsic motivations and deflect attention to work for rewards (Hamari et al. 2014; O'Donovan 2012). Organizational maturity should be sufficient to reap positive business outcomes beyond employee enjoyment from gamification efforts (de Boer et al. 2013).

8.3 Service Desk Business

8.3.1 Service Desk Explained

The Service Desk is an organizational function that provides services to resolve incidents (or outages), questions about IT usage, requests relating to IT usage, personal computer provisioning for new employees, services to access protected or auditable data, or events that encompass monitoring for potential IT failures (Conger and Probst 2013). In a Service Desk, patterns of problems recur daily. Explicit knowledge on past computer outages is codified into a "known errors database"

(KEDB), which is a searchable online database accessible by all Service Desk support staff that summarizes issues, outages, and their resolutions or workarounds. When an outage occurs or a request is made, they are recorded in a request ticket monitoring application. For outages, the KEDB is checked to determine if a solution or workaround already exists. When found, the solution is applied and verified as working. When no solution is found, the expertise of the Service Desk staff worker in the form of tacit knowledge takes over. Then, the worker reviews his past experience to determine similar situations and tries to resolve the issue based on that past experience (Conger and Probst 2013). Alterations and improvised solutions based on experience may result. Ideally, then, the new solution should be able to be codified and added to the KEDB.

Service Desk expertise is not a given. Rather, Service Desk staff begin as novices, develop skills, and become journeymen, eventually becoming expert. The levels of development can apply to Service Desk work domain, the Service Desk computer-mediated environment, or the company and its applications. Progress is made through skills development in all areas, which can come from training, on-the-job coaching, or self-motivated learning. The levels of achievement to attain expertise are consistent with creation of a "journey" for gamified encouragement (Burke 2013).

A systems approach to Service Desk services requires evaluation of the tasks based on input, process, output, and feedback mechanisms (Churchman 1978; Conger 2012). The inputs are issues, outages, requests, or operational events. Processes include ticket logging, searching a known errors database (KEDB), troubleshooting, conversing with the client, possibly discussing the issue with vendors, and escalating if no solution is found. Service Desk outputs that affect customers are a return to normal operations or a successful resolution to a request. Additional outputs are updating a ticket-tracking application and possibly updating the KEDB. Feedback to regulate the process takes the form of metrics on Service Desk operations (Conger 2012), including first-contact resolution (FCR), customer satisfaction, and so on. Typically, Service Desks strive for 75 % or higher FCR, but the U.S. national average remains under 65 % (Bomgar 2010). FCR often hinges on finding a KEDB entry matching the problem. When no KEDB resolution is found, the process usually relies on tacit knowledge, that is, personal expertise of the individual Service Desk employee.

8.3.2 Service Desk Characteristics That Make Gamification Attractive

The average Service Desk employee handles 10–100 requests per day with great variability on both the number, complexity, and repetitiveness of the requests (Tourless 2014). When a significant change to the operational environment is made, the next several days result in the same issues arising repetitively. When the operational environment is stable, the issues are likely to vary considerably. Thus, gamification is more attractive in the stable, variable environment as it requires mentoring, knowledge sharing for new entries to the KEDB, and a broader range of experience, skill, and knowledge to handle the highly variable environment. This does not imply that gamification should be suspended during times of operational change, only that benefits might be made more visible during other times.

8.4 Gamification of Service Desks

This section first describes a process for gamification and then analyzes the characteristics of Service Desks and their employees to develop a gamified Service Desk design.

8.4.1 Process of Gamification

Defining of game elements to be used is a critical activity. The general process is as follows (Adapted from Aparicio, et al. 2012; Fogg 2009a; Marczewski 2013; Conger 2011):

1. Evaluate the individual processes to determine if they require improvement. Improve any process deemed needy
2. Develop an overall goal or set of goals and desired outcomes for each level of expertise.
3. Identify the methods of obtaining outcomes in terms of the work being gamified, and link them to the goal set.
4. Evaluate game characteristics, social interactions, and element alternatives for each of the work methods, and identify a possible set of applicable game elements.
5. Define measures of success for each game element. In addition, identify the point at which the element will be deemed to have become ineffective.
6. Decide on whether or not a platform should be created. Alternatives include, for instance, "Badgewille, PubPharm, Bugdoor, and others" (Marczewski 2013, 123).
7. Develop and evaluate a prototype with a range of individuals to prove the concepts both apply and are effective.
8. Iterate through the steps to improve or replace any game elements that do not have the desired outcome or that evoke negative outcomes by the test group.

8.4.2 Analysis of Gamification Characteristics

The process in Sect. 8.4.1 is applied in this section to create gamification elements to be included for initial Service Desk work. The problem with this completely rational approach to game element selection and deployment is that there are no known heuristics for selecting one or another of the game elements. There are caveats from various authors on what to do or not do as general rules of thumb, but these are inconsistent and contradictory. Thus, the reasoning applied is accompanied by the rationale for each game element's selection with pros and cons of its inclusion identified.

8.4.2.1 General Game Goals and Outcomes

The goals and outcomes expected of the Service Desk should drive the gamification initiative. In an example taken from a 2013–14 consulting engagement, the goals included

- Provide 75 % FCR by December 31, 2015
- Provide 99.5 % resolution in-house by December 31, 2015
- Provide 99 % customer satisfaction at the "satisfied" or "very satisfied" levels by December 31, 2015
- Grow the KEDB to include 80 % of new outages by December 31, 2015
- Provide zero-defect provisioning 100 % of the time by December 31, 2015

Each of these Service Desk goals will next be considered for game needs and the elements appropriate to service them as well as the expected behaviors for each level of expertise.

8.4.2.2 General Game and Reward Elements

This section discusses the work required to complete each of the goals. Table 8.8 shows the goals, a short description of the work required to realize the goal, and activities expected of each level of expertise.

Novices and journeymen should be evaluated on their efficient and effective use of databases, success of troubleshooting, and ability to seek answers from colleagues. In addition, recognition of milestones for training, demonstration of expertise growth, breadth of areas mastered, organizational socialization (e.g., becoming familiar with experts' areas of expertise), and so on should be considered. Experts should be evaluated on their resolution of escalated issues, contributions to the KEDB, participation in training, mentoring of junior staff, and other areas of expected citizenship. Key indicators should be decided because if too many measures are taken, they demotivate or are ignored.

The FCR, in-house resolution, and customer satisfaction goals all relate to current functioning of the Service Desk. These tasks should be accomplished first and together so that if process redesign, new software, or other changes are required, all current effects can be managed. Therefore, these efforts would also be the first for gamification and could be used to test the concepts and design in the operational Service Desk environment.

FCRs are accomplished by junior staff and are individual interactions of Service Desk staff with their customers. Thus, FCR can use individual accomplishments for

Table 8.8 Service desk goals and work descriptions

Goal	Work description	Novice	Journey-man	Expert
95 % FCR	Converse with user via multiple methods, determine priority, create ticket, use KEDB, troubleshoot, escalate if not resolved	Converse, prioritize, update DBs, use KEDB (end if FCR)	Not applicable	Not applicable
99.5 % resolution in-house	The work is similar to FCR except that if not resolved on the first call, a junior person escalates the issue to a more senior person. Only experts are allowed to update the KEDB or work with vendors on items not resolved in-house	Converse, prioritize, update DBs, use KEDB, escalate	Converse, prioritize, update DBs, use KEDB, trouble-shoot, work with experts, escalate	Update DBs, use & update KEDB, trouble-shoot, work with vendors, work with junior staff
99 % customer satisfaction	Discuss service as group, discuss quality process and product, develop scriptlets and training to improve quality of customer interactions, develop standard phrases, sentences, etc. for email and Ticket System entries	Customer inter-actions are cordial, caring, accurate, respectful, complete	Customer inter-actions are cordial, caring, accurate, respectful complete	Customer and vendor inter-actions are cordial, caring, accurate, respectful complete
KEDB to include 80 % of new outages	Ad hoc journeyman and expert teams analyze novel outages, test potential KEDB entries, experts document and update KEDB		Analysis team, testing team	Analysis team, testing team, document and update KEDB
Zero-defect provisioning	Process redesign, obtain and use ghosting software	Use ghosting software, setup equip-ment, install software and equipment as needed	Use ghosting software, setup equip-ment, install software and equipment as needed	

rewards and recognition. FCR rates can be tracked for each person and entered to a leaderboard with the top five staff recognized and their FCR rates shown. Every person's FCR rates for the last week could be displayed as they log into the system. In this way, they can track progress, compare themselves to the other staff privately, and gain a form of feedback they might not otherwise have.

Customer satisfaction can be measured in terms of the process, that is, interactions with staff, and the product and success of the customer's request. At least 10 % of every Service Representative's requests should be polled for satisfaction and quality of the interactions. These numbers too could be shown for a week on a rolling basis and tracked over time. A leaderboard could be used, but it might be more effective to rate the group, rather than individuals, on customer satisfaction as the group rating is the goal. By tracking group customer satisfaction, the lowest and highest ratings of the week might also be shown but without identifying the Service Representative involved. In this way, the laggards can be compared to the best, and depending on the outcomes, the whole group, or only individuals who do not improve over time, can undergo added service training. If an individual's customer satisfaction ratings drop by more than 5 % in any week, or an individual is under an acceptable threshold, or there is no progress 3 weeks running, the Service Desk manager could be notified to evaluate the individual's workload and work. As needed, a mentoring system could be set up to assist junior people in improvement efforts. Other measures for tracking might include number of days or weeks of more than 90 % customer satisfaction rates. In addition, when anyone received some unacceptable rating, for instance, a rating under 80 % or one that included negative comments on interactions, they should be provided immediate feedback on how they might improve. An example might be "Customer expect you to provide a status update at least once every day until an issue is resolved."

To attain 99.5 % resolution in-house, different, more social aspects of Service Desk might be enhanced. Often, escalations are due to a lack of experience and knowledge. Therefore, as the gamification analysis is being conducted, an assessment of the tools, resources, and knowledge bases available to the Service Desk staff should also be evaluated (Conger 2014). All application and vendor documentation should be up to date and for the version of software in production. If this is not the case, these should be procured, and training for their use and key aspects of the packages or software should be conducted. In addition, a mentoring system could be established for senior support staff, who may be in different departments, to mentor more junior Service Desk staff. The game elements that might be applied to the mentoring of work could include monitoring of time spent mentoring, the expected decreases in time of resolution, and/or accuracy of resolution for the mentees as a result. For each 5 % increase in in-house resolution, some group recognition, possibly singling out outstanding performances when they occur, could be provided. For instance, an ad hoc pizza party luncheon, an early release from work, or other reward might be devised. Any monitoring activity should track the group with, for example, starting, month-to-date, and year-to-date numbers to show trends. A social blog could be set up for user coproduction, information sharing of mentoring activities, or tips that come to light during the mentoring activities. The entry of these items should become the responsibility of expert Service Desk staff. Thus, the Service Desk staff should be more sensitive to the usefulness of advice they are giving and then share the best advice via the blog. Rewards for information sharing might be provided until the practice becomes routine.

Finally, for the first three items, entries to the KEDB should be evaluated to ensure that as solutions are being found, the individual finding the solution enters all of the relevant information to the KEDB. This type of activity likely will identify a few stars in the staff who are more observant or better troubleshooters. They can be recognized for their attainment of new knowledge and skills and also for their sharing of the knowledge in the KEDB. Rather than use badges, etc., small but significant, e.g., $200 bonuses might be paid annually. Or, a computation of Service Desk time saved as a result of the solution's availability could be computed and the staff member given a percent of the saving. These rewards should be given publicly to provide recognition for the staff but could also be recognized as a one-time event that may not recur in the same way. By doing this, the staff can still be incented to participate but should not be diverted to acting solely from a monetary incentive (Burke 2014).

8.4.2.3 Game Player Identity and Personality Elements

A Service Desk requires integrity and honesty on the part of the staff in their interactions with customers. As a result, identity that differs from the individual's work identity is not recommended.

Personalities can be attended to in several ways. First, reward systems and metrics can be customized to the individual by providing a selection list and allowing individuals to choose the ones that most appeal to them. To ensure that the rewards and metrics are appealing and meaningful, a committee of several personality types should be provided guidelines, e.g., monetary value, and allowed to develop lists of potential rewards from which selections would be made. The team making final selections should be encouraged to get the input of the whole group either through a survey of preferences or through voting on the potential items to be provided.

Another accommodation for differing personality types is to specifically identify journeymen and experts who like the searching or goal aspects of their jobs best. Then, these individuals should be encouraged to streamline and develop subprocesses for more junior people to use as best practices (for instance, for searching the KEDB or troubleshooting). Matching mentors, if mentoring is used, based on placing different personality types together can help them understand each other better but also can get the best of what each person has to offer in terms of the search, solution identification and testing, and other aspects of the work. Teams can be encouraged to share their processes and working methods with others to help them in their mentoring efforts as well. These can be evaluated as citizenship activities and could be voted on by the Service Desk team to identify the best performers.

8.4.2.4 Game Metrics

Metrics report on goal attainment. Therefore, all of the efforts described should be analyzed and measured to ensure that they are meeting the desired goals and that the individuals involved are, in fact, more engaged in work, more productive, and improving on building (or sharing) expertise, FCRs, in-house resolutions, and customer satisfaction. Measuring individual perceptions is best done with surveys, focus groups, or free-form discussions, depending on the openness of the environment. If the organization is starting in a poor position, with lower maturity, lack of trust, and lacking collaboration, surveys might be best as they provide anonymity and are most likely to obtain honest answers. However, if the environment is trusting and fairly mature to start, the other more casual arrangements could work to also identify areas for improvement or rethinking more easily and faster than a survey.

8.5 Discussion

This chapter sought to develop gamification alternatives for IT Service Desk. Before gamifying, the business processes involved should be evaluated to determine if they need updating. Once the process is accepted, goals and measures of success should be defined (McCormick 2013; Muntean 2011; Simões et al. 2013). Then, for each goal, desired behaviors should be identified, and the type, thresholds, and frequency reporting and rewards should be decided. These key initial activities provide the basis for Service Desk gamification. Measures, expectations, and possibly rewards should differ for levels of expertise and for expected job behaviors. Positive feedback should be provided both when milestones are reached and also when behavior is less than expected.

No research found makes explicit recommendations of game features to be used in a Service Desk. Since first user contacts are with novice Service Desk staff, FCR rates depend on novices' ability to find information in the KEDB, seek out senior staff with needed expertise to get advice, troubleshoot, and recommend a resolution to a user. Since FCR is a critical metric of Service Desk success, each step of novice work should be tracked with, if possible, real-time suggestions on next steps or senior staff who may have requisite expertise. Once a novice obtains a predefined level of expertise, they should be progressed to the journeyman category and the monitoring and reward structures adjusted accordingly. Similarly, when a journeyman obtains a level of expertise to be recategorized as an expert, the monitoring and reward structures should again be adjusted.

Ideally, rewards and metrics kept can be customized to the individual with some that are provided for everyone. A list of potential metrics and rewards could be developed by an ad hoc committee of Service Desk staff, and the whole staff could vote on those most motivating or meaningful to themselves (de Boer et al. 2013; Muntean 2011; Simões et al. 2013; Viola 2011).

Recommendations relating to definition of idiosyncratic avatars and individual identities are not fully consistent with Muntean (2011), who recommends that such customization be allowed. But customization can be allowed while still requiring accurate individual identities as a basis for building trust with the user community. Two types of research support this accuracy. First, the potential for antisocial names is mitigated by requiring accurate representative names (Simões et al. 2013). Second, the potential for names that render the Service Desk more game than business, thus rendering it both unfit for its purpose and also motivating the wrong aspects of behavior, is avoided (O'Donovan 2012; Schell 2012).

The recommended actions do not provide much opportunity for customizing game elements to individual personality types. Rather, the recommendations focus of reward variety that is designed to meet the preferences of the different personality types (Muntean 2011; Simões et al. 2013; and Viola 2011). In addition, mentoring assignments that match different types of personalities should provide useful cross-training (O'Donovan 2012).

One aspect of work not discussed by any of the research found to date is the potential for backlash or jealousy from departments that are omitted from gamification efforts (Schell 2012). For instance, the Service Desk, as the primary customer-facing organization for an Information Technology (IT) function in an organization, exhibits work elements that are amenable to gamification. However, IT also includes software acquisition, operations, database, telecomm, and other departments and specializations that might feel slighted if gamification efforts single out only the Service Desk. As a result, some attention should be paid to providing recognition and rewards for other parts of the organization such that they feel jealousy is mitigated. To some extent, inclusion of achievements and public rewards could become part of all IT work to minimize jealousy and imminent loss of productivity by other IT departments.

Gamification works best when participation is voluntary (Hamari et al. 2014). Some discussion and thought should be given to making participation in any public recognition or award systems voluntary. Everyone should still be measured for FCR, customer satisfaction, and participation in group activities. But people who opt out of participating can be managed privately by managers in a more traditional way. In this way, the disengaged, apathetic workers might obtain more attention and be turned into more productive individuals or might be counseled to seek a different position that is more interesting to them.

Care must be taken to ensure that gamification does not create play in the Service Desk (Webster 1988). Labeling of work as "play" or a "game" would negatively affect the participants, especially in organizations that do not support play at work (Starbuck and Webster 1991).

8.6 Conclusion

This chapter develops concepts of gamification and relates them to potential uses in the workplace. A specific example of how to develop gamified rewards, measures, and task structures that meet the social needs of Service Desk work was defined.

Gamification at work is expected to grow to the point that all work will be redesigned to more specifically elicit desired behaviors and to incorporate motivating, enjoyable, gamified aspects of work.

References

Alattar M (2012) Neuroscience helps explain how we handle money. Fredericksburg.com, March 30. Downloaded on May 15 2014 from http://news.fredericksburg.com/healthyliving/2012/03/30/neuroscience-helps-explain-how-we-handle-money/

Aparicio AF, Vela FLG, Sánchez, JLG, Montes, JLI (2012) Analysis and application of gamification. In: Proceedings of the 13th international conference on Interacción Persona-Ordenador, ACM, New York, October, p 17

Bartle RA (2004) Designing virtual worlds. New Riders Press, Indianapolis

Blohm I, Leimeister JM (2013) Design of IT-based enhancing services for motivational support and behavioral change

Bogost I (2011) Persuasive Games: Exploitationware. Gamasutra Mei, May 3. Downloaded on May 14 2014 at http://www.gamasutra.com/view/feature/6366/persuasive_games_exploitationware.php

Bomgar (2010) HDI Industry Benchmark Report Series, Help Desk International (HDI). Downloaded on October 5 2014 from www.bomgar.com/Documents/resources/hdi-financial.pdf

Burke B (2013) The gamification of business. www.forbes.com/sites/gartnergroup/2013/01/21/thegamification-of-buisness/. Checked on 1(12), 2014.

Burke B (2014) Gamify: how gamification motivates people to do extraordinary things. Brookline Village, MA

Churchman CW (1978) Foreword. In: van Gigch JP (ed) Applied general systems theory, 2nd edn. Harper & Row, New York, pp ix–x

Conger S (2011) Process mapping and management. Business Expert Press, New York

Conger S (2012) Service quality: state of research and future considerations. In: Kajan E, Dorloff F-D, Bedini I (eds) Handbook of research on e-business standards and protocols: documents, data and advanced web technologies. IGI Global, Hershey, pp 537–566

Conger S (2014) Research proposal for remote rural internet assignments, The Council for Scientific and Industrial Research, Pretoria, South Africa

Conger S, Probst J (2013) Knowledge management in service desk decision making. In: M. Mora M, Gomez JM, Garrido L, Perez FC (eds) Engineering and management of IT-based service systems: an intelligent decision-making support systems approach. Springer, London, pp 1–18

Davenport TH (2011) Rethinking knowledge work: a strategic approach. McKinsey Q 1(11):88–99

de Boer J, Geerts A, Adriani, P (2013) Game maturity model. Compact Magazines. Downloaded May 15 2014 from http://www.compact.nl/artikelen/C-2013-4-Boer.htm

de Boer J, Geerts A, Adriani P (2015) Game maturity model. Compact_2013, 40 Years of Compact, 48-55, Downloaded on July 22, 2015 from http://www.compact.nl/pdf/C-2013-4-Boer.pdf

Deterding S (2011). Situated motivational affordances of game elements: a conceptual model. In: Gamification: using game design elements in non-gaming contexts. A workshop at CHI

Deterding S, Khaled R, Nacke LE, Dixon D (2011a) Gamification: toward a definition. In: CHI 2011 gamification workshop proceedings, ACM, New York, May

Deterding S, Dixon D, Khaled R, Nacke L (2011b) From game design elements to gamefulness: defining gamification. In: Proceedings of the 15th international academic MindTrek conference: envisioning future media environments, ACM, New York, 9–15 September, pp 9–15

Digital Leaders (2014) Productivity game. P. 30–31. Downloaded on May 15 2014 from www.bcs.org/content/ConMediaFile/23494

Fitz-Walter Z, Tjondronegoro D, Wyeth, P (2011) Orientation passport: using gamification to engage university students. In Proceedings of the 23rd Australian computer-human interaction conference, ACM, November, pp 122–125

Fogg BJ (2002) Persuasive technology: using computers to change what we think and do. Morgan Kaufman, Burlington

Fogg BJ (2009a) Creating persuasive technologies: an eight-step design process. Persuasive April, p 44
Fogg BJ (2009b) The behavior grid: 35 ways behavior can change. In: Proceedings of the 4th international conference on persuasive technology, ACM, NY, April, p 42
Fogg BJ (2014) How to create long-term change from short-term motivation. Keynote speech at the Gamification Summit, San Francisco, 10–13 June
Fogg BJ, Cuellar G, Danielson D (2002) Motivating, influencing, and persuading users. In: The human-computer interaction handbook: fundamentals, evolving technologies and emerging applications. L. Erlbaum Associates Inc., Hillsdale
Gartner (2011) Gartner predicts over 70 percent of global 2000 organisations will have at least one gamified application by 2014. The Gartner Group, September. Accessed 14 May 2014 at http://www.gartner.com/it/page.jsp?id=1844115
Goasduff L, Pettey C (2011) Gartner says by 2015, more than 50 percent of organizations that manage innovation processes will gamify those processes
Hamari J, Koivisto J, Sarsa H, Hamari J (2014) Does gamification work. In: A literature review of empirical studies on gamification. In: Proceedings of the 47th Hawaii international conference on system sciences, Hawaii, 6–9 January, pp 3025–3034
Hardiman LT (1997) Personality types and software engineers. Computer 30(10):10
Kapp KM (2012) The gamification of learning and instruction: game-based methods and strategies for training and education. Wiley.com
Malone TW (1981) Toward a theory of intrinsically motivating instruction. Cogn Sci 5(4):333–369
Malone TW (1982) Heuristics for designing enjoyable user interfaces: lessons from computer games. In: Proceedings of the 1982 conference on human factors in computing systems, ACM, NY, March, pp 63–68
Malone TW, Lepper MR (1987) Making learning fun: a taxonomy of intrinsic motivations for learning. Aptitude Learn Instr 3:223–253
Marczewski A (2013) Gamification: a simple introduction. Andrzej Marczewski
Martocchio JJ, Webster J (1992) Effects of feedback and cognitive playfulness on performance in microcomputer software training. Pers Psychol 45(3):553–578
McCormick T (2013) Anthropology of an idea gamification. Foreign Policy, July/August, 26–27
Muntean CI (2011) Raising engagement in e-learning through gamification. In Proceedings of the 6th International Conference on Virtual Learning ICVL, October, pp 323–329
O'Donovan S (2012) Gamification of the games course. Acesso em, 17
Rumburg J, Zbikowski E (n.d.) The seven most important performance indicators for the Service Desk, Service Desk Institute (HDI). Downloaded on October 6, 2014 from http://www.thinkhdi.com/~/media/HDICorp/Files/Library-Archive/Rumburg_SevenKPIs.pdf
Schell J (2010) Visions of Gampocalypse, Verba Buena Center for the Arts, Verba Buena, July 27
Schell J (2012) When games invade real life. TED Talks, Apple Computer, Cupertino. Accessed on 14 May 2014 at http://www.ted.com/talks/Jesse_Schell_when_games_invade_real_life
Scott-Mackay L (2014) Gamification: game on! In: Proceedings of the ITSMF-New Zealand conference, Wellington, New Zealand, 5–7 May
Simões J, Redondo RD, Vilas AF (2013) A social gamification framework for a K-6 learning platform. Comput Hum Behav 29(2):345–353
Starbuck WH, Webster J (1991) When is play productive? Account Manag Inf Technol 1(1):71–90
Tourless (2014) Average support calls per IT employee, Spiceworks.com, October 4. Master's thesis, University of Utrech, Utrech. Downloaded on October 5, 2014 from http://community.spiceworks.com/topic/597102-average-support-calls-per-it-employee?source=topic&pos=11responsibility
Viola (2011) Gamification I videogiochi nella vita quotidiana, published by Arduino Viola Von Ahn

Webster J (1988) Making computer tasks at work more playful: Implications for systems analysts and designers. In: Proceedings of the ACM SIGCPR conference on management of information systems personnel, ACM, New York, May, pp 78–87
Webster J (1989) Playfulness and computers at work. Ph.D. dissertation, New York University, New York. UMI order no: GAX89-11170
Webster J, Martocchio JJ (1993) Turning work into play: implications for microcomputer software training. J Manag 19(1):127–146
Witt M, Scheiner C, Robra-Bissantz S (2011) Gamification of online idea competitions: insights from an explorative case. Informatik schafft Communities, 192

Part III
Empirics on Emerging Work Practices

Chapter 9
Work Design Characteristics of Mobile-Intensive Workers: Implications for Future Work Design

Hyejung Lee and Jun-Gi Park

Abstract Modern Work Design Theory (WDT) presumes that different characteristics of work (motivational, social, and contextual) influence attitudinal outcomes of workers such as job satisfaction, thus work needs to be designed carefully with these characteristics taken into consideration. Moreover, increased adoption of ICT also changes these work characteristics as it provides capability to overcome physical limitations such as time and place. Recent rapid infiltration of smart devices connected to the Internet brings telecommuting and flexible time back into reality, hence "smart work" and "work smart" are becoming another catchphrase of consulting firms. This study extends the work design theory with ICT use. WDT variables are empirically tested against two different ICT user groups: one with mobile messenger use and another with PC messenger use. Mobile messenger use is treated as the surrogate of mobile working, expecting mobile messenger users are more subjected toward smart work while PC messenger users are relatively traditional workers at a fixed place. Meaningful differences are found in terms of motivational, social, and contextual work characteristics. Also, job satisfaction is found to be critically high for smart workers. Autonomy and interdependence are much higher for mobile messenger users while complexity of work is found to be much higher for PC-based messenger users. Results indicate the work design theory developed in industrial setting may also be applicable in information- and knowledge-based smart work setting. Further research and limitations are discussed at the end with practical implications.

Keywords Work design theory • Motivational characteristics • Social characteristics • Attitudinal outcomes • Smart work • Autonomy • Job complexity • Interdependence • Satisfaction

---

H. Lee
Center for Work Science, Yonsei University, Seoul, South Korea
e-mail: h.jlee@yonsei.ac.kr

J.-G. Park (✉)
IT Policy and Strategy Research Institute, Yonsei University, Seoul, South Korea
e-mail: warren.pak@gmail.com

J. Lee (ed.), *The Impact of ICT on Work*, DOI 10.1007/978-981-287-612-6_9

9.1 Introduction

Since the beginning of industrialization, employers as well as academics took interest in improving the efficiency and the productivity of employees (Babbage 1935; Smith 1776). According to research on early industrial societies, specialization was one of the best solutions in maximizing efficiency of workers (Gilbreth 1911; Taylor 1911). However, specialization which refers to simplified and repetitive tasks decreased the employees' work satisfaction and increased stress, which further resulted in increased absence and quitting work (Hackman and Lawler 1971). These side effects make people think about jobs that need to be designed to increase internal motivation for effective performance as well as the task organizing or systemizing for the employee's job (Hackman and Lawler 1971). In this regard, the work design theory had been proposed specifying the conditions under which employees would become internally motivated to perform effectively on their jobs (Hackman and Oldham 1975; Herzberg et al. 1959; Turner and Lawrence 1965). This work design theory has been recently expanded to emphasizing the social relations among employees and the physical working environment in addition to the originally proposed motivational factors (Humphrey et al. 2007; Taber and Taylor 1990).

Historically, the nature of work has been changing whenever related technologies advance. Current type of work and form of work had been mostly settled after the Industrial Revolution. It took a while for our society to stabilize 9-to-5, 5-days-a-week work schedule aligning the characteristics of technologies with work characteristics. Now, the technologies are information and communication technologies (ICT). Similar to the way in which the tools used in agricultural society were replaced by steam engines in the industrial era, as societies move into informational societies, the work of the industrial age that people performed in factories and offices that were routine and repetitive has been mostly replaced by information technology. Office workers have started using computers in carrying out their tasks. Automated computing systems and machines have taken over most simple and repetitive tasks, and tasks of humans at work become more nonrepetitive and knowledge intensive. In particular, sophisticated communication technology such as the Internet has helped workers to communicate with each other beyond time and space. With the help of ICT, workers today are now able to perform their tasks whenever and wherever they wish. In addition to phone, fax, and email, workers are using instant messengers, teleconferences, cloud, etc. This "anywhere, anytime" work style based on ICT (Information Communication Technology) is called "smart work" in the Republic of Korea (Lee and Lee 2012).

As emphasized by the work design theory, work characteristics are important in motivating workers to work hard. Originally, five core dimensions of job design had been identified in human resource studies: skill variety, task identity, task significance, autonomy, and feedback (Hackman and Oldham 1976). These studies about jobs have been extended into, later, "Work Design Theory (WDT)." WDT classifies motivational, social, and work context as critical work characteristic dimensions that may affect work outcomes, such as performance, satisfaction, organizational commitment, etc. Autonomy may refer to the flexibility of work scheduling management and choices of work method in smart work contexts with ICT use. Social characteristics of WDT may be extended to workers networking and sharing information resources while work context refers to mobile and contingent workplaces.

In this regard, several research questions arise. Does the WDT hold true in smart work environments in which ICT is extensively used? As ICT relieves workers from mundane and repetitive tasks, autonomy may increase. With real-time networking capabilities provided by ICT, the interdependence felt by workers may be different. Are the pictures drawn by the WDT different in smart work contexts compared to traditional work contexts?

9.2 Literature Review

9.2.1 Work Design Theory

"From the early time and motion studies of Taylor (1911) to the intense interest in motivational aspects of work in the 1970s (Hackman and Oldham 1975), literally thousands of studies have been conducted examining work design issues (Morgeson and Humphrey 2006, p. 1321)." Hackman and Oldham (1976) proposed the Job Characteristics Model (JCM) positing that enriched or complex jobs may increase employee motivation and work outcomes. They have identified five core job characteristics: skill variety, task identity, task significance, autonomy, and feedback from job, which influence three critical psychological states of workers: experienced meaningfulness of the work, experienced responsibility for outcomes of the work, and knowledge of the actual results of the work activities. They also have posited that these psychological states are mediating variables between job characteristics and behavioral outcomes of workers. Subsequently, Fried and Ferris (1987) reviewed around 200 relevant studies on job characteristics and applied meta-analytic procedures to validate 5 core variables. Results of the study confirmed the psychological states as a mediating role.

After 20 years, Morgeson and Humphrey (2006), developed the work design questionnaire (WDQ) to measure work characteristics and validated WDQ with empirical data. WDQ has two motivational dimensions: task and knowledge characteristics. Task characteristics consist of autonomy, task variety, significance, task identity, and feedback form job. Knowledge characteristics are job complexity, information processing, problem solving, skill variety, and specialization. They have added two more dimensions: social characteristics and work context. Social support, initiated interdependence, received interdependence, interaction outside organization, and feedback from others are the social characteristics. Work context dimension includes ergonomics, physical demands, work conditions, and equipment use.

Humphrey et al. (2007) also conducted a meta-analytic research just as Fried and Ferris (1987 #49) and proposed theoretical extension of work design model with job characteristics. Their study provides 14 more variables in addition to 5 core job characteristics. Extended work design model they proposed consists of three dimensions: motivational, social, and work context. The motivational dimension consists of task and knowledge characteristics adopted from the WDQ of Morgeson and Humphrey (2006). Social and work context characteristics are exactly the same as Morgeson and Humphrey (2006) except equipment use. Three psychological states are still treated as critical mediators in their research. Outcome variables are lined up in more detail in their studies: behavioral outcomes (performance, absenteeism, and turnover intentions), attitudinal outcomes (satisfaction, organizational commitment, job involvement, and internal work motivation), role perception outcomes (role ambiguity and role conflict), and well-being outcomes (anxiety, stress, burnout/exhaustion, and overload).

There is a longitudinal investigation of work design theory and IT system implementation (Griffin 1991). In this study, task perceptions were measured with five core motivational characteristics from the job characteristic model: task variety, autonomy, feedback, significance, and identity. Also, attitudinal variables like job satisfaction and organizational commitment and behavioral variables like performance, absenteeism, and propensity to quit were measured as outcomes. The results showed that IT system implementation increased employees' job motivational factors significantly. Also, job satisfaction and organizational commitment were found to be increased in the early stages of IT adoption, but after 24 months after adoption, these were reverted back to the original level. Worker productivity was stable during the early stages of the IT adoption but critically improved when measured at 24 and 48 months after implementation. Job satisfaction and organizational commitment were stabilized after a while, but productivity increased as time went by.

9.2.2 *Smart Work and Work Smart*

ICT allow workers to work anywhere anytime using remote databases and information systems available in real time 24 h a day (Lee et al. 2014). Recently, the term "smart work" showed up among policy researchers in Korea (Lee and Lee 2012), reflecting the changing nature of work using smart devices. Though the term was coined recently, it points to and includes the various work systems proposed previsously, such as telework, telecommuting, flexible work, and mobile work (Lee and Lee 2012). In the literature, authors are focusing on the flexibility provided by ubiquitous computing technologies (Lee and Lee 2012). In this line of research, primary job design characteristics such as autonomy and flexibility are found to be increased by the smart work.

Although the workplace is changing from the fixed office work environment using desktop PCs to mobile office environment using smart devices like smartphone, laptop, and smartpad, only a few studies had been conducted comparing fixed and flexible work environment (Botha et al. 2009). O'Neill et al. (2009) compared variables related to performance and satisfaction between teleworkers and office workers; there are different effects on autonomy, job complexity, and satisfaction. Hence, teleworkers showed high task autonomy and low task complexity; due to its high autonomy, teleworkers had a higher level of work satisfaction.

Belanger and Collins (1998) explained that various flexible work policies have been enabled by ICT. They attempted to provide what outcomes individuals, organizations, and society expect from smart work. There are several results about smart work success. An antecedent variable, "interdependence" is a significant work characteristic in flexible work environment. At the organizational level, it was the improvement of productivity, and at the individual level, it was the increase of satisfaction, improvement of worker individual productivity, decrease of stress, balancing of work life and personal life, etc.

Lee et al. (2014) studied the phenomenon of work fragmentation in smart work environment using ICT. ICT can not only disrupt the continuity of work but also increase work efficiency; so this study explores the types of work fragmentation and their characteristics. The data about fragmentation and work characteristics including autonomy, complexity, flexibility, and usage of ICT were collected by online survey. They proposed four types of work fragmentation: concentrated, temporally distributed, spatially distributed, and fully fragmented.

9.2.3 Computer-Mediated Communication

Computer-Mediated Communication (CMC) is becoming very popular with the Internet. Email systems that deliver text had been the only feature of CMC at the beginning, but now options are abundant (Hiltz and Johnson 1990; Riva and Riva 2002). CMC, now, includes any form of digital file exchange (video, audio, text) that requires the use of computing system (Dietz-Uhler and Bishop-Clark 2001). The advantage of CMC is the lack of temporal or spatial constraints. CMC can occur at any time and in any place (Kiesler et al. 1984; Kiesler and Sproull 1992; Kiesler 1997). Dietz-Uhler and Bishop-Clark (2001) assessed the effects of real-time CMC like Messenger and not-real-time CMC like email on subsequent face-to-face discussions. The results showed that face-to-face preceded by both real-time and not-real-time CMC were perceived to be more enjoyable than not preceded by CMC.

CMC researchers explained the reason of email or messenger acceptance as followed by the acceptance or success of MIS. So computer-mediated communication system usage is simply examined by analysis of user satisfaction with CMC and user performance with CMC just like MIS success (Hiltz and Johnson 1990; Walther and Bunz 2005).

9.3 Research Methodology

9.3.1 Research Model

The research model posits that the expanded work design theory (Humphrey et al. 2007) is composed with the understanding of the influence of motivational factor, social characteristics, and work context characteristics on attitudinal outcome and satisfaction. Work design factors were independent variables. Autonomy and job complexity came from motivational characteristics, and interdependece was chosen among the social ones. System quality was considered as a work context factor. The research model is diagrammed in Fig. 9.1.

Usually, communication devices are used for contacting others in order to carry out tasks, and the type of device is chosen accordingly; there is a tendency to use the communication device to fit the characteristic of the work (Kim et al. 2007). Online messenger is considered one of the ubiquitous computing applications one can use in anywhere, at any place, and real time. But there is an obvious limitation in mobility for PC messengers and PC-based communication as it can only be used on a PC. Meanwhile, mobile messengers are based on the notion of mobility, which is another point to focus on. Furthermore, it is important to remember that there are apparent differences in PC performance and the possible functions of smartphones. This research differentiates messenger users into the groups of PC environment and mobile environment; it works with the hypothetical setup of the respective variables of Work Design Theory and differences in the degree of influence.

In the research of Griffin (1991) and O'Neill et al. (2009), it is asserted that in order to make workers satisfied with their job, there needs to be preceding motivational factors. Motivational factors include autonomy and job complexity. Autonomy

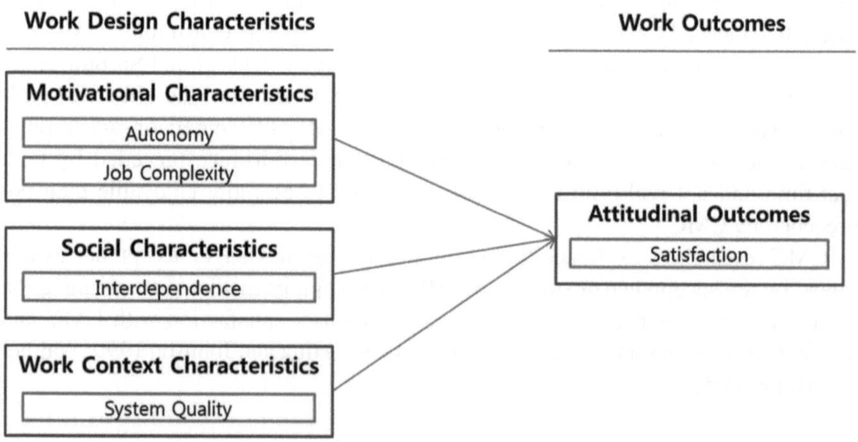

Fig. 9.1 Research model

consists of three subdimensions: work scheduling autonomy, work method autonomy, and decision-making autonomy. Also, it explains that if the task is too simple or easy, it can have a negative effect on motivation, so when designing a job, raising complexity can lead to higher satisfaction than when the complexity is too low. By considering the relation of motivational factors and attitudinal outcomes in the context of usage environment of PC messengers and mobile messengers, the authors make the following hypotheses. More so than a PC environment, a mobile environment allows greater freedom to choose the time and location of carrying out tasks: *(hypothesis 1) as autonomy has a positive impact on workers' satisfaction, there will be a difference in perception of PC messenger users and mobile messenger users.*

So far, there is a limitation to usage of software and performance for smartphones when compared to PCs. It is relatively more advantageous and fitting to use PC messengers when dealing with tasks that are complex and require difficult skills and to use mobile messengers when simple and fast movement of information is required or quick decision-making is necessary. Hence *(hypothesis 2), as job complexity has a positive effect on workers' satisfaction, there will be a difference in perception of PC messenger users and mobile messenger users.*

There are three dimensions of interdependence as a social work characteristic: scope, resources, and criticality (Kiggundu 1981). In the case of scope, interdependence occurs when one task ends and another begins; there is a connection, and the boundary is interdependent. Resource interdependence is when various tasks require the sharing of materials, tools, and capital (including human capital and information). Criticality interdependence appears when a task or various tasks influence more important work (Qu et al. 2009). Interdependence is treated more importantly in the cases of teamwork (Guzzo and Dickson 1996; Ilgen 1999). When work interdependence rises, employees must communicate about what is necessary for the task and what they expect. As this occurs, opportunity to communicate with each other increases, and the number of times they contact each other also increases (Humphrey et al. 2007). This research assumed that workers who perform work of high-level interdependence would make efforts to exchange materials and communicate with each other to carry out their tasks regardless of the time and location. Therefore *(hypothesis 3), as interdependence has a positive effect on workers' satisfaction, there will be a difference in perception of PC messenger users and mobile messenger users.*

IT devices are the essence of conducting smart work. In this research, PC messengers and mobile messengers become tools in accomplishing tasks. Thus, system quality becomes a significant precedence factor of the environment of individual tasks. According to Park et al. (2013), the user perception of system quality of IT service influences the satisfaction of the IT user. The research (Park et al. 2014) makes the point that depending on IT quality, there is change in the psychological mechanism of the individual users; in actuality, this implies the need for uniformity and consistency in IT quality. Hence *(hypothesis 4), as system quality has a positive effect on workers' satisfaction, there will be a difference in perception of PC messenger users and mobile messenger users.*

9.3.2 Data Collection

We conducted a survey during January 2013; the survey targeted PC messenger and mobile messenger users through snowball sampling, which includes the person with which the respondent usually communicates. In the survey, the respondents were told to choose either PC messenger or mobile messenger as the messenger used most when carrying out their tasks. In order to maintain the objectivity of the statistical data, the anonymity of the respondents was guaranteed; the surveys that were not completely filled out or the surveys that showed inconsistency and insincerity in its answers were left out. For the analysis, a total of 289 respondents were included.

Out of the total respondents, there were 158 (54.7 %) workers who used PC messengers and 131 (45.3 %) workers who used mobile messengers while carrying out their tasks. The sample collected was in accordance with this ratio. As for field of work, there were 115 (39.8 %) workers who were in the R&D department, 70 (24.2 %) workers in the Manufacturing/Purchase/Distribution department, and 60 (20.8 %) workers in the Marketing/Sales department. The average work experience was about 2.44 years (with a standard deviation of 1.22); in terms of work experience, there were 81 (28.0 %) workers who had less than 3 years, 80 (27.7 %) workers with 3–5 years, 69 (23.9 %) workers with 6 ~ 10 years, and overall there was an even separation of work experience under 10 years.

When examining the surveys by respondents' characteristics in its groups of PC messenger and mobile messenger users, there is a noticeable difference in the field of work: the most PC messenger users were in the marketing/operations department with 56 (35.4 %) workers, followed by the productivity/purchase/quality/distribution department with 42 (26.6 %) workers, and the research/development department with 36 (22.8 %) workers. On the other hand, when looking at the divisions of mobile messenger user workers, the research/development department had the highest with 79 (60.3 %) workers, and the marketing/operations department had only 4 (3.1 %) workers; this revealed a starkly different result from the PC messenger user tendencies. Other detailed statistics are shown in Table 9.1.

9.3.3 Measurement

In order to test the hypothesis, this research performed field experiments. With the help of literature review, this study used a valid surveying method with items that were specifically fitted for the purpose of the study: there were a total of 14 measurement items, and it scored a 7 on the Likert Scale. First, the three items of measurement for work autonomy were based on Langfred (2005) and Humphrey et al. (2007) that defined work autonomy through the degree of freely carrying out a task. Second, the two measurement items of job complexity, similar to the way it was defined in the research of Humphrey et al. (2007), were described by the complex and nonrepetitive task that requires a high level of skills. Third, interdependence was defined as a degree of dependence on department or coworker as defined in

Table 9.1 Respondents demographics

Category		PC messenger users (%)	Mobile messenger users (%)	Total
Departments	Planning/Finance	15(9.5)	13(9.9)	28(9.7)
	HR/Operations	9(5.7)	4(3.1)	13(4.5)
	Mfg/Purchase/Distrib	42(26.6)	28(21.4)	70(24.2)
	Marketing/Sales	56(35.4)	4(3.1)	60(20.8)
	R&D	36(22.8)	79(60.3)	115(39.8)
	Others	–	3(2.3)	3(1.0)
Experience	Less than 3 years	50(31.6)	31(23.7)	81(28.0)
	3~5 years	41(25.9)	39(29.8)	80(27.7)
	6~10 years	37(23.4)	32(24.4)	69(23.9)
	11~15 years	19(12.0)	20(15.3)	39(13.5)
	Over 15 years	11(7.0)	9(6.9)	20(6.9)
Total		158	131	289

Table 9.2 Measurement items

Variables		Items	References
Autonomy	AUT1	I freely decide the method of carrying out tasks.	Humphrey et al. (2007) and Langfred (2005)
	AUT2	I can complete my tasks as I wish.	
	AUT3	I can choose my tasks.	
Job complexity	JCX1	In order to carry out the task, I need a high level skill.	Humphrey et al. (2007)
	JCX2	My task is complex and non-repetitive.	
Interdependence	INT1	My task is only possible with help from others.	Humphrey et al. (2007) and Langfred (2005)
	INT2	In order to carry out my task, I need to receive information from another person.	
	INT3	My task is highly related to the department goal.	
System quality	SQ1	It is easy to use the system that I need to use to carry out my task.	Parasuraman (2005)
	SQ2	The system that I need to use to carry out my task is convenient.	
	SQ3	The system that I need to use to carry out my task is simple.	
Satisfaction	SAT1	I am satisfied with my tasks.	Humphrey et al. (2007)
	SAT2	I like the advantages of my tasks.	
	SAT3	I am suitable for my current tasks.	

Langfred (2005) and Humphrey et al. (2007) and was measured in three items. Fourth, system quality was defined as system usage simplicity, according to Parasuraman (2005), which defined system as servicing quality, and was measured in three items. Lastly, satisfaction was defined as degree of satisfaction of task as suggested in Humphrey et al. (2007) and was measured three times. The control definitions of measuring tools and measuring items are suggested in Table 9.2.

9.4 Results

In this research, analysis of validity and reliability, as well as the independent sample t-test and regression analysis, analyzing average difference between two groups, were conducted using SPSS 18.0.

9.4.1 *Factor Analysis and Reliability*

In order to analyze the validity of the measurements, factor analysis took place. If the size of the factor loading regarding measuring item's associate variable is .70 or greater, it was evaluated as having secured measuring item's conceptual validity. As shown in Table 9.3, all associated loadings were over .70. In order to examine internal consistencies within measuring items, reliability analysis was carried out. As a result, Cronbach's alpha values of each variable were over the reference value of .70 and thus indicated reliability.

9.4.2 t-*Test Results Between Groups*

After dividing the workers into a group who primarily work using a PC messenger and a group who primarily work using a mobile messenger, and after analyzing the differences of average values of each variable, the following

Table 9.3 Results of factor analysis and reliability analysis

Items	Factor analysis					Reliability
	1	2	3	4	5	Cronbach's α
INT3	.944	.057	.196	.170	−.026	
INT2	.942	.062	.160	.145	−.032	.966
INT1	.907	.078	.217	.142	−.027	
SQ3	.093	.971	.005	.015	.056	
SQ2	.026	.938	−.006	.015	.149	.949
SQ1	.062	.928	.041	−.034	.060	
SAT1	.155	.000	.909	.169	−.129	
SAT3	.163	−.011	.895	.235	−.180	.905
SAT2	.398	.072	.737	.191	−.147	
AUT2	−.005	−.002	.158	.881	−.068	
AUT1	.296	.023	.145	.855	−.085	.869
AUT3	.207	−.026	.221	.838	.015	
JCX2	−.016	.107	−.178	−.079	.922	.886
JCX1	−.055	.135	−.160	−.033	.921	

Table 9.4 *t*-test results of variables

Variables	Mean(S.D)		t value	p-value
	PC messenger user group	Mobile messenger user group		
Autonomy	3.73(1.36)	4.54(1.35)	−5.069	0.000
Job complexity	5.20(1.16)	3.65(1.47)	9.813	0.000
Interdependence	5.21(1.40)	5.54(1.08)	−2.216	0.027
System quality	5.23(1.29)	5.09(1.24)	0.956	0.340
Satisfaction	4.28(1.35)	5.72(1.12)	−9.848	0.000

results are shown in Table 9.4. The mobile messenger group (M=4.54, SD=1.35) had greater task autonomy than the PC messenger group (M=3.73, SD=1.36), and it was analyzed that the differences between the two groups seemed significant. As for job complexity, the PC messenger group (M=5.20, SD=1.16) seemed to be higher than the mobile messenger group (M=3.65, SD=1.47), and differences between the two groups also seemed meaningful. Regarding interdependence of duty, the PC messenger group (M=5.21, SD=1.40) was lower than the mobile messenger group (M=5.54, SD=1.08), and their differences also seemed relevant. There did not seem to be much significance regarding system quality between the two groups, and with regard to task satisfaction, the PC messenger group (M=4.28, SD=1.35) was much higher than the mobile messenger group (M=5.72, SD=1.12), showing great significance between the two groups.

Next, the mean and standard deviations of each survey item and the difference between the two groups were analyzed as seen in Table 9.5. Task autonomy understood by workers using mobile messenger was higher overall, and while the two groups have significant differences, the survey item "…can complete my tasks as I wish" had the greatest difference, and the mean of survey item "…freely decide the method of carrying out tasks" was 4.85, being the highest of the three items. In items asking about the job complexity, the average differences recognized by PC messenger workers and mobile messenger workers were 1.465 and 1.644, respectively, showing a significant difference in recognizing job complexity. With mobile messenger workers, the mean was around 3 points, showing a tendency of recognizing a job as not complex. While it was analyzed as mobile messenger workers seeming to perceive higher interdependence, both groups showed a high mean over 5 points in each item. As for system quality, both groups are satisfied for both scored an overall 5 points, and there seemed to be no differences in the two groups regarding each item. Lastly, indicators measuring the satisfaction of tasks show that mobile messenger workers were extremely satisfied, displaying an average of 5.68, 5.78, and 5.69. Of all survey items, "I like it because of the advantages of the job" showed the highest mean within the mobile messenger worker group.

Table 9.5 *t*-test of each survey item

Items	Mean(S.D)		Average difference	t value	p-value
	PC messenger user group	Mobile messenger user group			
AUT1	4.11(1.45)	4.85(1.52)	−.741	−4.167	.000
AUT2	3.40(1.66)	4.55(1.59)	−1.151	−5.976	.000
AUT3	3.67(1.50)	4.21(1.39)	−.543	−3.164	.002
JCX1	5.19(1.30)	3.73(1.55)	1.465	8.574	.000
JCX2	5.21(1.25)	3.56(1.54)	1.644	9.801	.000
INT1	5.16(1.38)	5.50(1.12)	−.339	−2.267	.024
INT2	5.23(1.49)	5.53(1.18)	−.299	−1.904	.058
INT3	5.25(1.46)	5.58(1.09)	−.333	−2.217	.027
SQ1	5.33(1.30)	5.18(1.32)	.146	.939	.349
SQ2	5.20(1.37)	4.92(1.29)	.273	1.73	.085
SQ3	5.16(1.39)	5.15(1.29)	.012	.075	.941
SAT1	4.20(1.56)	5.68(1.24)	−1.483	−9.024	.000
SAT2	4.74(1.51)	5.78(1.14)	−1.038	−6.653	.000
SAT3	3.91(1.52)	5.69(1.24)	−1.776	−10.941	.000

9.5 Analysis of Research Model

This research confirmed that variable differences exist by analyzing the differences between PC messenger users and mobile messenger users, based on Work Design Theory. Therefore, in order to evaluate this research model, regression analysis of each model was conducted, and from the differences between models, the hypothesis was verified. An analysis of the general model that includes both groups showed autonomy ($b=0.281$, $t=5.545$), job complexity ($b=-0.281$, $t=5.762$), and interdependence ($b=0.328$, $t=6.444$) turned out to have significant influence, yet system quality measured as environmental factor did not have significant influence. Measured values are shown in Fig. 9.2.

Next, after distinguishing the PC messenger worker group and the mobile messenger worker group, regression analysis was conducted. As seen in Fig. 9.3, which shows the model that measured the PC messenger group, autonomy ($b=0.280$, $t=3.687$) and interdependence ($b=0.349$, $t=4.515$) showed significant influence on satisfaction but were different from the general model analysis results, as job complexity did not have significant influence.

On the other hand, with regard to job character and the satisfaction of the mobile messenger group, results were analyzed to be similar to the general model analysis results in which autonomy ($b=0.173$, $t=2.180$), complexity ($b=-0.171$, $t=2.152$), and interdependence ($b=0.394$, $t=5.007$) seemed to have relevance to satisfaction while system quality did not have a significant effect on satisfaction (Fig. 9.4).

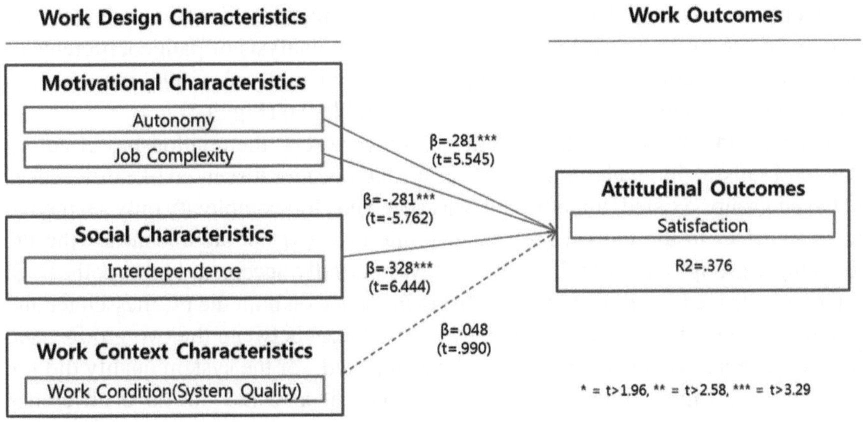

Fig. 9.2 Regression results for general model

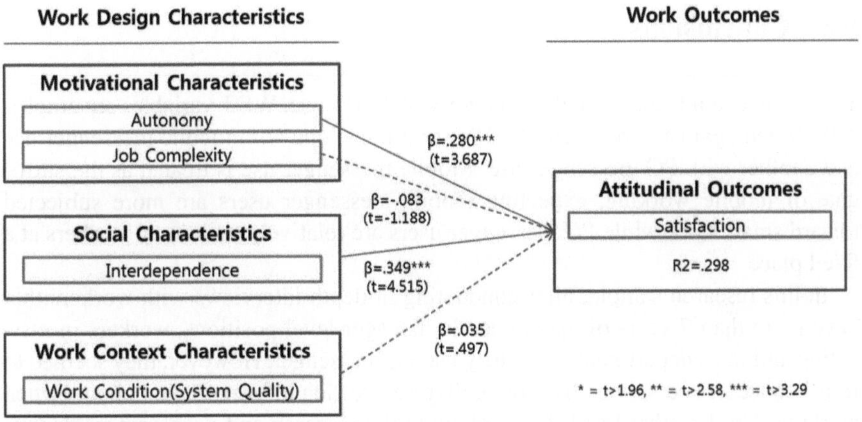

Fig. 9.3 Regression results for PC messenger user group ($N=158$)

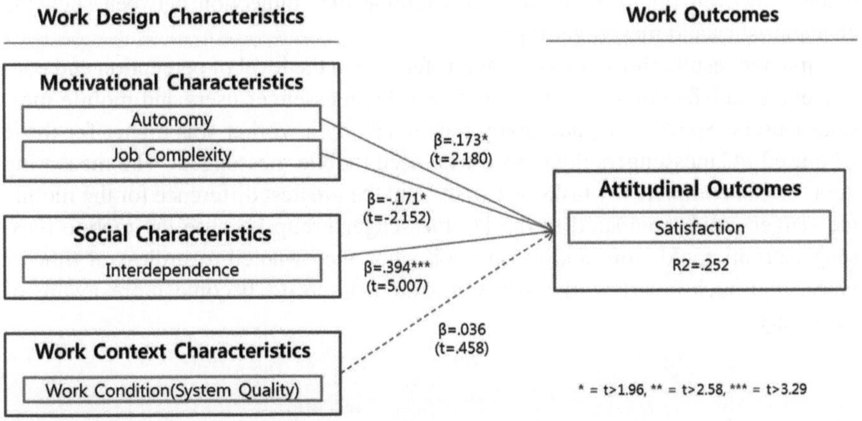

Fig. 9.4 Regression results for mobile messenger user group ($N=131$)

In order to examine the differences between the relationships of variables of the two groups to evaluate the hypothesis, a difference analysis of path coefficients of each group was conducted. A formula proposed by Chin et al. (1996) was used, as shown below. Analysis results are indicated in Table 9.6 (Fig. 9.5).

For both PC messenger and mobile messenger users, the relationship of autonomy and satisfaction had a significant effect, and because it seemed like differences between groups existed, hypothesis 1 was accepted. Job complexity only seemed to have an effect in the mobile messenger group and was not significant for the PC messenger group; therefore, hypothesis 2 was partially accepted. For hypothesis 3, interdependence turned out to have a strong influence on both the PC messenger and mobile messenger groups, and there were differences between the two groups, and it was therefore accepted. Hypothesis 4 was rejected, for the system quality did not have any relevance to satisfaction, and because it also did not have difference between two groups.

9.6 Conclusions

This study extends the work design theory with ICT use. WDT variables are empirically tested against two different ICT user groups: one with mobile messenger use and another with PC messenger use. Mobile messenger use is treated as the surrogate of mobile working, expecting mobile messenger users are more subjected toward smart work while PC messenger users are relatively traditional workers at a fixed place.

In this research sample, after conducting in-depth interviews with workers that have more than 7 years of experience in manager-level positions, workers in marketing and sales departments primarily use PC messenger. However, they seemed to fulfill concentrated service by having diverse and rich information on clients when working. On the other hand, for workers in the research and development department, in order to creatively perform a task, they actively interact with their coworkers in real time to exchange information and tend to work regardless of time and place. However, this research did not examine the connection between such job characteristics and messenger type.

First, the results showed significant difference in the level of perception and consequential satisfaction of job tasks between PC messenger users and mobile messenger users. Specifically, autonomy recognized by a worker was higher for those who used PC messengers than those who used mobile messengers. The measuring item "…can complete my tasks as I wish" had the greatest difference for the mobile messenger group compared to the PC messenger group because the mobile messenger group could work and finish a job when they wanted regardless of time or place, and such smart work quality allows workers to become more aware of autonomy.

Table 9.6 Results for the difference analysis of path coefficients of each group

Hypothesis	Path name	PC messenger user group		Mobile messenger user group		t-value for path coefficient difference	Evaluation
		Path coefficient	Standard error	Path coefficient	Standard error		
H1	Autonomy → Satisfaction	0.280***	0.074	0.173*	0.082	11.650	Accepted
H2	Job complexity → Satisfaction	–0.083	0.081	–0.171*	0.060	10.308	Partially accepted
H3	Interdependence → Satisfaction	0.349***	0.074	0.394***	0.082	–4.900	Accepted
H4	System quality → Satisfaction	0.035	0.074	0.036	0.072	–0.116	Rejected

* $p<0.05$, ** $p<0.01$, *** $p<0.001$

$$t_{ij} = \frac{p_1 - p_2}{\sqrt{\frac{n_1 - 1}{n_1 + n_2 - 2} \times SE_1^2 + \frac{n_2 - 1}{n_1 + n_2 - 2} \times SE_2^2} \times \sqrt{(\frac{1}{n_1} + \frac{1}{n_2})}}$$

Fig. 9.5 Formula for the difference analysis of path coefficients of each group (p_i:i-th path coefficient, n_i : i-th sample size, SE_i :i-th S.E. of path coefficient)

Second, regarding job complexity, differences between the two groups were greater than other variables not because the workers simply recognize their tasks as being complex but because PC messenger users recognize their job as being extremely complex while mobile messenger users recognize their job as being not as complex. When a job is complex or needs advanced skills, different types of programs are used simultaneously. And various types of data also need to be processed. In the current working environment, using stable networks and computer power to connect smoothly to databases in order to process various information at the same time at the office is more convenient in such cases. When using a smartphone, simultaneous processing of vast data has technical limitations, and a mobile phone's small and limited screen could add to the inconvenience of smoothly handling tasks. Therefore, workers who primarily use mobile messengers tend to engage in less complex tasks and do not need advanced skills.

Third, interdependence shows a high average, over five points, in both groups, and this could be interpreted as that the act of using a messenger itself is caused by the high interdependence of the job. Also, the result of mobile messenger users recognizing interdependence more often is the same as the results from Belanger and Collins (1998). In other words, workers who perform tasks with high interdependence tend to interact and exchange information regardless of time and place, and mobile messenger users showed a higher tendency of this behavior.

Fourth, our study showed that the mobile messenger group was much more satisfied than the PC messenger group with regard to job satisfaction. Not only does this refer to the satisfaction of the job itself, but it also refers to the fact that the benefits of the job scored the highest. This is the same result of Belanger and Collins (1998), O'Neill et al. (2009), and Lee H.J. and Lee J.W. (2012), that flexibility in work such as time and place brings greater satisfaction from workers, therefore suggesting that smart-work workers tend to be more satisfied than office workers regarding their job.

Through regression analysis of the research model, the work design theory was additionally evaluated. As with the work design theory, the more autonomy and less complexity there was in a job, the greater the positive effect that motivation characteristics had on worker satisfaction, and the higher the interdependence, the greater the positive effect that social characteristics had on satisfaction. Here, system quality is suggested as there was not a significant difference of situational characteristics between groups, yet this study did show the same over-average recognition. This was shown not only in the general model but in all the group regression analysis as it was rejected. This could be interpreted as that system quality did not impact satisfaction as a situational variable, but it acted as a control variable. In other words, because there were no differences in system quality between the two groups, results were acquired while other factors were not influenced by system quality differences. Especially with group regression analysis, in a PC messenger setting, job complexity did not have a significant effect on satisfaction while in a mobile messenger setting, significances existed. In other words, when using a mobile messenger, the degree of satisfaction varied depending on the degree of complexity recognized by the worker.

This research has a few limitations. First, it does not explain whether the workers voluntarily selected different IT systems or if this is entirely due to work characteristics of the Work Design Theory. Therefore, there is a need to analyze the reason through in-depth interviews or research on IT system choice. Second, because not all variables but partial variables were selected from the Work Design Theory, to say the theory is supported would be untrue. Therefore, a follow-up study evaluating each characteristic from all variables including parameter is necessary. Third, in this study, groups were divided into PC messenger users and mobile messenger users to examine their differences. However, to label PC messenger users as non-smart-work workers only because they do not use mobile messengers would be insufficient. Therefore, designing a study to classify smart-work work environment in detail and conduct a similar study would be a more meaningful endeavor. If such a study is conducted, evaluating the relationship between Work Design Theory variables for smart-work workers would also be possible.

Acknowledgment This work was partially supported by the National Research Foundation of Korea Grant funded by the Korean Government (NRF-2012S1A3A2033474).

References

Babbage C (1935) On the economy of machinery and manufactures. Knight, London

Belanger F, Collins RW (1998) Distributed work arrangements: a research framework. Inf Soc 14(2):137–152

Botha RA, Furnell SM, Clarke NL (2009) From desktop to mobile: examining the security experience. Comput Secur 28(3–4):130–137

Chin W, Marcolin B, Newsted P (1996) A partial least squares latent variable modeling approach for measuring interaction effects: results from a Monte Carlo simulation study and voice mail emotion/adoption study. Paper presented at the seventeenth international conference on information systems, Cleveland, Ohio

Dietz-Uhler B, Bishop-Clark C (2001) The use of computer-mediated communication to enhance subsequent face-to-face discussions. Comput Hum Behav 17(3):269–283

Fried Y, Ferris GR (1987) The validity of the job characteristics model: a review and meta-analysis. Pers Psychol 40(2):287–322

Gilbreth FB (1911) Motion study. Constable, London

Griffin RW (1991) Effects of work redesign on employee perceptions, attitudes, and behaviors: a long-term investigation. Acad Manag J 34(2):425–435

Guzzo RA, Dickson MW (1996) Teams in organizations: recent research on performance and effectiveness. Annu Rev Psychol 47:307–338

Hackman JR, Lawler EE (1971) Employee reactions to job characteristics. J Appl Psychol 55(3):259–286

Hackman JR, Oldham GR (1975) Development of the job diagnostic survey. J Appl Psychol 60(2):159–170

Hackman JR, Oldham GR (1976) Motivation through the design of work: test of a theory. Organ Behav Human Perform 16(2):250–279

Herzberg F, Mausner B, Snyderman BB (1959) The motivation to work. Wiley, New York

Hiltz SR, Johnson K (1990) User satisfaction with computer-mediated communication systems. Manag Sci 36(6):739–764

Humphrey SE, Nahrgang JD, Morgeson FP (2007) Integrating motivational, social, and contextual work design features: a meta-analytic summary and theoretical extension of the work design literature. J Appl Psychol 92(5):1332–1356

Ilgen DR (1999) Teams embedded in organizations – some implications. Am Psychol 54(2):129–139

Kiesler S (1997) Preface. In: Kiesler S (ed) Culture of the internet. Lawrence Erlbaum Associates, Publishers, Mahwah, pp 4–16

Kiesler S, Sproull L (1992) Group decision making and communication technology. Organ Behav Hum Decis Process 52(1):96–123

Kiesler S, Siegel J, McGuire TW (1984) Social psychological aspects of computer mediated communication. Am Psychol 39(10):1123–1134

Kiggundu M (1981) Task interdependence and the theory of job design. Acad Manag Rev 6(3):499–508

Kim H, Kim GJ, Park HW, Rice RE (2007) Configurations of relationships in different media: FtF, email, instant messenger, mobile phone, and SMS. J Comput-Mediat Commun 12(4):1183–1207

Langfred CW (2005) Autonomy and performance in teams: the multilevel moderating effect of task interdependence. J Manag 31(4):513–529

Lee H, Lee J (2012) Developing a policy framework for smartwork: task, technology, people, organization and management. J Digital Policy Manag 10(11):145–164

Lee S, Park JG, Lee J (2014) ICT and the changing nature of work: work fragmentation. Inf Policy 21(1):35–56

Morgeson FP, Humphrey SE (2006) The work design questionnaire (WDQ): developing and validating a comprehensive measure for assessing job design and the nature of work. J Appl Psychol 91(6):1321–1339

O'Neill TA, Hambley LA, Greidanus NS, MacDonnell R, Kline TJB (2009) Predicting teleworker success: an exploration of personality, motivational, situational, and job characteristics. N Technol Work Employ 24(2):144–162

Parasuraman A (2005) ES-QUAL: a multiple-item scale for assessing electronic service quality. J Serv Res 7(3):213–233

Park JG, Lee H, Jang J, Lee J (2013) Roles of technical and functional service quality, and cognitive and affective trust in IT service encounter. J Next Generation Inf Technol 4(8):312–321

Park JG, Lee H, Lee J (2014) Explicating moderating effects of conflict in the psychological mechanism in IT service engagement. J Korea Soc IT Serv 13(1):1–18

Qu HM, Li N, Li H (2009) Moderating role of environment uncertainty on the relationship between interdependence and relationship performance. In: ICSSSM '09. 6th international conference on. at the service systems and service management, 2009

Riva G, Riva (2002) The sociocognitive psychology of computer-mediated communication: the present and future of technology-based interactions. Cyberpsychol Behav 5(6):581–598

Smith A (1776) An inquiry into the nature and causes of the wealth of nations. Strahan W& Cadell T, London

Taber TD, Taylor E (1990) A review and evaluation of the psychometric properties of the job diagnostic survey. Pers Psychol 43(3):467–500
Taylor FW (1911) The principles of scientific management. Norton, New York
Turner AN, Lawrence PR (1965) Industrial jobs and the worker. Harvard University Press, Boston
Walther JB, Bunz U (2005) The rules of virtual groups: trust, liking, and performance in computer-mediated communication. J Commun 55(4):828–846

Chapter 10
Work Longer Or Live Smarter? Striving for Desirable Work Time Arrangements in Diverse Cultural Contexts

Luo Lu

Abstract The long working hours and their noxious effects seem to be more prevalent in today's competitive global business world. This chapter thus explores the joint role of personal choice and social welfare provision in the context of working hours and work attitudes across a wide range of countries with diverse levels of economic development, cultural background, and welfare regimes.

Secondary analysis was employed using data collected from the International Social Survey Program (ISSP), with a sample of 8,525 employees from nine countries. These countries represent four types of social welfare regimes: the social democratic welfare (Denmark, Sweden, and Norway), liberal welfare (United States and Australia), conservative corporatist welfare (France and Germany), and the East Asian welfare (Taiwan and South Korea).

I found that the fit between desired and actual working hours was associated with higher job satisfaction and organizational commitment. However, this association did vary across different social welfare regimes. Logistic regression further revealed that compared against the East Asian welfare regime, employees in countries with social democratic, conservative, and liberal welfare systems were more likely to experience a fit between personal preferences and actual choices of working hours. Furthermore, after controlling for the macro-level social institutional factors and micro-level demographics, personal financial needs of "wanting to earn less" could still predict the state of misfit.

Recommendations are thus made to organizations to facilitate a state of fit between individual preferences and available choices through supplying multiple options to employees.

Keywords Working hour • Personal choice • Social welfare regime • Cross-national comparison • Work attitudes

---

L. Lu (✉)
Department of Business Administration, National Taiwan University, Taipei, Taiwan, ROC
e-mail: luolu@ntu.edu.tw

J. Lee (ed.), *The Impact of ICT on Work*, DOI 10.1007/978-981-287-612-6_10

10.1 Working Longer: Combined Pressure of Economic Recession and Cultural Sanction

10.1.1 Job Insecurity: The Economic Drive to Work Longer

Fierce global competition and worldwide economic recession over the years have resulted in fundamental changes in the employment relationship, such as layoffs, early retirement, and temporary employment (Sparks et al. 2001; Worrall and Cooper 2013). Afraid of losing jobs, most employees work harder than before; however, more working time leads to increased strain (Dekker and Schaufeli 1995; Lu 2011). The advance of Information and Communication Technologies (ICT) is also changing the nature of work, in two seemingly contradictory ways. On the one hand, ICT brings in more flexibility in terms of place and time of work, which can make work arrangements more accommodating to diverse personal needs and lifestyles. On the other hand, the widespread use of ICT easily trespasses the demarcation of work and life. One consequence of such a blurring of the line between work and nonwork is the increasing "invisible" working hours when employees are constantly bombarded with instructions and queries sent through ICT by their employers outside the official working time. Some governments (e.g., Taiwan) are now considering amendments to the labor law to forbid such invasion of employers into workers' personal time and space, or to compensate workers for these "invisible" working hours with overtime pay.

Hours of work have long been recognized to have a marked effect on the way an individual and his family lives (Dankert et al. 1965). Findings and theories from predominantly Western nations have suggested a clear link between working hours and health symptoms (Sparks et al. 1997). Long working hours have also been associated with both work- and nonwork-related accidents (Kirkcaldy et al. 1997; Trimpop et al. 2000), elevated job-related stress (Cooper et al. 1982), and decreased job satisfaction (Trimpop et al. 2000). Despite the vast amount of literature concerning working hours and various strain outcomes, the majority of studies have been conducted in North American and European countries, as evident by the studies included in the comprehensive review on the topic (Sparks et al. 1997). Employees in Asia on average work longer hours (Taiwan: 41.6; South Korea: 44.2; Japan: 35.4) than do North Americans (United States: 33.9; Canada: 31.7) and Europeans (Germany: 34.2; UK: 31.6) (Directorate-General of Budget 2012). Do they fare worse than people in the West?

10.1.2 Cultural Values: The Social Sanction to Work Harder

The Confucius culture, which still has a strong hold on societies such as mainland China, Hong Kong, Taiwan, Japan, Korea, and Singapore, has traditionally sanctioned "hardworking" as a virtue, and working long hours is a norm in these contemporary societies of the so-called Confucius Circle (Kanai 2009; Lu 2011). However, compared to individualists in the West, collectivists such as the Chinese and Japanese are more flexible in viewing work and family issues, and the demarcation between work and family is far from rigid in daily life (Yang et al. 2000). A recent qualitative study revealed that Taiwanese employees often view work as a means of maintaining and improving the living standards for their families, or as a way of fulfilling their duties and commitments to glorify the family name (Lu et al. 2012). In other words, working long hours and working hard are not only practicing a deep-rooted cultural teaching but also instrumental in consolidating the value of family as a building block of the society. Indeed, a few studies found that Chinese employees took a more integration rather than segmentation approach to work and family issues, and were more tolerant of spillover between the two domains (Yang et al. 2000; Olson-Buchanan and Boswell 2006). These cultural expectations and flexible role boundaries have further fueled the "norm of working long hours" in these Asian societies, and thus little research has been conducted in this part of the world on the potential adverse effects of long working hours (Lu et al. 2011 being an exception).

In addition to the indoctrination of cultural values such as diligence, one consistent finding in the past studies is that employees in different countries exhibit different responses to work stress dependent on the availability of social resources at the macro level, such as social welfare institutions. For example, Spector et al. (2004) found a significant relationship between working hours and physical health for Chinese but not for Anglo workers.

10.1.3 The Present Study: A Multinational Analysis Combining Economic and Social Factors

The purpose of this chapter is thus to extend the literature on working hours in the following ways. First, I examined the effects of *choice* or *fit*, rather than the mere length of working time (i.e., the number of working hours) on work outcomes. Specifically, I took into account personal preference of working hours, which has largely been overlooked in previous studies. Second, I explored whether the above effects varied in societies of different welfare regimes as a proxy of the availability of macro-level social resources. Specifically, I conducted a multinational analysis comparing nine countries encompassing a comprehensive classification scheme of social welfare systems, which has never been done before in the literature on working hours. Finally, I tested the effects of personal drive (i.e., financial needs) on the choice of working hours, after controlling for societal resources. This is the first study combining individual and societal factors in explaining the choice of working hours across cultural borders.

10.2 Choice Matters: The Benefit of Fit Between Preferred and Actual Working Hours

10.2.1 Fit as a Game Changer in the Linkage Between Working Hours and Strains

Although the connection between working hours and strains (e.g., work–family conflict, job dissatisfaction, and ill health) has been established, the effect size is uniformly small for Western employees (Bruck et al. 2002; Kirkcaldy et al. 2000; Sparks et al. 1997). This suggests that the mechanisms through which working hours produce strains remain largely unknown and critical factors may have been overlooked. Barnett et al. (1999) argued that "fit" may be one such factor, namely, whether an employee wants to dedicate these hours that he or she does to work. The congruence between personal needs and situation supplies correlates highly with improved job satisfaction and performance (Caldwell and O'Reilly 1990), strengthened organizational identification, and a strong intent to stay in the organization (Edwards and Cable 2009). This suggests that the fit between desired and real working hours may be an important explanatory factor for different work outcomes observed in the literature. However, personal preferences were rarely considered in the relationship between working hours and strains. The construct of working hours as typically measured fails to capture employees' motivation and/or desire to do so. This lacking may explain the weak correlations with strains. More importantly, a person's choice in time expenditure should be respected to enhance both personal well-being and societal welfare. Although employment is widely seen to promote social inclusion and societal values, integration and stability in society are also facilitated by living according to the same norms and values as other members of society. The family is a major integrating structure protecting both the physical and mental well-being of people (Stack and Eshleman 1998). The same holds true for other forms of social participation, such as voluntary associations and leisure activities (Argyle 2001; Lu 2012; Lu and Hu 2005). Therefore, if people are allowed to choose between spending time on paid employment and on family living or other activities, a state of fit so achieved can enhance both role satisfaction in diverse life domains and general well-being.

10.2.2 The Demand–Discretion Model

The issue of *choice* can also be understood within the framework of the demand–discretion model (Karasek 1979; Karasek and Theorell 1990). According to this work stress model, strain is highest among those who endure high work demands (e.g., long working hours) and suffer from a lack of control over work (e.g., lack of autonomy regarding working hours). For those who endure high work demands but enjoy high decision latitude, work may represent more of a challenge than drudgery.

A recent study based on a nationwide sample confirmed that autonomy in deciding working time (i.e., on- and off-time) was positively related to increased organizational commitment among Taiwanese employees (Lu et al. 2008). The issue of personal choice and control in relation to work schedule therefore merits further attention.

Applying the notion of personal choice and fit, Costa et al. (2006) compared the effects of two aspects of the flexible arrangement of working hours on health and well-being. They distinguished *variability*, which is subject to company control and decision, from *flexibility*, which is related to individual discretion and autonomy. Analyzing data from the Third European Survey on working conditions involving 21,505 workers, they concluded that the most favorable effects were associated with high flexibility and low variability. Furthermore, analyses of the impact of background variables such as demographics and working and social conditions revealed that flexibility is the most important factor influencing job satisfaction and the second important factor affecting family and social commitment. Therefore, suitable arrangements for flexible working time, taking employees' needs and desires into account, appear to benefit employees' health, role satisfaction, and general well-being, with positive results too for the company and for the society.

10.2.3 Voluntarily Working Longer: "Moonlighting"

Other studies have also produced evidence underlining the beneficial effects of personal choice. Literature on "moonlighting" has produced two hypotheses: the "energic/opportunity hypothesis" and the "deprivation/constraint hypothesis" (Jamal 1986). The term "moonlighting" typically refers to workers who have a day job (typically salaried) but then take on further personally contracted work during their nonworking hours in the evenings or weekend: thus, they can be distinguished from regular night-shift workers. The first hypothesis proposes that moonlighters are a special breed, having more energy and higher socioeconomic expectations than others. To satisfy their higher aspirations, they voluntarily exert more energy and effort in their work than non-moonlighters. Thus, they may take a second evening or weekend job to earn extra. The "deprivation/constraint hypothesis," in contrast, proposes that moonlighters are generally financially underprivileged and socially disadvantaged and thus resort to moonlighting as a means of survival. In other words, those people take a second evening job to make ends meet because they could not find a decent-paying day job. In a review of the literature, Baba and Jamal (1992) concluded that empirical evidence supports the "energic/opportunity hypothesis," thereby suggesting that moonlighters *choose* to work a second job or the night shift to increase their income. Moonlighters may not suffer negative health consequences from working long or unusual hours because they have chosen to work extra hours or unroutine schedules. Therefore, compared to non-moonlighters, moonlighters were not subject to increased ill-health consequences.

10.2.4 The Person–Environment Fit (P-E Fit) Theory

In the work stress literature, person–environment fit (P-E Fit) theory emphasizes the interaction between the individual and the environment (Caplan 1983; French et al. 1982). The core premise of P-E Fit theory is that stress arises not from the person or the environment alone but rather from the fit between the two. People who work for the hours they want are in a state of fit and thus are satisfied and content. Conversely, people who work *more* or *less* hours than they would like represent a state of misfit, which is likely to cause strains and ill-being.

Applying the P-E Fit theory to *choice* and working hours, Hall and Savery (1986) found that employees' ability to control their hours of work influences perceived stress levels. Kirkcaldy et al. (2000) found that, for people with a Type A tendency (hard-driving) and a stronger focus of internal locus of control, working long hours produced positive results, presumably because they *chose* to work so hard. *Choice* may thus differentiate people on their manifest strains and well-being.

10.2.5 The Present Study: Testing for the Ubiquity of Fit Effects

Although it is intuitive to infer that the fit of working hours should have beneficial effects on employees' work outcomes, previous studies have mostly all focused on stress and strains as the dependent variables, rather than work-related attitudes. Furthermore, few researchers have examined the effects of fit in non-Western countries (Lu 2011 as an exception). Thus, it is imperative to empirically test the ubiquity of the effects of fit in a large representative sample of employees across different nations, focusing on work outcomes as dependent variables. I thus hypothesized that

Hypothesis 1: People who have a fit between desired and actual working hours experience higher job satisfaction and organizational commitment compared to those who experience a misfit in working hours, regardless of the countries they reside.

10.3 Social Welfare Institutions as Providers of Macro-level Resources

10.3.1 Societal Environment: Another Game Changer?

Cable and Edwards (2004) noted that P-E Fit is a subjective experience which can be influenced by individual differences and elements found in the social environment (Cooper et al. 2001; Lazarus and Folkman 1984). In a rare large-scale comparative cross-cultural study, Spector et al. (2004) found significant correlations between working hours and psychological health for both Anglo (Australia, Canada, England, New Zealand, and the United States) and Chinese employees (Hong Kong, mainland China, and Taiwan). They also found a significant relationship between working hours and physical health for Chinese but not for Anglo workers. These small and inconsistent effects ($r = 0.01 \sim -0.09$) suggest that people in diverse social environments may respond differently to the pressure of working long hours and/or the fit or misfit of P-E. Research on the transactional stress model (Lazarus and Folkman 1984) has already noted that avowed cultural values (c.f., Hofstede 1991) as individual-level psychosocial resources play an important role in employees' reactions to the work environments (Lu et al. 2010, 2011).

Furthermore, Erlinghagen (2008) stated that social systems (e.g., political, economic, tax, and social welfare regimes) as macro-level resources protecting and sustaining the lives of society members also need to be considered in explaining cross-cultural differences in employees' work outcomes. Labor market regulations and state welfare provisions in particular influence people's work preferences and attitudes (Ginn and Fast 2006; Lu 2010). Erlinghagen (2008) proposed a fourfold typology of policy sets, typified by four welfare regimes (Aspalter 2006; Esping-Andersen 1999), based on a combination of labor market and social protection policies. I thus explore this specific dimension of the social environment, *social welfare*, as a proxy of the availability of macro-level resources.

10.3.2 The Four Social Welfare Systems

Esping-Andersen (1999) and Aspalter (2006) proposed a fourfold scheme of welfare systems including social democratic, liberal welfare, conservative corporatist, and East Asian welfare. The tenet of the theory is to classify social welfare systems along four focal dimensions: decommodification, social stratification, marketization, and welfare serving economic development. Specifically, *decommodification* is the strength of social entitlements and citizens' degree of immunization from market dependency. Decommodification is the process of viewing utilities as an entitlement, rather than as a commodity that must be paid or traded for. *Social stratification* is the categorization of people into rankings of socioeconomic tiers based on factors like wealth, income, social status, occupation, and power. Stratification is the relative social position of persons in a given social group, category, geographic region, or other social unit. *Marketization* is a restructuring process that enables state agencies to operate as market-oriented enterprises by changing the legal environment in which they operate. In the social welfare context, marketization refers to the creation of a functioning market system for the provision of various welfare services. Finally, *welfare serving economic development* refers to the purposive intention of the government in pushing forward economic progress through the provision of welfare services. A brief comparison of the four welfare systems can be found in Table 10.1 along these four dimensions, and a more detailed explanation follows.

In *social democratic welfare* states, such as the Nordic countries, governments encourage people to work. For instance, governments implement policies and supply resources to care for young children and senior citizens, charge high taxes, and enhance job retention and reemployment opportunities to maximize manpower. Every citizen has an equal right to apply for welfare payment if he/she becomes unemployed or disabled. *Liberal welfare* states such as the United States and Australia, as opposed to social democratic welfare states, regard work as a civil obligation and set liberal markets with minor governmental intervention. Welfare payment applies only to minority groups who have passed strict reviews by the government agencies. In *conservative corporatist* states such as Spain, France, and Germany, men are still the main providers of the family, and women often choose peripheral jobs or stay at home (Ginn and Fast 2006). Since women are the major support providers to families, state welfare provision is typically limited and mainly available to men excluding unemployed women. Similar to conservative corporatist welfare states, East Asian countries such as Taiwan and South Korea emphasize the value of family, and support is provided mainly by family members. Furthermore, contrary to Western concepts of social welfare, *East Asian welfare* is construed as a tool for developing a nation's economy, rather than protecting its citizens. It needs to be noted that while the first three types of welfare systems are well documented and researched, the last (East Asian welfare) is less clearly defined and more elusive. However, its evolving nature makes it more interesting to chart and compare against the others. Furthermore, as it evolves, it has the potential to serve as an exemplar for other developing countries in different geographic regions other than East Asia.

Table 10.1 A brief comparison of the four welfare systems

	Key dimensions				
Welfare systems	De-commodification	Social stratification	Marketization	Welfare serving economic development	Representative countries
Social democratic	High	Low	Low	Low	Nordic countries
Liberal	Low	Medium	High	High	United States, Australia
Conservative corporatist	Medium	High	Medium	Medium	Spain, France, Germany
East Asian	Low	High	Medium	High	Taiwan, South Korea

Adopted from Lee and Ku (2003)

10.3.3 The Present Study: Social Democratic Welfare Is the Best?

Based on the above description of the four welfare types, I believe that the social democratic welfare system provides the safest and most hopeful social environment for employees, reducing anxiety in the search for jobs and reemployment. Research has indeed shown that in social democratic welfare states, employees can afford to allocate more time to spend with families and friends compared to those in conservative corporatist and liberal welfare states (Ginn and Fast 2006). A study by Anderson and Pontusson (2007) also confirmed the benefits of social security in reducing negative reactions to job threats. However, no study has yet included East Asian welfare countries in comparison alongside the three Western social welfare regimes. I thus hypothesized that

Hypothesis 2: The effects of fit of desired and actual working hours (P-E Fit) on work attitudes (work satisfaction and organizational commitment) vary across different welfare regimes, such that the positive effect in a social democratic welfare regime is stronger than those of the other three welfare systems.

10.3.4 Financial Needs: To Earn More but Work Longer?

In addition, I explored the effect of personal financial needs on the state of fit between desired and actual working hours, over and beyond that of the macro-level social security provision. Many employees work longer hours in the current competitive business world because of increased workloads, job insecurity, performance pressure, and the rising cost of living (i.e., pressure to earn more). Lu (2010, 2011) showed that the state of personal/family finance played an important role in employees' preferences regarding working hours. Driven by the needs of merchandise consumption and maintaining living standards in the global economic recession, people worked harder than ever before. Recent studies found that the increase in nonstandard or contingent employment contracts, the decline of unions, and the widespread use of subcontracting all fueled financial strains and hardship (Green et al. 2000; Worrall and Cooper 2013). Furthermore, employees push themselves to report to work even when they are sick, in fear of financial (wage) loss, tarnished image which may lead to job loss, and other social repercussions (Lu et al. 2013). This is the rising phenomenon of "sickness presenteeism" in the modern working world (Johns 2012). The financial need to earn more or lack of it will be a proximal predictor of one's decision on working hours. I thus hypothesized that

Hypothesis 3: People who want to earn more or earn less will result in a state of misfit of desired and actual working hours, after controlling for the effects of social welfare regimes.

10.4 Method

10.4.1 Selection of Countries and Participants for Cross-Cultural Comparisons

I conducted a secondary analysis using data collected in the International Social Survey Program (ISSP) with a theme on *work orientation*. The ISSP, which involves 40 countries worldwide, is an annual survey that uses a uniform questionnaire with a stratified random sample from each country, addressing a different theme each year. Thus in theory, every country sample is a representative sample of the nation's general population. In the context of this study, it is worth noting that respondents were citizens of a particular country, not "guest workers" in that country. For example, if a person is from Denmark but is working in the United States, he would be classified in the *social democratic* welfare cluster (as for Denmark, see below). Constrained by the nature of the ISSP (surveying citizens), I could only focus on where the person is from, not where the person is working.

Also, in my exercise I included in analysis only respondents claiming that they held full-time or part-time jobs, identified by a particular question in the survey. Because of varying work demands and labor regulations in different countries, identical indices of working hours for full-time jobs were unavailable. To further complicate matters, in some Asian countries (e.g., Taiwan), the self-reported average working hours in credible anonymous research surveys exceed the government regulatory cap on working time, attributable to the covert practice of the "invisible working time" (i.e., employees working unrecorded unpaid overtime out of social pressure) (cf. Lu 2011). However, within the ISSP framework, full-time employment is defined as a workweek of minimum 30 h, and part-time employment is defined as a 10–29-h workweek (Ginn and Fast 2006). Using this type of grouping eliminates unwanted variations in working hours and thus avoids discrepancies between self-declared employment statuses and the actual time expenditure in paid positions. Consequently, the current representative national sample comprised of 8,525 respondents from 9 countries. Based on the fourfold scheme of welfare systems, I classified these countries into four clusters: *the social democratic* welfare cluster ($n=2{,}339$) including Demark, Sweden, and Norway; *the liberal* welfare cluster ($n=2{,}121$) consisting of the United States and Australia; *the conservative corporatist* welfare cluster ($n=1{,}875$) including France and Germany; and *the East Asian* welfare cluster ($n=2{,}190$) consisting of Taiwan and South Korea.

10.4.2 Measures Used for the Study Variables

As an established ISSP practice, questionnaires were administered in face-to-face home interviews by trained interviewers (cf. Ginn and Fast 2006; Lu 2010, 2011). The data analyzed in this study were derived mainly from the following parts of the survey.

10.4.2.1 Actual Working Hours and Personal Preference

Two aspects of time expenditure were assessed: (a) *actual working hours* pertaining to the kind of job the participant held in the present (full-time vs. part-time) and (b) *desired working hours* expressed by the personal preference to choose either a full-time or a part-time job, without considering financial returns. Specifically, for the question *"If you could choose your working hours, and if you had only one choice, which of the following would you choose?"* participants were instructed to select one of the following options: (a) full time (work more than 30 h) or (b) part time (work 10–29 h). Note that both desired and actual working hours were assessed using the same discrete response options as above, rather than measured in the number of hours. To reiterate, this study is really about the fit (preferred vs. actual) between full-time or part-time work mode (because that is the data available) and not about the number of working hours (because the data are neither available nor compatible across countries). However, I keep the term "working hours" because it is not only the wording used in the original survey (see above) but also the terminology used in the relevant literature. The *fit* index in the present study was thus the congruence between the "current employment status" and the "desired option" of employment choice. Consequently, the following groups were identified:

Group A—fit: correspondence between desired and actual working hours, e.g., holding a full-time job and wanting a full-time job

Group B—misfit—wanting more: preferring more working hours than he/she actually does, e.g., holding a part-time job but wanting a full-time job

Group C—misfit—wanting less: preferring less working hours than he/she actually does, e.g., holding a full-time job but wanting a part-time job

10.4.2.2 Work Attitudes

In the survey, participants were asked to rate their (a) *job satisfaction* with the question "How satisfied are you with your job?" (1 = *completely dissatisfied* to 7 = *completely satisfied*) and (b) *organizational commitment* with three items tapping the affective, normative, and continuance aspects of commitment (Meyer and Allen 2001). Five-point rating scales were used, ranging from 1 (*strongly disagree*) to 5 (*strongly agree*), with high scores representing high levels of organizational commitment. The internal consistency of this three-item scale was 0.78 in the current sample, which is quite acceptable considering the limited number of items used.

10.4.2.3 Personal Financial Needs

Personal financial needs were measured with the item "If you had only one of these three choices, which of the following would you prefer?" (*1* = *work longer hours and earn more money*, *2* = *work the same number of hours and earn the same amount of money*, or *3* = *work fewer hours and earn less money*).

10.4.2.4 Control Variables

Information on gender (0 = *male*, 1 = *female*), age, seniority (tenure on the job), marital status (0 = *married*, 1 = *not married*), rank (0 = *manager*, 1 = *nonmanager*), as well as the gross domestic product (GDP), unemployment rate, social security rate, and the legal working hours of these states was also collected. These variables are often included in sociological studies of work and employment (e.g., Ginn and Fast 2006).

10.5 Results

10.5.1 The Beneficial Effects of "Fit" on Work Attitudes Across Countries

To explore the relationship between P-E Fit and work attitudes and the variation of this relationship across different welfare systems, a series of ANOVAs was conducted, with the fit between desired and actual working hours as the independent variable and job satisfaction and organizational commitment as the dependent variables (see Table 10.2 for results). As can be seen in the first row of results in Table 10.2, for the entire sample, the main effects of the "fit" between desired and actual working hours were significant on both job satisfaction and organizational commitment. Post hoc comparisons further revealed that employees with a fit between desired and actual working hours (Group A) had the *highest* job satisfaction and organizational commitment, followed by those who wanted to work more hours (Group B) and those who wanted to work fewer hours (Group C). Consistent with my *Hypothesis 1,* the fit group (Group A) generally fared better than the two misfit groups (Groups B and C).

10.5.2 The Finer-Tuned Effects of "Fit" on Work Attitudes in Different Countries

However, when I decomposed the results within each of the four social welfare systems, the pattern was somewhat different in each sector (see results in Rows 2–5 of Table 10.2). Rearranging the three groups according to their level of work attitudes, shown in the last column of Table 10.2, it is noted that for employees in the *social democratic* and *liberal* welfare countries, Groups A and C reported the highest job satisfaction. For employees working in the *conservative corporatist* and *East Asian* welfare systems, Groups A and B had the highest job satisfaction. Mirroring the results on job satisfaction, in a *social democratic* welfare system, Groups A and C had the highest organizational commitment. In the *conservative corporatist*

Table 10.2 ANOVA: Effects of fit between desired and actual working hours on work outcomes

		1. fit (n=5,463)		2. misfit-wanting more (n=2,068)		3. misfit-wanting less (n=994)		F	df	Post hoc Scheffe test
		M	SD	M	SD	M	SD			
All	JS	4.27	1.05	4.08	1.08	4.08	1.13	29.60 ***	8,359	1>2=3
	OC	10.10	2.44	9.79	2.43	9.27	2.70	47.03 ***	7,775	1>2>3
Social democratic	JS	4.36	0.99	4.11	1.03	4.52	1.05	19.73 ***	2,306	1=3>2
	OC	9.80	2.36	9.10	2.33	9.85	2.41	20.47 ***	2,073	1=3>2
Liberal	JS	4.43	1.07	4.16	1.23	4.30	1.16	9.35 ***	2,078	1=3>2
	OC	10.57	2.42	10.30	2.47	10.33	2.50	2.44	2,041	
Conservative corporatist	JS	4.30	1.04	4.14	1.20	4.04	1.10	9.94 ***	1,815	1=2>3
	OC	9.55	2.57	9.05	2.71	8.18	2.58	41.88 ***	1,649	1=2>3
East Asian	JS	3.93	1.04	3.99	1.00	3.73	1.07	5.25 ***	2,157	1=2>3
	OC	10.42	2.27	10.30	2.25	10.19	2.42	1.07	2,009	

Notes: (1) *** $p<.001$
(2) *JS* job satisfaction, *OC* organizational commitment

welfare system, employees in Groups A and B had the highest organizational commitment. However, employees in the *social democratic* welfare system did not show higher organizational commitment than the others. Therefore, *Hypothesis 2* was only partially supported.

10.5.3 The Interrelations Among all Study Variables: Individual-Level and Societal-Level

As a supplementary analysis, I computed the correlation matrix including all the research variables for the entire sample. Results are presented in Table 10.3. In this analysis, East Asian welfare regime was set as the comparison target for each of the other three systems. As can be seen in the table, compared against the East Asian welfare regime, the *social democratic* system and the *liberal* system correlated positively with employees' job satisfaction. Again, compared against the East Asian welfare regime, the *liberal* system correlated positively, while the *social democratic* system and the *conservative corporatist* system correlated negatively with employees' organizational commitment. These results corroborated the findings from the ANOVAs (cf. Table 10.2), showing that employees' work attitudes might vary in different social welfare regimes.

10.5.4 The Predictors of "Fit" of Work Hours: Individual-Level and Societal-Level Variables

To test *Hypothesis 3*, I used logistic regression, which allowed the criterion to be a categorical variable (fit or misfit). I used three steps to predict the fit status (0 = fit, 1 = misfit). First, I entered the country-level control variables for national differences (i.e., GDP, legal working hours, the unemployment rates, social security rates, and the type of social welfare regimes). Second, I entered individual-level demographics as control variables (i.e., gender, age, number of dependent children, and marital status). Third, I entered personal financial needs as predictors. The results showed that employees wanting to earn less money had a higher tendency to experience a misfit between desired and actual working hours (see Model 3 in Table 10.4). Furthermore, when all the individual-level and societal-level variables were taken into account in the same model (Model 3), employees in countries of lower unemployment rates, higher social security rates, longer legal work hours, social democratic welfare, liberal welfare, conservative welfare and employees who were female and nonmanagers also had a higher tendency to experience a misfit between desired and actual working hours.

Table 10.3 Correlation among all variables

	M	SD	1	2	3	4	5	6	7	8	9	10	11	12	13
1. Unemployment rates	11.67	12.79	1												
2. GDP	32635.18	11049.46	–.12 ***	1											
3. Social security rates	19.38	7.46	.67 ***	.36 ***	1										
4. Legal work hours	41.71	3.52	.94 ***	–.28 ***	.47 ***	1									
5. Social democratic v.s. East Asian	.27	.45	–.28 ***	.49 ***	.44 ***	–.36 ***	1								
6. Liberal v.s. East Asian	.25	.43	–.31 ***	.41 ***	–.26 ***	–.45 ***	–.35 ***	1							
7. Conservative v.s. East Asian	.22	.41	.99 ***	–.12 ***	.61 ***	.95 ***	–.33 ***	–.31 ***	1						
8. Gender	.52	.50	–.03 **	–.04 ***	–.07 ***	–.02 *	–.03 *	–.01	–.04 **	1					
9. Age	42.01	11.84	–.04 ***	.10 ***	.03 **	–.07 ***	.08 ***	.04 ***	–.04 ***	.05 ***	1				
10. Marital status	.76	.43	–.05 ***	.04 ***	.03 *	–.07 ***	.07 ***	.02 *	–.05 ***	.01	.41 ***	1			
11. Job position	.35	.48	.07 ***	.05 ***	.04 **	.04 **	–.06 ***	.07 ***	.07 ***	.17 ***	.06 ***	.08 ***	1		
12. Job satisfaction	4.20	1.07	.02 *	.15 ***	.09 ***	–.00	.05 ***	.09 ***	.01	.00	.07 ***	.06 ***	.11 ***	1	
13. Organizational commitment	9.94	2.49	–.16 ***	.03 *	–.22 ***	–.13 ***	–.09 ***	.14 ***	–.16 ***	.08 ***	.10 ***	.09 ***	.18 ***	.51 ***	1

Notes: (1). * $p<.05$; ** $p<.01$; *** $p<.001$
(2). Social democratic vs. East Asian: Social democratic = 1, else = 0; Liberal vs. East Asian: Liberal = 1, else = 0; Conservative vs. East Asian: Conservative = 1, else = 0; Gender: female = 0, male = 1; Marital status: single = 0, married = 1; Job position: employee = 0, supervisor = 1

Table 10.4 Predicting the state of P-E Fit: Logistic regression results

	Misfit vs. Fit		
	Model 1	Model 2	Model 3
	Beta	Beta	Beta
Constant	−1.60	−.40	−.60
Unemployment rates	−.90 ***	−.85 ***	−.86 ***
GDP	.00	.00	.00
Social security rates	.10 ***	.11 ***	.11 ***
Legal work hours	.17 ***	.14 **	.14 *
Social democratic vs. East Asian	4.20 ***	3.71 ***	3.55 ***
Liberal vs. East Asian	3.59 ***	3.17 ***	3.11 ***
Conservative vs. East Asian	26.21 ***	24.82 ***	24.78 ***
Gender		−.72 ***	−.72 ***
Age		.00	.00
Marital status		.08	.06
Job position		−.14 **	−.17 **
Wanting to earn more			−.04
Wanting to earn less			1.02 ***

Notes: (1) * $p<.05$, ** $p<.01$, *** $p<.001$
(2) Misfit vs. Fit: Misfit = 1, Fit = 0; Social democratic vs. East Asia: Social democratic = 1, else = 0; Liberal vs. East Asian: Liberal = 1, else = 0; Conservative vs. East Asian: Conservative = 1, else = 0; Gender: female = 0, male = 1; Marital status: single = 0, married = 1; Job position: employee = 0, supervisor = 1

10.5.5 *The Predictors of "Misfit" of Work Hours: The Finer-Tuned Analysis Contrasting the Two Different States of Misfit*

Repeating the above procedures, I conducted an additional analysis to predict personal misfit status of "misfit—wanting more" (1 = wanting more, 0 = else) and "misfit—wanting less" (1 = wanting less, 0 = else) respectively. As displayed in Table 10.5 (Model 6), people who wanted to earn more were more likely to experience the misfit state of working fewer hours than preferred, namely, wanting to work more hours. In contrast, as shown by Model 3 in Table 10.5, people who wanted to earn less were more likely to experience the misfit state of working more hours than preferred, namely, wanting to work fewer hours. Therefore, *Hypothesis 3* was supported, that is, personal financial needs contributed to a misfit between desired and actual working hours, after controlling for macro-level factors and individual-level demographics.

Table 10.5 Predicting the type of P-E misfit: Logistic regression results

	Misfit-wanting less			Misfit-wanting more		
	Model 1	Model 2	Model 3	Model 4	Model 5	Model 6
	Beta	Beta	Beta	Beta	Beta	Beta
Constant	.90	1.40	1.96	−7.59 *	−5.88	−6.88
Unemployment rates	−.44 ***	−.39 ***	−.36 ***	−1.25 ***	−1.22 ***	−1.26 ***
GDP	.00	.00	.00	.00	.00	.00
Social security rates	.06 *	.06 **	.07 **	.12 *	.12 *	.12 *
Legal work hours	.03	.02	.00	.32 **	.28 **	.30 **
Social democratic vs. East Asian	2.27 **	1.87 *	1.38	4.85 **	4.43 *	4.91 **
Liberal vs. East Asian	1.49 *	1.13	.80	5.18 ***	4.87 ***	5.23 ***
Conservative vs. East Asian	11.40 ***	9.80 ***	8.79 **	37.56 ***	36.88 ***	38.00 ***
Gender		−.65 ***	−.64 ***		−.51 ***	−.55 ***
Age		.00	.00		.00	.01
Marital status		.21 **	.18 *		−.16	−.16
Position		.05	.00		−.42 *	−.41 ***
Wanting to earn more			.06			.54 ***
Wanting to earn less			.09 ***			−.02

Notes: (1) * $p<.05$, ** $p<.01$, *** $p<.001$
(2) Misfit-wanting less: wanting less = 1, else = 0; Misfit-wanting more: wanting more = 1, else = 0; Social democratic vs. East Asian: Social democratic = 1, else = 0; Liberal vs. East Asian: Liberal = 1, else = 0; Conservative vs. East Asian: Conservative = 1, else = 0; Gender: female = 0, male = 1; Marital status: single = 0, married = 1; Job position: employee = 0, supervisor = 1

10.6 Discussion

10.6.1 A Summary of Main Research Findings

In this study, I examined the fit between desired and actual working hours and its association with employees' job satisfaction and organizational commitment in a world undergoing rapid social and economic changes, focusing on the comparison of various welfare regimes. I also explored the relationship between personal financial needs and the state of fit/misfit between personal preferences and actual working hours. A brief summary of the tested hypotheses and results can be found in Table 10.6. Specifically, it is found that (1) for the entire sample, the main effects of the "fit" between desired and actual working hours were significant on both job satisfaction and organizational commitment, thus *Hypothesis 1* was fully supported;

Table 10.6 A summary of hypotheses and their test results

Hypotheses	Test results	Description of the findings	Results presented
1. People who have a fit between desired and actual working hours experience higher job satisfaction and organizational commitment compared to those who experience a misfit in working hours, regardless of the countries they reside.	Supported	For the entire sample, the main effects of the "fit" between desired and actual working hours were significant on both job satisfaction and organizational commitment.	Table 10.2
2. The effects of fit of desired and actual working hours (P-E Fit) on work attitudes (work satisfaction and organizational commitment) vary across different welfare regimes, such that the positive effect in a social democratic welfare regime is stronger than those of the other three welfare systems.	Partially supported	The effects of fit did vary across different welfare regimes, but the beneficial effect of fit in a social democratic welfare regime is not uniformly stronger than those of the other three welfare systems.	Table 10.2
3. People who want to earn more or earn less will result in a state of misfit of desired and actual working hours, after controlling for the effects of social welfare regimes.	Partially supported	People who want to earn less money had a higher tendency to experience a misfit between desired and actual working hours.	Table 10.4

(2) the effects of fit did vary across different welfare regimes, but the beneficial effect of fit in a social democratic welfare regime is not uniformly stronger than those of the other three welfare systems, thus *Hypothesis 2* was only partially supported; and finally (3) people who want to earn less money had a higher tendency to experience a misfit between desired and actual working hours, thus *Hypothesis 3* was again partially supported. Below is the more detailed description and explanation of these main findings embedded in the contemporary literature.

10.6.2 The Confirmed Benefit of Choice and "Fit" on Workers' Well-Being Across Countries

Using the multinational samples in this study, I found that employees' work attitudes varied depending on the state of fit between desired and actual working hours. This finding resonated with the positive relationship between P-J Fit (person–job fit) and work attitudes found in a meta-analysis (Kristof-Brown et al. 2005). The thrust of the present research is to underline the fit of *working hours* as an important aspect of the generic concept of P-E Fit, in addition to ability and needs. Furthermore, I extended the existing research to demonstrate that the importance of this particular aspect of P-E Fit is universal, regardless of culture and social infrastructures. Although researchers have identified fit as a mediator between working hours and burnout in Western countries (Barnett et al. 1999), the potential beneficial effects of personal choice and the resultant state of fit pertaining to working hours have rarely been empirically tested for non-Western countries. To remedy this shortcoming, I included two economically viable East Asian societies, South Korea and Taiwan, in the present study. What I found involving a cross-nation sample of nine diverse countries are similar to those obtained by Lu (2011) among Taiwanese workers, showing that those who enjoyed a state of fit between desired and actual working hours generally had a better attitude toward work and lower strains, compared to those who were in a state of misfit, regardless of whether they wanted to work more or fewer hours. Together, these findings support the ubiquity of the favorable effects of achieving the psychological state of fit in one's choice of working hours.

10.6.3 Does Social Welfare Really Help? The Role of Family and the Responsibility of the State

In the present study, I found that the relationship between desired/actual working hours and work attitudes did vary across different social welfare types. Contrary to my expectations, employees who experienced congruence between personal preference and actual supply did not report the most positive attitudes toward work under the social democratic welfare system. It may be noted that the welfare regimes fell into two clusters, in terms of their influence on the association between the fit of working hours and work outcomes: social democratic and liberal welfare combined as one cluster and the other cluster consisting of conservative corporatist and East Asian welfare. Esping-Andersen (1999) and Lee and Ku (2003) did point out that the conservative corporatist and East Asian systems shared some common characteristics, wherein men were the main providers of the family and women provided the majority of caretaking and home maintenance. More importantly, societies adopting both the conservative corporatist and East Asian welfare systems greatly emphasize the value of the family as a "social safety net" and discourage their citizens to rely on state welfare/security. Under the threat of economic recession and organizational restructuring, people feel the even greater need to be employed and work more hours, thus earning more money to support the family. Hardworking and monetary successes are traditionally regarded as top priorities in the East Asian life. In accordance with the Confucian cultural heritage, workers in Taiwan and South Korea work harder and longer to provide their families a respectable living standard and to glorify their family names with career successes (Lu et al. 2011). It is conceivable that employees in East Asian and conservative corporatist systems may avow higher levels of positive work attitudes to increase their job opportunities.

Our findings corroborate the link between working hours and health consequences established for Western (Sparks et al. 1997) and Chinese (Lu 2011; Spector et al. 2004) workers, thus the impact of long working hours on both the employee and his/her family deserves more research attention and managerial interventions. Considering the early warning by Dankert et al. (1965), that working hours affect not only the individual but also the family, any arrangements in working time should include both support for employees who are coping as well as the needs and responsibilities of their family life. Despite the existence of daycare and nursing homes, as well as assistance and training for reemployment supplied by Nordic countries to assist workers, employees were still struggling to maintain a full-time job and at the same time trying to spend more time to be with family and friends (Ginn and Fast 2006).

10.6.4 Important Determinants of Choice of Working Hours: Monetary Drive or Other Personal Needs?

In the present study, logistic regression was conducted to examine the association between personal financial needs and the state of fit between desired and actual working hours. As expected, I found that those with lower economic needs (i.e., wanting to earn less) had more chance of slipping into misfit of the desired and actual working hours. Supplementary analysis did confirm that some people wanted to earn more but had options to work less time than they desired. However, there may be critical factors other than financial needs contributing to the state of fit pertaining to work hours. Caplan (1987) proposed that an individual's ability and aspiration could be the most important factor influencing the fit between a person and the environment. Costa et al. (2006) also found that European workers considered individual autonomy in deciding working hours the most important factor affecting job satisfaction. These diverse human needs other than earning more money deserve more systematic examination in relation to working hours and well-being in future studies.

10.6.5 Limitations of the Present Study

Before drawing conclusions, certain methodological limitations should be noted. First, the present study was essentially an exercise in secondary data analysis, which has inherent limitations. For example, established theory-based multi-item measures of job satisfaction and organizational commitment should have been adopted. Multi-item scales for these variables were not used because of space constraints for a large-scale social survey with an embedded international core module. The true extent of the relationship between desired and actual working hours and work attitudes may thus be obscured by the use of single-item or lean-item measures; therefore, due caution should be exercised in interpreting the results.

Second, the missing variable bias may pose a threat to the generalizability of the findings. As mentioned above, certain factors other than financial needs should have been taken into account but unfortunately were not included in the original design of the ISSP survey to enable a cross-cultural comparison.

Finally, personal financial needs in this study were measured with the item "If you had only one of these three choices, which of the following would you prefer?" (*1 = work longer hours and earn more money*, *2 = work the same number of hours and earn the same amount of money*, or *3 = work fewer hours and earn less money*). One may argue that "*work the same number of hours and earn more money*" is another realistic scenario, which is not captured. This is because the researchers who designed the original survey seemed to assume that it is human nature to maximize gains while minimizing costs, thus including the abovementioned option would create unwanted confound in the study.

However, considering the scarcity of cross-national probability samples and high-quality data collection in the field, the present study makes a contribution by bridging certain knowledge gaps regarding the issue of working hours and work attitudes from a cross-national comparative perspective.

10.6.6 Practical Implications of the Findings

Findings of this study offer useful insights to inform management practices. I found that the fit between desired and actual working hours was associated with higher job satisfaction and organizational commitment. However, misfit exists and may hinder work attitudes. In fact, a substantial proportion of the sample (43.32 %) wanted to work either more (29.32 %) or fewer hours (14 %). To respond to those who want to increase their monetary returns via working more hours, companies should review their compensation schemes to raise employees' tolerance to extended working hours. In addition, providing employees with a say in deciding their working hours can foster perceived organizational support and individual control at work, which can consequently promote job satisfaction, organizational commitment, and work–family integration (Lu et al. 2008).

Indeed, situating the present study in the wider context of work–family integration, further suggestions and enlightenment may be drawn from the findings. The ultimate value of scientific research is to better human life. For some time now, researchers in the developed West (e.g., Scandinavian countries) have lobbied and successfully promoted family-friendly organizations (Dikkers et al. 2005). Incidentally, these are countries with social democratic welfare systems as identified in the present study. However, work–nonwork arrangements are an alien concept in most East Asian organizations (Chang et al. 2012), where working "extra-hour" is the social norm, such as in Taiwanese (Lu 2011) or Japanese (Kanai 2009) work settings. It is thus imperative to raise awareness of work–family integration basing on rigorous empirical research on work–family interference (WFI), and to further promote effective coping with WFI in traditionally hardworking East Asian societies.

To reiterate, although the Confucian cultural values promote diligence at work, the extraordinarily long working hours have been linked to heightened stress and WFI for the Taiwanese workers (Lu 2011; Lu et al. 2008), and even premature death in Japan (Kanai 2009). Thus, organizations need to redesign the working hour arrangements to bring in more flexibility and personal control over the work schedule. Discretion pertaining to working hour arrangements has been proved to ameliorate the negative impact of WFI for Taiwanese workers (Chang et al. 2012). Autonomy in deciding working hours was found to be the most important factor affecting job satisfaction for European workers (Costa et al. 2006). Alternatively, organizations need to provide fairer compensations for those working long hours through personal choice, either out of financial necessity or social sanction. In East Asian countries, people may not yet have the luxury of working fewer hours than they do, or fear for tarnished image if they fail to conform to the hardworking norm. Then, better compensation for working extra-hour is at least some consolation and a "goodwill" gesture from the employer. Getting fair pay for working extra-hour is also conducive to "providing for the family through hardworking" mentality rooted in the traditional Confucian value system, which could offset detrimental effects of long working hours on well-being (Lu et al. 2012; Yang et al. 2000).

10.7 Conclusions

To conclude, both working hours and personal choices should be considered when devising suitable working time schedules to maximize employees' well-being, organizational commitment, and societal integration. At the same time, societal macro-level provisions of support (e.g., social welfare system) need to be carefully designed and implemented to facilitate both economic growth and individual need fulfillment. The challenge in the contemporary world for organizations and individuals is to blend work and family needs and demands, to create a constructive circle of harmony and enrichment for every working individual, every operating organization, in every thriving human society. Taking into account the various needs of individuals and organizations, and the responsibilities of the state, using the social welfare system as a societal infrastructure should enable us to find a personal balance point in work and family, and help organizations survive and strive in the current global economic competition.

Acknowledgment The empirical data in Taiwan were collected with the support of a grant from the National Science Council, Taiwan (NSC94-2420-H-001-008-B1). In writing this chapter, the author was supported by another grant from the Ministry of Science and Technology, Taiwan (MOST103-2410-H-002-195-SS3).

References

Anderson CJ, Pontusson J (2007) Workers, worries and welfare states: social protection and job insecurity in 15 OECD countries. Eur J Polit Res 46(2):211–235

Argyle M (2001) The psychology of happiness, 2nd edn. Routledge, London

Aspalter C (2006) The East Asian welfare model. Int J Soc Welf 15:290–301
Baba VV, Jamal M (1992) How much do we really know about moonlighters? Public Pers Manag 21:65–73
Barnett RC, Gareis KC, Brennan RT (1999) Fit as a mediator of the relationship between work hours and burnout. J Occup Health Psychol 4:307–317
Bruck CS, Allen TD, Spector PE (2002) The relation between work-family conflict and job satisfaction: a finer-grained analysis. J Vocat Behav 60:336–353
Cable DM, Edwards JR (2004) Complementary and supplementary fit: a theoretical and empirical integration. J Appl Psychol 89:822–834
Caldwell DF, O'Reilly CA (1990) Measuring person-job fit with a profile comparison process. J Appl Psychol 75:648–657
Caplan RD (1983) Person-environment fit: past, present, and future. In: Cooper CL (ed) Stress research. Wiley, New York, pp 35–78
Caplan RD (1987) Person-environment fit theory and organizations: commensurate dimensions, time perspectives, and mechanisms. J Vocat Behav 31(3):248–267
Chang TT, Lu L, Kuo CY (2012) Effects of work resources on work-to-family conflict and work outcomes. Organ Manag 5:101–135
Cooper CL, Davidson MJ, Robinson P (1982) Stress in the police service. J Occup Med 24:30–36
Cooper CL, Dewe P, O'Driscoll MP (2001) Organizational stress: a review and critique of theory, research and applications. Sage, Thousand Oaks
Costa G, Sartori S, Akerstedt T (2006) Influence of flexibility and variability of working hours on health and well-being. Chronobiol Int 23:1125–1137
Dankert CE, Mann FC, Northrup HR (1965) Hours of work. Harper & Row, New York
Dekker SWA, Schaufeli WB (1995) The effects of job insecurity on psychological health and withdrawal: a longitudinal study. Aust Psychol 30(1):57–63
Dikkers JSE, den Dulk L, Geurts SAE, Peper B (2005) Work-nonwork culture, utilization of work-nonwork arrangements, and employee-related outcomes in two Dutch organization. In: Poelmans SAY (ed) Work and family: an international research perspective. Lawrence Erlbaum Associates, Mahwah, pp 147–172
Directorate-General of Budget (2012) Year book of manpower statistics. Executive Yuan, Taipei
Edwards JR, Cable DM (2009) The value of value congruence. J Appl Psychol 94(3):654–677
Erlinghagen M (2008) Self-perceived job insecurity and social context: a multi-level analysis of 17 European countries. Eur Sociol Rev 24:183–197
Esping-Andersen G (1999) Social foundations of postindustrial economies. Oxford University Press, Oxford
French JRP Jr, Caplan RD, Harrison RV (1982) The mechanism of job stress and strain. Wiley, New York
Ginn J, Fast J (2006) Employment and social integration in midlife: preferred and actual time use across welfare regime types. Res Aging 28:669–690
Green F, Felstead A, Burchell B (2000) Job insecurity and the difficulty of regaining employment: an empirical study of unemployment expectations. Oxf Bull Econ Stat 62:857–885
Hall K, Savery LK (1986) Tight rein, more stress. Harvard Business Review. 64(1):160–164
Hofstede G (1991) Culture and organizations: software of the mind. MaGraw-Hill, London
Jamal M (1986) Moonlighting: personal, social, and organizational consequences. Hum Rel 39:977–990
Johns G (2012) Presenteeism: a short history and a cautionary tale. In: Houdmont J, Leka S, Sinclair R (eds) Contemporary occupational health psychology: global perspectives on research and practice, vol 2. Wiley, Malden, pp 204–220
Kanai A (2009) "Karoshi (Work to Death)" in Japan. J Bus Ethics 84:209–216
Karasek R (1979) Job demands, job decision latitude and mental strain: implications for job redesign. Adm Sci Q 24:285–306
Karasek R, Theorell T (1990) Healthy work. Basic Books, New York

Kirkcaldy BD, Trimpop R, Cooper CL (1997) Working hours, job stress, work satisfaction, and accident rates among medical practitioners and allied personnel. Int J Stress Manag 4:79–87
Kirkcaldy B, Levine R, Shephard RJ (2000) The impact of working hours on physical and psychological health of German managers. Eur Rev Appl Psychol 50:443–449
Kristof-Brown AL, Zimmerman RD, Johnson EC (2005) Consequences of individual's fit at work: a meta-analysis of person-job, person-organization, personal group, and person-supervisor fit. Pers Psychol 58(2):281–342
Lazarus R, Folkman S (1984) Stress, appraisal, and coping. Springer, New York
Lee YJ, Ku YW (2003) Another welfare world? A preliminary examination of the developmental welfare regime in East Asia. Taiwan J Sociol 31:189–241
Lu L (2010) Employment among older workers and inequality of gender and education: evidence from a Taiwanese national survey. Int J Aging Hum Dev 70(2):145–162
Lu L (2011) Working hours and personal preference among Taiwanese employees. Int J Workplace Health Manag 4(3):1–21
Lu L (2012) Aging and quality of life in Taiwan. J Altern Med Res 4(3):233–243
Lu L, Hu CH (2005) Personality, leisure experiences and happiness. J Happiness Stud 6:325–342
Lu L, Kao SF, Chang TT, Wu HP, Cooper CL (2008) Work/family demands, work flexibility, work/family conflict, and their consequences at work: a national probability sample in Taiwan. Int J Stress Manag 15:1–21
Lu L, Siu OL, Lu CQ (2010) Does loyalty protect Chinese workers from stress? The role of affective organizational commitment in the Greater China region. Stress Health 26:161–168
Lu L, Kao SF, Siu OL, Lu CQ (2011) Work stress, Chinese work values, and work well-being in the greater China. J Soc Psychol 151:767–783
Lu L, Chang TT, Chang YY (2012) The meanings of work and family and their roles in coping with work and family conflict: practicing the Chinese bicultural self. Indigen Psychol Res Chin Soc 37:141–189
Lu L, Lin HY, Cooper CL (2013) Unhealthy and present: motives and consequences of the act of presenteeism among Taiwanese employees. J Occup Health Psychol 18(4):406–416
Meyer JP, Allen NJ (2001) Affective, continuance, and normative commitment to the organization: a meta-analysis of antecedents, correlates, and consequences. J Vocat Behav 61:20–52
Olson-Buchanan JB, Boswell WR (2006) Blurring boundaries: correlates of integration and segmentation between work and nonwork. J Vocat Behav 68:432–445
Sparks K, Cooper C, Fried Y, Shirom A (1997) The effects of hours of work on health: a meta-analytic review. J Occup Organ Psychol 70:391–408
Sparks K, Faragher B, Cooper CL (2001) Well-being and occupational health in the 21st century workplace. J Occup Organ Psychol 74:489–509
Spector PE, Cooper CL, Poelmans S, Allen TD, O'Driscoll M, Sanchez JI, Siu OL, Dewe P, Hart P, Lu L et al (2004) A cross-national comparative study of work/family stressors, working hours, and well-being: China and Latin America vs. the Anglo world. Pers Psychol 57:119–142
Stack S, Eshleman JR (1998) Marital status and happiness: a 17-nation study. J Marriage Fam 60:527–536
Trimpop R, Kirkcaldy B, Athanasou J, Cooper CL (2000) Individual differences in working hours, work perceptions and accident rates in veterinary surgeries. Work Stress 14:181–188
Worrall L, Cooper CL (2013) The effect of the recession on UK managers: the quality of working life 2007–2012. Res Appl Psychol 59:23–48
Yang N, Chen CC, Choi J, Zou Y (2000) Sources of work-family conflict: a Sino-U.S. comparison of the effects of work and family demands. Acad Manage J 43:113–123

MIX
Papier aus verantwortungsvollen Quellen
Paper from responsible sources
FSC® C105338

If you have any concerns about our products,
you can contact us on
ProductSafety@springernature.com

In case Publisher is established outside the EU,
the EU authorized representative is:
Springer Nature Customer Service Center GmbH
Europaplatz 3, 69115 Heidelberg, Germany

Printed by Libri Plureos GmbH
in Hamburg, Germany